FROM CURING TO HEALING

A Plastic Surgeon's Journey Through Palliative Care - Reflections

Cherian Koshy

Made with ♥ on the Notion Press Platform
www.notionpress.com

Foreword

I felt overwhelmed when requested to write a Foreword for Cherian Koshy's Oeuvre. This thought-provoking essay compilation has a spiritual underpinning with philosophical spinoffs. Dr Koshy's wealth of information and fund of knowledge navigating the nuances and intricacies, the nitty-gritty of plastic surgery, cancer surgery, and palliative medicine and his foray into linguistics have made this book, which I could read at the manuscript stage to be one seamlessly woven between prose and poetry, punctuated by the parenthetical periods of his involvement and experience in different fields. This book is a real feat!

More than two decades back, I could interact with him for the multi-professional training in Palliative Care at St Christopher's London. I was amazed at his skills in creating a tapestry of information from Plastic Surgery to Pain to Politics or Palliative Medicine with consummate ease - obviously, he wields the pen and scalpel and guitar strings with equal dexterity.

I was amazed at his grasp of several languages, including Latin, when he remarked, '*Divinium est Sedare Dolorum*' (Blessed are they who treat pain-it is divine to alleviate pain)

His journey is from scalpel and sutures to songwriting, serenity, and solace to the less fortunate.

In fact, I coaxed and cajoled him to organise his thoughts into print and bequeath them to another generation, and it has happened!

This book on his transition from plastic surgery to palliative medicine is an excellent and exceptionally well-argued, analysed, and articulated narrative.

Dr Cherian Koshy is a thought leader, an orator, and a good teacher who believes in and practices a low-tech, high-touch practice of medicine.

I recommend this as a keepsake to be read by as many as possible.

Marinella Murg Rotariu

Director Emmanuel Hospice, Oradea, Romania, Member of the National Council of the National Association of Palliative Care in Romania, Palliative Care Trainer in Eastern Europe.

Contents

Dedicated to those who could.

Undress my Mind

Slowly unzip my imagination

Reach and caress my intellect

Unbutton My Thoughts

And tickle my brilliance

Strip me bare of all obtuseness and

Make my sagacity pulse.

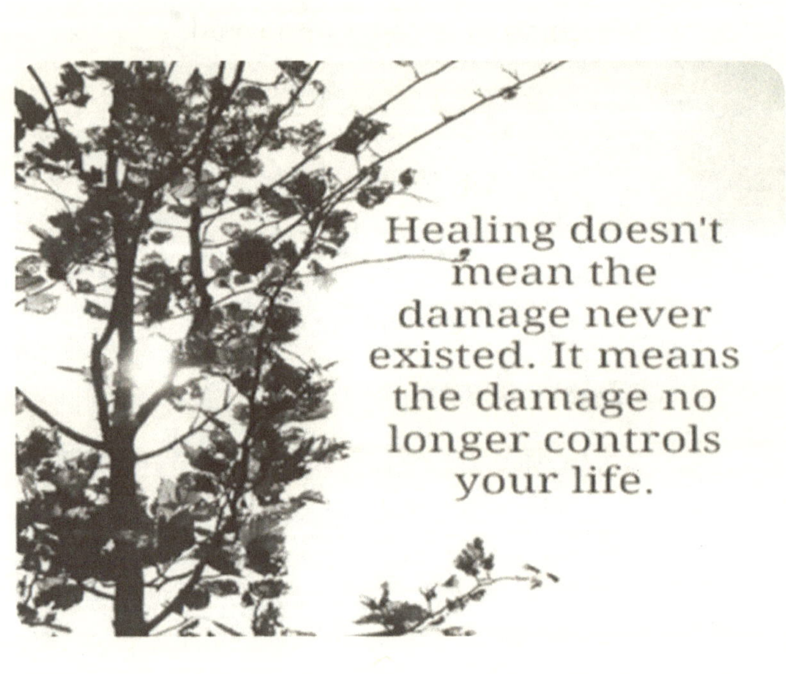
Healing doesn't mean the damage never existed. It means the damage no longer controls your life.

Preface

A Journey Through Medicine: From Trivandrum to the World

It was fifty years ago, in November 1974, that I had the privilege of stepping into the hallowed precincts of a Medical School in Trivandrum, the capital city of Kerala, inaugurated by Pandit Jawaharlal Nehru the first Prime Minister and Rajkumari Amrit Kaur the then Health Minister in 1951. Fondly called 'God's Own Country' and 'the Bride of the Arabian Sea', Kerala has a deep and storied history, a land where spirituality and science often intertwine. It is here, two millennia ago, that the Apostle Thomas, doubting no more, landed to spread his message, greeted by a flute-playing Jewish girl. This juxtaposition of ancient tradition and modern aspirations reflects Kerala's essence, and it is in this culturally rich environment that my journey in medicine began.

St Thomas Day is Celebrated on July 3rd, (July 3rd 72 AD – the day he was martyred at Mylapore. Chennai)

On St. Thomas Day, the twilight gleams,

A day of doubt and faith, of dreams.

The sceptic's heart, with questions rife,

Finds in the end a path to life.

His fingers touched the wounds so real,
A moment where the heavens kneel.
From doubt emerged a faith so pure,
In the risen Lord, a truth secure.

O Thomas, blessed in your quest,
Your doubt has led us to the best.
In every heart that questions still,
Your story strengthens, binds, and fills.

On this day, let faith and reason blend,
In a quest for truth that never ends.
For in the shadows, light is born,
And with the dawn, new hope adorns.

Coming from a family with several doctors, particularly on my mother's side, the path to becoming a physician was almost an inherited one. Medicine was not just a profession; it was a calling passed down through generations, a way of life rooted in the commitment to healing. Growing up surrounded by conversations about patients, diagnoses, and treatments, I was immersed in the world of medicine long before I set foot in medical school. It was the only path that made sense to me, and with this lineage came an expectation that only the brilliant few would make it—a standard that I was determined to meet.

By the time I turned thirty, my journey in medicine had already reached significant milestones. I had not only completed my MBBS but also specialized in General Surgery and super-specialized in Plastic Surgery (M.Ch). These years were filled with rigorous training, long hours, and an unyielding dedication to mastering my craft. The field of surgery, particularly plastic surgery, attracted me because of its intricate blend of science and artistry. It was more than just a technical discipline; it was a field where precision met creativity, where the restoration of form and function could dramatically improve a patient's quality of life.

Between these accomplishments, I had the opportunity to work as a House Doctor (Junior Resident) at St. Stephen's Hospital in Delhi in 1981. This experience was a formative one, exposing me to the diverse and often challenging realities of healthcare in a bustling metropolitan hospital. From the unique medical cases to the constant flow of patients, St. Stephen's was a place of learning and growth. It was here that I honed my skills, gained confidence, and developed a deep appreciation for the complexities of patient care.

My journey continued with a five-year tenure at the prestigious St. John's Medical College in Bangalore. This institution, known for its commitment to excellence in medical education and patient care, provided me with an environment that fostered both professional and personal growth. St. John's was a place where the ethos of compassionate care and cutting-edge medical practice coexisted, and it was here that I further solidified my foundation as a surgeon. The diverse patient population and the range of medical challenges I encountered only deepened my passion for the field. My passion is to see the villager and farmer where he belongs 'with 'warts and all' and their living conditions and health issues took me to rural areas of Gujarat, Maharashtra, Karnataka, West Bengal (to see the schedule at Nirmal Hriday of Mother Teresa in Kolkata) and rural Tamil Nadu and in the Himalayas at Manali.

In 1996, after gaining invaluable experience and honing my skills, I joined the renowned Regional Cancer Centre in Trivandrum. The transition to a specialized cancer treatment facility marked a significant chapter in my medical career. Here, I had the opportunity to focus on oncology, particularly the surgical aspects of cancer treatment, which presented unique challenges and required a different level of empathy and precision. Working at the Regional Cancer Centre allowed me to contribute to a cause larger than myself—helping patients navigate the complex and often overwhelming journey of cancer treatment.

My career also took me overseas, where I gained a broader perspective on medicine and healthcare. These experiences exposed me to different healthcare systems, medical practices, and cultural approaches to healing. The insights I gained during these years abroad enriched my understanding of global medicine and provided me with new tools and techniques to bring back to my practice in India.

Looking back on the past five decades, I realize that my journey through medicine has been shaped by a combination of inherited legacy, personal dedication, and the wisdom gained from a diverse range of experiences. From the early days at Trivandrum Medical School to my time at St. Stephen's, St. John's and the Regional Cancer Centre, each step has been a building block in the tapestry of my career. The lessons learned, the patients treated, and the lives touched along the way have all contributed to the physician I am today.

Medicine, for me, has never been just a profession. It has been a lifelong journey of learning, healing, and growing. It has been about balancing science with compassion, skill with empathy, and expertise with the humility to understand that healing is not always in our hands alone. As I reflect on these fifty years, I am grateful for the privilege of being part of this sacred field and for the opportunity to serve as a healer in a world that continues to need compassionate care more than ever. I've learnt from patients and their stories much more than what I gleaned from books, particularly about their 'Total Pain' – and often obliged their requests regarding the change of my primitive Nokia mobile to a smartphone or even had to accede to their 'pleas' for my hair colouring. Yes, intimacy causes freedom in a relationship,

My Ambition to Author a Book

Writing a book has long been an ambition of mine, a dream that lingered in the back of my mind even as I navigated the demanding world of surgery and medicine. Despite having written columns for prominent newspapers like the New Indian Express, Deccan Chronicle, and The Hindu, the idea of organizing my thoughts into a cohesive manuscript seemed like a distant, almost unattainable goal. Yet, over time, this aspiration has evolved from a mere idea into a project that is finally taking shape—a journey that has been inspired, in part, by my experiences and the people I have encountered along the way.

One such person who has had a profound impact on my literary ambitions is our Member of Parliament from Trivandrum, Dr Shashi Tharoor. He is a man of many talents—an erudite scholar, a prolific author, a former Under Secretary General at the United Nations, and perhaps one of the most sought-after motivational speakers and debaters in India. I had the privilege of sharing the stage with him during his visit to the Regional Cancer Centre, where his eloquence and depth of knowledge were on full display. His ability to weave words into powerful narratives left a lasting impression on me, igniting a spark that would fuel my own desire to write.

Dr Tharoor's influence on my journey to authorship goes beyond mere admiration. In the preface of his book Bookless in Baghdad, he writes, "For me, books are like the Toddy Tappers hatchet that cuts through the rough husks that enshroud our minds to tap into the exhilaration that ferments within." This metaphor resonated deeply with me, capturing the essence of why I, too, have felt compelled to write. Books have the power to cut through the noise and confusion of life, allowing us to tap into the core of our thoughts and emotions. They offer a way to distil complex experiences into something meaningful, something that can be shared with others.

As an avid reader and a bibliophile, though not as voracious, or reckoned or regarded as this great legend as Dr Tharoor, I have always found solace and inspiration in the written word. Books have been my companions through both the quiet and chaotic moments of life, providing insights and perspectives that have shaped my understanding of the world. The idea of contributing to this vast repository of human knowledge and experience has always appealed to me, but the challenge has been in finding the time and clarity to bring my thoughts together in a way that does justice to the stories I want to tell.

The journey of writing a book is, in many ways, akin to the practice of medicine. Both require patience, precision, and a deep sense of empathy. Just as a surgeon must carefully navigate the complexities of the human body, a writer must skillfully weave together ideas and experiences to create a narrative that resonates with readers. And just as every patient is unique, so too is every story—each with its own set of challenges and rewards.

For me, this book is not just a collection of words on a page; it is an opportunity to share the lessons I have learned over the course of my career, particularly in the realms of plastic surgery, oncology, and palliative medicine. It is a chance to explore the themes of healing, suffering, and the human experience in a way that goes beyond the clinical environment. Through this book, I hope to provide insights not only into the world of medicine but also into the broader questions of life, death, and what it means to live with dignity and purpose.

As the book begins to take shape, I find myself drawing on the inspiration of those who have come before me—writers, thinkers, and leaders like Dr Tharoor, who have shown me that the power of the written word is as vital as the power of the scalpel. Writing requires a different kind of discipline, one that demands introspection, creativity, and a willingness to be vulnerable. But it is also a deeply rewarding process, one that allows for the exploration of ideas in a way that can touch lives and spark change.

In many ways, this book represents the culmination of my life's work, not just as a doctor but as a human being who has borne witness to the full spectrum of the human experience- the battles of the mind and cries of the heart. It is an attempt to distil the wisdom gained from years of working with patients who have faced unimaginable challenges and to share that wisdom with a broader audience. It is a testament to the resilience of the human spirit and a tribute to the countless lives that have touched mine over the years.

Ultimately, my ambition to author a book is about more than just putting pen to paper. It is about creating something lasting, something that can serve as a source of knowledge, comfort, and inspiration for others. It is about leaving a legacy that goes beyond the operating room and the hospital walls, reaching out to those who seek understanding and connection in the face of life is most difficult questions.

With each passing day, the dream of writing this book becomes more of a reality. And while the process is challenging. It is also exhilarating—much like the thrill of surgery, but with the added depth of reflection and introspection. I am excited to see where this journey will take me and hopeful that, in the end, it will lead to something that can make a difference in the lives of others, just as books have done for me.

These following pages have been divided into two parts – my unforgettable goose bump creating professional experience and how, through it all, I could find answers to the hard questions that accompany humankind – pain and suffering and Theodicy – which is vindicating God in the presence of suffering.

We 'Enter Life at Birth, we leave Life at Death in between is the Enterprise of Life' जीवन और मृत्यु के बीच जीवन का उद्यम है

Therefore, we need to give the same care to those who 'leave life' the care that we gave to them when they entered life- 'Living' before 'leaving' Honing in and consolidating my accumulated wisdom and wealth of experience – to be immodestly articulating – I hope to keep you engaged with whatever God has Blessed me with.

To tinker with God's Creation Is a privilege denied to many.

Dr Cherian Koshy, MS, M.Ch (Plastic Surgery)

Former Assistant Professor Plastic and Reconstructive Surgery, St Johns Medical College, Bangalore, Alumnus Leadership Training HI Institute Maui Hawaii, USA, National and International Faculty Palliative Medicine, Retired Additional Professor Department of Surgical Sciences and Head of Palliative Medicine Regional Cancer Centre, Trivandrum, Kerala, India, (https://www.rcctvm.gov.in/) Presently Professor of Surgery, SUTAMS, Trivandrum

Email cherianrcc@gmail.com

10th November 2024

1

Career is What One is Paid For; Calling is What One is Made For: Drawing the Fault Line

In the intricate tapestry of our lives, career and calling often become intertwined threads, yet they represent fundamentally different concepts. A career is typically defined by the work one undertakes in exchange for financial compensation. It is a practical pursuit, governed by economic necessity and often shaped by market demands. Calling, however, transcends the material; it is a profound sense of purpose, a pursuit driven by inner conviction and personal fulfilment. The distinction between career and calling is crucial, as conflating the two can lead to a life where our hands reach for the purse while our hearts yearn for the pulse of genuine passion and meaning.

To explore this dichotomy, consider the example of individuals who excel in their careers but remain unfulfilled. These individuals might achieve financial success, secure prestigious positions, or gain societal recognition. Yet, despite these external markers of success, they may find themselves wrestling with a persistent sense of dissatisfaction, an aching void. This dissatisfaction often arises from a misalignment between their daily work and their deeper sense of purpose. While their careers provide financial stability, they might lack the intrinsic rewards of pursuing a calling.

Conversely, those who have identified and embraced their calling often experience a profound sense of satisfaction that transcends monetary compensation. A calling is not merely about choosing a profession; it is about aligning one's work with one's values, passions, and intrinsic motivations with an overarching integrity, sincerity propelled by a sense of purpose towards excellence, munificence, and beneficence. It involves pursuing work that resonates with one's deepest sense of purpose and identity. For such individuals, the act of working becomes a form of self-expression and fulfilment rather than a mere obligation.

Drawing the fault line between career and calling is not an exercise in negating the value of financial compensation. Rather, it is about recognising that a truly fulfilling life often requires balancing economic needs with the pursuit of what one is genuinely made for. This balance ensures that our efforts are not solely directed towards material gain but are also aligned with our personal values and passions.

In my own journey, I have come to recognise the profound difference between these concepts. While my career in medicine has provided financial stability and professional respect, it is my calling within this field that has given my work deeper meaning, particularly the transcendence of spirituality. My calling emerged from a profound sense of purpose: to alleviate suffering, to offer compassionate care, and to contribute to the broader understanding of palliative medicine. This calling has guided my decisions, driven my passion, and provided me with a sense of fulfilment that goes beyond the confines of my professional role.

Identifying one's calling requires introspection and self-awareness. It involves understanding what truly motivates and inspires us, beyond external rewards. It is about finding that intersection where our skills, passions, and values converge. For me, this journey of self-discovery has been both enlightening and transformative. It has taught me that true satisfaction in one's career comes not just from what one does, but from how well it aligns with one's deeper sense of purpose.

In conclusion, drawing a clear fault line between career and calling is essential for a fulfilling and meaningful life - a life of fulfilment - with a good sleep each day as the 'softest pillow is a clear conscience'. While careers provide financial support and societal status, callings offer profound personal satisfaction and alignment with one's true self. By understanding and pursuing our calling, we ensure that our hands reach not only for the purse but also for the pulse of genuine purpose and passion. In this balance lies the key to a life well-lived, where work becomes more than a means to an end—it becomes a reflection of who we truly are

Career Versus Calling

In the realm of work where many strive,

A career's path is often driven by

The lure of gold, the quest for fame,

A steady rhythm, a well-known name.

Yet beyond the office, through the day's grey haze,

Lies a calling's light, a soul's true blaze.

It whispers soft, with purpose clear,

A deep, intrinsic path to steer.

A career pays the bills, it's true.

But it may not light the heart's own view.

It charts a course through need and gain,

While the calling sings a sweeter strain.

A career can mould and shape our day,

But calling charts a broader way.

Where passion stirs and dreams take flight,

It turns the mundane into pure delight.

In the balance, find your own sweet song,

Where careers duties and calling belong.

For hands that reach for purse alone,

Miss the pulse of purpose fully known.

So, heed the call beneath your skin,

Where true fulfilment's light burns within.

Let career support, but calling guide,

In this harmony, let your spirit abide.

2

Curing to Healing: A Journey Beyond Medicine

In the realm of medicine, two verbs—curing and healing—carry profound significance, yet their nuances are often-overlooked. While both are integral to the practice of medicine, they represent fundamentally different processes. Curing implies an external, often measurable intervention, focused on the eradication of disease or the correction of a physical malady. Healing, on the other hand, transcends the physical domain, embodying a deeper, often unquantifiable restoration of wholeness and well-being. Each verb carries its own valency and transitivity, revealing distinct layers of engagement between the physician and the patient, the body and the soul, the external and the internal.

Curing: The Pursuit of External Resolution

Curing is a verb that implies direct action upon an object, making it highly transitive. In this sense, it is the application of medical knowledge and technology to remove a disease, repair tissue, or restore function. The relationship is clear-cut: the physician acts upon the patient to resolve a defined problem. Whether it's excising a tumour, setting a broken bone, or prescribing antibiotics for an infection, curing operates within the realm of observable outcomes. Success in curing is measured in test results, the absence of symptoms, or the return to normal function.

Curing is largely rooted in the biomedical model of health, where the focus is on the biological processes that can be corrected, fixed, or eliminated. In this paradigm, the patient's body is seen as a machine that can be repaired when broken. However, curing is inherently limited by the boundaries of physical health. Not every illness can be cured, and not every cure leads to complete well-being. This is where the concept of healing begins to diverge.

Healing: The Restoration of Wholeness

Healing, in contrast, is less about direct action and more about a process of becoming whole. Unlike curing, healing is not solely the domain of the physician; it is an internal journey undertaken by the patient. It is often intransitive; in that it doesn't always involve the direct application of a force upon an object. Instead, healing reflects a state of balance, peace, and restoration that may or may not coincide with the resolution of a physical condition.

Healing addresses the interconnectedness of body, mind, and spirit. It recognises that true well-being encompasses more than the absence of disease; it includes emotional, psychological, and existential dimensions. A person with a chronic illness, for example, may never be cured, but they can experience healing through acceptance, emotional support, and finding meaning in their journey. Healing involves a deeper engagement with the patient's life, acknowledging that suffering is not only physical but also emotional and spiritual.

'Nobody dies cured - but people died healed' – the paraplegic who is at a coffee vending machine or a blind person navigating his way are not cured but perhaps more healed than most of us who are health and wellness oriented!

The transitivity of healing is often mutual or reflexive. It's a shared process between the healer and the patient, and sometimes the healer must facilitate the conditions in which the patient can heal themselves. Healing requires empathy, presence, and an openness to the complexities of the human experience, moving beyond the scientific to embrace the personal and the sacred.

The Limits of Curing and the Need for Healing

In modern medicine, the focus on curing can sometimes overshadow the importance of healing. The relentless pursuit of cures, especially in the context of terminal illness or chronic disease, can lead to what Dr Eric Cassell calls "the suffering of treatment." Patients may undergo aggressive interventions that promise a cure but deliver suffering instead, leaving them physically alive but spiritually and emotionally depleted.

This is where healing becomes crucial. Healing allows for the acceptance of death, the management of chronic conditions, and the restoration of dignity even in the face of incurable disease. Healing recognises that life is finite and that, ultimately, the quality of life matters more than its length. In palliative care, for example, the focus shifts from curing to healing, as the goal becomes to alleviate suffering, enhance quality of life, and support patients and families in their final journey.

Curing and Healing: A Complementary Relationship

Although curing and healing are distinct, they are not mutually exclusive. In fact, they are often complementary. A cure can facilitate healing, just as healing can support a cure. For instance, a successful surgery may cure a patient's physical ailment, but the healing process—addressing the emotional trauma, adjusting to a new body image, or dealing with the existential questions that arise—requires time, compassion, and support.

Similarly, healing can occur even when curing is not possible. A patient in the final stages of cancer may not be cured, but through palliative care, they can find healing in the form of pain relief, emotional peace, and spiritual reconciliation. Healing, in this context, is about helping the patient to live well until they die, to experience a "good death" that respects their dignity and values.

Embracing Healing in the Practice of Medicine

The journey from curing to healing reflects a broader understanding of what it means to care for patients. Medicine, in its highest form, must embrace both. Curing addresses the immediate, physical needs of the patient, but healing attends to the whole person. It recognises that health is not just the absence of disease but the presence of well-being in all its dimensions.

As a physician who has walked this path from curing to healing, especially in the field of palliative care, it becomes clear that the true art of medicine lies in balancing both. Curing is a vital part of medicine, but healing is where the deeper, more transformative work happens. Together, they form a holistic approach to care that honours the complexity of the human experience.

The Valency of Verbs: Distinctions Between Curing and Healing

In medicine and care, language is not just a means of communication—it reflects the complexity and depth of human experience. The terms "curing" and "healing" are often used interchangeably in everyday discourse, but they carry distinct meanings, especially when we analyse them through the lens of linguistics and verb valency.

Verb valency refers to the number of arguments (subject, object, etc.) that a verb can take. This concept is crucial in understanding how language shapes our perceptions and actions. In the context of Curing a narrow Disease Centric Valency of these verbs reflects their different roles in medicine and human well-being.

Curing - A narrow Disease Centric Valency

The verb "cure" typically implies a direct action on a disease or condition, often focusing on eliminating the underlying cause. It tends to have a narrow valency, usually involving a subject (the medical practitioner) and a direct object (the disease or patient). For example:

The doctor cured the patient of the infection.

Here, the verb "cured" takes the doctor as the subject, the patient as the object, and the disease (infection) as an indirect argument. The emphasis is on the removal of a pathological condition, suggesting a clear and measurable outcome. The valency in this case is constrained to the technical aspects of disease eradication, with little room for broader considerations of the patient's overall well-being.

Curing, in this sense, is a clinical and objective process. It involves the application of medical knowledge, technology, and techniques to remove or neutralise a specific threat to the body. The verb's valency does not typically extend to the emotional, psychological, or spiritual dimensions of the patient's experience.

3

Healing: A Broader, Holistic Valency

In contrast, the verb "heal" encompasses a wider range of human experience. Healing is not limited to the removal of disease but involves restoring wholeness and balance to the individual. The valency of "heal" is broader, often taking multiple arguments that reflect physical, emotional, psychological, and even spiritual dimensions. For example:

"The nurse helped heal the patient after surgery."

"Time healed his emotional wounds."

In these examples, the verb "heal" involves not just the medical practitioner and the patient but also an array of other elements—time, emotional support, and internal processes. The process of healing is not confined to the body alone; it extends to the mind and soul. The valency of "heal" can accommodate various indirect arguments, including intangible factors like love, care, time, and resilience. Healing is often a subjective experience, unique to each individual, and it may continue long after the medical treatment has concluded.

Unlike curing, healing is not always about achieving a definitive outcome. While curing aims for the eradication of disease, healing seeks the restoration of well-being and personhood, even if the disease persists. A person may be healed in spirit or mind even if their body remains incurably ill. This broader valency reflects the complexity of the human experience and recognises that health and well-being are multidimensional.

The Art of Healing

Curing is a task of skill,

A battle fought with steadfast will.

It mends the body, bone, and skin,

It seals the wounds that lie within.

Yet healing is a gentler art,

It touches deeper in the heart.

It whispers softly through the mind,

In places cure cannot find.

For curing is a task of hands,

A science every mind understands.

But healing, subtle, cannot be forced.

It takes its own uncharted course.

Curing mends what eyes can see,

It fights disease with strategy.

But healing speaks to what we feel,

A power far beyond the real.

Curing's reach is finite, true.

It ends where science cannot view.

But healing is transcendent light,

That shines through every darkest night.

So as we cure, remember still,

That healing moves beyond the will.

It touches the soul and spirit deep,

And helps the heart in peace to keep.

The Philosophical and Ethical Implications of Verb Valency in Curing and Healing

The distinction in valency between "curing" and "healing" also reveals underlying philosophical and ethical considerations. In medical practice, focusing solely on curing can sometimes lead to a reductionist view of patients, where they are seen primarily as biological entities in need of repair. This narrow focus can neglect the broader aspects of their humanity—such as their emotional and psychological needs, their social connections, and their spiritual well-being.

Healing, with its broader valency, aligns more closely with a holistic approach to care. It acknowledges that patients are not just bodies to be fixed but individuals with complex needs that extend beyond the physical. Healing requires attention to the person as a whole, addressing their suffering in all its forms. This is especially relevant in fields like palliative care, where curing may no longer be possible, but healing in the form of comfort, dignity, and peace remains paramount.

To conclude, the valency of the verbs "cure" and "heal" reflects their different roles in medicine and care. Curing, with its narrower valency, focuses on the removal of disease and often involves a direct, measurable outcome. Healing, on the other hand, has a broader valency that encompasses the whole person, addressing physical, emotional, psychological, and spiritual dimensions.

Understanding these distinctions is crucial for medical practitioners and caregivers alike. While curing is an essential aspect of medicine, healing reminds us of the need to care for the person behind the disease. The broader valency of "healing" challenges us to consider how we can support patients not just in their bodies but in their entire being, fostering a deeper sense of well-being that transcends the limitations of medicine alone.

Curing Versus Healing

Curing is a transitive touch,

A focused skill, precise and such.

It bends the body back to form,

And fights the tides of flesh-born storm.

It's something we can grasp and do,

A verb with action, swift and true.

Curing seeks the wound, the pain,

To cleanse the blood and clear the stain.

Yet healing, softer, moves within,
A journey where the soul begins.
It has no object, force, or speed.
But meets us in our deepest need.

For curing tendons, bones, and skin,
But healing speaks to what's within.
A quiet balm, unseen, it flows,
Where only spirit truly knows.

Curing binds what eyes can see,
But healing sets the spirit free.
It doesn't aim to fix or mend,
But gently helps the heart to bend.

In curing, we take up the fight,
With hands that labour in the light.
In healing, we release control.
And trust the process of the soul.

So let us care where care can be,

But honour heals mystery.

For body, mind, and spirit blend,

In ways that only time can mend.

4

Years at St John's Medical College Bangalore Entry 1989 - Fly by Wire, Die by Fire - The Crash of an A-320 Airplane

---

This ominous phrase dominated the headlines of leading Indian newspapers on February 15th, 1990, serving as a grim reminder of the flaws that had emerged in the "fly-by-wire" technology. On the morning of February 14th, 1990, while I was attending to patients in the Plastic Surgery outpatient department at St. John's Medical College in Bangalore, I received alarming news: an Indian Airlines Boeing A320 had crashed. The medical college hospital, known for its expertise in trauma and burns management, was being prepared to receive victims of the air disaster.

It was a ghastly, gory gruesome, grisly sight - all my senses were benumbed and assaulted - seeing the cruel red fire, the billowing black smoke, the dalliance of metal and mortar, hearing the cries and screams, and the stench of burning flesh - a Boeing Aircraft broken into two like a child's toy - 'Man after all is a mortal coil' (Hamlet - Shakespeare) "As flies to wanton boys are we to the gods;- they kill us for sport" (King Lear by William Shakespeare. Gloucester says this line while wandering on the heath after being blinded by Cornwall and Regan) We could only assist in triage and become team leaders and cheer leaders!

Around 90 passengers perished in the crash, and those who were fortunate enough to survive and make it to the hospital, located less than ten kilometres away, had sustained severe burns, inhalation injuries, and multiple traumas. Tragically, many of these patients later succumbed to their injuries. Among them were members of an Indian family from London, who were eventually evacuated by a Swiss ambulance aircraft flown in specifically for the purpose. As I helped transfer the family from St. John's Medical College Hospital to the aircraft, I caught my first glimpse of the inside of a sleek, sophisticated flying ambulance. Despite the limited first aid and resuscitation facilities we had in Bangalore, I found some solace in knowing that we had done our best to assist in transporting this family back to London, where they belonged.

Sadly, the story did not have a happy ending. The family arrived alive in the UK, but when I followed up with my friends there, I learned that the eight-year-old girl I had so desperately wanted to save had died a few weeks later after spending a week on life support in London. Her pale face and hands, cold as metal, remain etched in my memory. When I touched her with my warm hands, she looked at me and smiled—a moment that lingers with me to this day.

Later, I came to understand that "fly-by-wire" refers to an electrically controlled signalling system. In essence, it is a computer-configured control system in which a computer is placed between the pilot and the aircraft's final actuators or surfaces. This system modifies and adjusts the pilot's manual inputs in accordance with the existing flight and landing parameters.

The Double Whammy

In a tragic twist of fate, our resource-strapped firefighters, with no fire drills and standard operating procedures lacking regular training and drills, inadvertently worsened the situation for the inhalation-injured passengers. Their high-powered water jets, intended to extinguish and douse the flames, further compromised the already fragile respiratory systems of the survivors. The result was an added insult to injury—death by drowning, instead of being saved.

What is Fly-by-Wire?

The evolution of aviation has been a remarkable journey from the simple mechanics of early planes to the highly sophisticated systems of modern aircraft. One of the most significant advancements in recent years has been the introduction of "fly-by-wire" technology. Fly-by-wire replaces traditional manual flight controls with electronic systems, offering greater precision, safety, and efficiency. However, as with all technological progress, there are inherent risks. The phrase "Fly-by-Wire, Die by Fire" captures both the marvel and the peril of relying on cutting-edge technology to defy gravity and traverse the skies.

The Revolution of Fly-by-Wire

Fly-by-wire technology has revolutionised modern aviation. In traditional aircraft, pilots controlled the plane's movements through a series of mechanical linkages—cables, pulleys, and rods. Fly-by-wire eliminates this complex, heavy system and replaces it with digital signals. When a pilot moves the joystick or rudder pedals, their commands are converted into electronic signals sent to the aircraft's control surfaces. These signals are processed by computers, which then determine the most efficient and safe way to execute the pilot's intentions. The computers also adjust for factors like wind speed, turbulence, and engine performance, allowing for smoother and safer flights.

This system has numerous advantages. It reduces the weight of the aircraft, improves fuel efficiency, and enhances manoeuvrability. It also introduces a level of precision that human reflexes alone could never achieve. For instance, fly-by-wire systems can make hundreds of adjustments per second, reacting to changes in the environment far faster than any pilot could. This increased precision is critical in high-stress situations, such as avoiding mid-air collisions or responding to sudden turbulence.

Fly-by-wire technology also introduces redundancy and safety features that were previously impossible. Multiple backup systems ensure that if one part of the system fails, others can take over, maintaining control of the aircraft. This redundancy has made modern aviation safer than ever before. Today, air travel is one of the safest modes of transportation, largely thanks to innovations like fly-by-wire.

The accident investigation revealed that the pilots inadvertently selected the wrong mode on the flight control system during the final approach. Instead of choosing the correct landing mode, they set the aircraft to "open descent mode" at a low altitude, which caused the engines to idle and reduced the plane's thrust. This led to a rapid descent that went unnoticed until it was too late to recover. The aircraft hit the ground short of the runway, breaking apart and catching fire.

Out of the 146 passengers and crew on board, 92 people died in the crash. The investigation emphasised issues with the pilots' familiarity with the A320's advanced flight control systems, as this model was relatively new to Indian Airlines at the time. This accident highlighted the importance of proper training on new aircraft technology and its integration into real-world operations.

The Indian Airlines Flight 605 crash on February 14, 1990, in Bangalore was caused primarily by pilot error during the landing approach. The Airbus A320, flying from Mumbai to Bangalore, was attempting to land at the old HAL Airport in Bangalore when it crashed on approach, about 2.5 kilometres short of the runway.

Fly-by-Wire, Die by Fire

(The A320 Crash, Bangalore, February 14th 1990)

In the hush of a dawning sky, it soared.

A bird of metal dreams on board.

Fly-by-wire, a marvel to trust,

Technology guiding, as we humans must.

Through clouds, it sliced with a silent hum,

Passengers bound for what's to come.

The future tethered to electric thread,

Hearts unwary, no thought of dread.

But fate, like a flame that flickers and shifts,

Broke through the veil of electronic gifts.

A descent too fast, a trust misplaced,

Error's hands in the cockpit traced.

The earth below did not forgive.

The field of death, where few would live.

Fire by air, fire by ground,

Twisted wreckage, no solace found.

Over ninety souls in flames did fly,

Dreams extinguished beneath that sky.

Bangalore wept, its air turned cold.

As the flight of progress took its toll.

Fly-by-wire, an elegant dream,

But in that moment, a lethal scheme.

For in our quest to master the air,

We must remember the risks we bear.

Technology failed, humanity cried,

In that fateful crash, where so many died.

A reminder etched in fire and flight,

That with each advance, we walk a thin line.

5

Industrial Hand Trauma and the Limits of Curing Without Healing: Reflections from St. John's Medical College, Bangalore

During my five years at St. John's Medical College, Bangalore, I was consumed by the complexities of industrial hand trauma, tendon injuries resulting from assault, burns, and maxillofacial trauma. This work was relentless, occupying my mind and hands around the clock. I was not just a surgeon but a restorer of function, a mender of bodies shattered by accidents or malevolent intent. My days were filled with intricate surgeries—repairing severed tendons, grafting skin on burns, and reconstructing faces after devastating trauma. Amid these urgent tasks, I also addressed scar revisions, congenital anomalies, and body sculpting, catering to both Indian and European patients seeking to regain some semblance of normalcy or enhance their appearances. The precision required in each procedure was immense, and I poured myself into every case, determined to achieve the best possible outcome.

The continuous flow of crushed hand injuries necessitated that I needed to team up with an orthopaedic colleague, and we published a landmark 'mini external fixator for phalangeal fractures' to restore the pincer grip, thumb to index, which could take care of most activities of daily living (ADL).

Yet, as I look back and ponder the countless hours spent in the operating room, stitching together torn bodies and damaged lives, it was not the surgical victories that defined my experience. Rather, it was the unsettling realisation that despite my ability to cure physical injuries, I could not always heal the emotional wounds that lay beneath. The watershed moments were not the technical successes of perfectly sutured tendons or meticulously reconstructed faces but rather the disturbing undercurrents of unresolved anger and desire for revenge that lingered in my patients' hearts.

One case in particular still haunts me—a young man whose tendons had been sliced in an assault. I meticulously sutured them, restored the function of his hand, and watched with satisfaction as he regained movement and strength. By all accounts, he was "cured." Yet, beneath the surface, there was no peace. He seethed with rage, consumed by thoughts of retribution against his assailant. He had regained the use of his hand, but his spirit remained wounded, driven by an insatiable thirst for revenge. My surgical success felt hollow in the face of this reality.

This experience became a turning point in my practice. I began to see that, while I could mend the body, true healing required more than physical restoration. The young man's venomous desire for reprisal became a stark reminder that the body and mind are intricately connected and that my role as a healer extended beyond the confines of the operating room. The aphorism, "An eye for an eye makes the whole world blind," echoed in my thoughts, and I realised that my work was being undone by forces far beyond my control.

From that day forward, I made it a point to counsel my patients, particularly those who had suffered trauma from assault. I carved out time to speak with them, not just as their surgeon but as someone who understood the complex interplay between physical injury and emotional pain. I sought to help them find a path to healing that went beyond their sutured tendons or reconstructed faces—a path that might prevent the cycle of violence from continuing. These conversations were often challenging, but they were essential. I began to see that true healing, the kind that mends both body and soul, required more than a surgeon's skill; it demanded empathy, patience, and a willingness to engage with the deeper wounds that lie beneath the surface.

In those five years at St. John's, I became not just a plastic surgeon but a witness to the human condition in its rawest form. The operating room was my domain, but the real work often began after the surgery was done. My time in Bangalore taught me that while curing is essential, healing is far more complex and elusive. It requires us to look beyond the immediate injury and address the underlying pain, fear, and anger that so often accompany trauma. Only then can we truly make a difference in the lives of those we serve.

Hands of Ruin, Hands of Hope

A moment's slip, a grinding fall,

The hand once strong, now shattered, small.

Bones like glass, they break apart.

Tendons torn from strength and art.

The fingers bent in a silent cry,

Soft tissues crushed; the nerves run dry.

No gentle grip, no steady hold,

The hand, a story dark and cold.

Yet deep within, a will remains,
To rise beyond the crushing pains.
Surgeon's tools, so sharp and fine,
Begin their work, a fragile line.

Pins and plates, with sutures threaded,
Knitting life where hope once bled.
Tendons grafted, nerves re-sewn,
In careful hands, new strength is grown.

But healing's not just flesh and bone,
It's in the mind, where fear is sown.
The hand remembers every tear.
The sudden loss, the deep despair.

Yet slowly, softly, life returns,
With every stretch, the spirit learns.
Through scars and pain, the hand revives,
A fragile flame that still survives.

Though bones were crushed, and flesh was torn,

The hand, once ruined, is reborn.

Its power lies not just in might,

But in the will that sparks the fight.

For even when the fingers fail,

And strength is but a distant tale,

The hand that heals, with time and grace,

Can touch the world and find its place

6

Treating Burns in Adults and Children: A Lifelong Struggle for Survival and Healing

---

My time in St.John's Medical College Hospital was a parenthetical period in my career treating maxillofacial trauma, hand injuries, and burns. Treating burn injuries, whether in adults or children, is a complex and prolonged medical challenge that involves not just the medical team but also the patient's family and society. Burns range from minor first-degree burns to life-threatening third-degree burns that can compromise major organ functions, especially when large areas of skin are involved. This is where the expertise of plastic surgeons becomes pivotal. The initial goal is survival—keeping the patient alive despite the trauma inflicted on the body. However, the road to recovery is fraught with physical, emotional, and financial struggles that can be overwhelming for both the patient and their loved ones.

The Immediate Battle: Survival

The first task when treating severe burns is ensuring that the patient survives the acute phase. Burns that cover more than 20% of the body surface area (BSA) can be fatal without prompt and aggressive treatment. The skin, the body's largest organ, acts as a protective barrier against infection and helps regulate body temperature and fluid balance. When this barrier is compromised, the risk of infection, dehydration, and hypothermia becomes life-threatening.

Patients with major burns often require intensive care, with continuous monitoring and interventions to stabilise their condition. Fluid resuscitation, typically guided by formulas like the Parkland formula, is critical in the early hours post-injury to prevent hypovolemic shock. Alongside this, managing the airway and breathing becomes crucial, particularly in cases of inhalation injury, which can lead to respiratory distress. Pain management is another critical component, as burns are among the most painful injuries a person can endure.

Patients admitted to Burns Wards necessitated an atmosphere with less microbial contamination; therefore, I did a study on 'Ionised Air in Burns Management – A Preliminary Report'. This found encouraging results, as bacterial counts from three levels - the wall, tabletop, and floor - before and after switching on the ioniser came down, as did infection rates[2].

I never bothered to patent it. However, our study has been xeroxed for marketing the so-called air purifiers for chambers of CEOs, Five-Star Hotels, and recently on Amazon for Homes and Car Interiors, and of course the ubiquitous celebrities and politicians as a necklace of honour to be shielded from microbes - post-COVID.

The Mammoth Struggle: Skin Grafting and Reconstruction

Once the patient survives the initial phase, the focus shifts to wound management and reconstruction, often involving skin grafting. This is where the long and agonising struggle truly begins. Burns can leave extensive raw areas that require skin grafting to promote healing and reduce the risk of infection. The process of skin grafting itself can be complex and fraught with challenges. Surgeons need to determine the best donor site, ensure that the graft will "take" (i.e., successfully adhere and integrate with the recipient site), and manage any complications that may arise, such as graft rejection or infection.

For the patient and their family, this period is one of immense emotional and physical pain. Repeated surgeries, dressing changes, and the constant battle against infection take a toll on the patient's strength and resilience. Families are drained, both emotionally and financially, as they watch their loved ones endure this suffering. The financial burden of burn treatment can be staggering, especially in countries where healthcare costs are largely out-of-pocket. Intensive care, multiple surgeries, prolonged hospital stays, and rehabilitation are all expensive, and many families find themselves selling assets, taking loans, or falling into poverty to afford the necessary care.

The Social Dimension: Acid Burns and Suicidal Attempts Beyond accidental burns, there are cases of burns caused by deliberate acts of violence, which add a tragic dimension to this already devastating condition. Acid attacks, often perpetrated by jilted lovers or business rivals, represent one of the most reprehensible forms of violence. The intent behind these attacks is not just to harm but to permanently disfigure and scar the victim, often a woman. Acid burns, particularly on the face, cause irreversible damage to the skin, eyes, and underlying tissues. Victims face a lifetime of surgeries, reconstructive procedures, and psychological trauma. The impact on their self-esteem, social life, and ability to earn a living can be devastating.

Similarly, burns resulting from suicide attempts, particularly by women facing marital harassment or dowry-related issues, highlight deep societal problems. Despite legal reforms and social campaigns, dowry-related violence continues to plague many parts of the world. Women who feel trapped in abusive marriages, with no other escape, may resort to self-immolation as a desperate plea for relief. These burns are often extensive, and even if the woman survives, she is left with debilitating scars—both physical and emotional.

The treatment of burns, whether accidental or deliberate, requires more than just medical intervention. It calls for a holistic approach that addresses the physical, emotional, and financial burdens placed on the patient and their family. Burn survivors need access to long-term rehabilitation, psychological support, and, in many cases, social reintegration programmes. Efforts to prevent deliberate burns, such as acid attacks and suicide attempts, must focus on changing societal attitudes, strengthening legal protections, and providing support systems for vulnerable individuals.

Burn treatment is not just a medical challenge—it is a societal one. The scars left by burns are not only skin-deep; they run deep into the fabric of families and communities. By addressing the root causes of burn injuries and improving access to comprehensive care, we can begin to heal these wounds, both visible and invisible.

A Burning Issue

The flame ignites, a moment's curse,

Turning life from calm to worse.

In seconds, flesh meets fire's embrace,

And the long road starts—an endless race.

A journey paved in pain and tears,

Where healing spans the slowest years.

Treatment begins with broken skin,

Layers of hope wrapped deep within.

Grafts and dressings, hands that mend,

But the toll exacts, without an end.

Each procedure is a costly toll,

Draining body, spirit, soul.

Resources thin as the wounds grow wide,

Doctors fight to turn the tide.

Yet for every battle fought and won,

Another scar, another one.

Death sometimes comes, silent, swift.

But deformity lingers, a lifelong gift.

The mirrors reflect a different face,

A twisted form that time won't erase.

Limbs contract, hands lose grace,

But in their hearts, a steady pace—

For those who heal must find their way,

In bodies changed, but souls that stay.

Families strain with funds and care,

The cost is too great, the load unfair.

Hospitals filled with cries and pleas,

A burning issue no one sees.

For the fight goes on, year by year,

With each victory measured in silent tears.

Yet through it all, they persevere.

Scarred but alive, conquering fear.

For though the flames may steal their skin,

They cannot burn the will within.

A story of survival told,

Where hope outweighs the pain of gold.

In every graft, in every scar,

A life restored, though changed by far.

And while the wounds may heal in time,

The cost of burns, a heavy climb.

7

The Contrast of Reconstructive Surgery: Cleft Lip and Palate Repair

Speech, Sucking, Swallowing are essential to existence. In contrast to elective cosmetic procedures, reconstructive surgeries such as cleft lip and palate repairs serve a profoundly different purpose. Cleft lip and palate are among the most common congenital deformities, affecting one in every 700 live births. These conditions can severely impact a child's ability to eat, speak, and breathe, and they often lead to social stigmatisation and emotional distress. For the families of these children, the prospect of surgery offers hope for a better future.

As a plastic surgeon, I have witnessed first-hand the transformative power of cleft repair surgery. The procedure not only restores function but also helps children integrate more comfortably into society, reducing the stigma they might otherwise face. For parents, the surgery is a beacon of hope—a chance for their child to lead a more normal life, free from the challenges posed by a visible deformity.

The gratitude and relief expressed by parents following a successful cleft repair are profoundly moving. Unlike elective cosmetic surgeries, where patients may seek perfection or enhancements, cleft repair surgery is about restoration and empowerment. It is about giving children the chance to smile, to speak clearly, and to be seen for who they truly are rather than being defined by a congenital deformity. The joy on a parent's face when they see their child's repaired lip for the first time is one of the most rewarding experiences a surgeon can have.

While body-sculpting surgeries may dominate the headlines, reconstructive surgeries like cleft lip and palate repairs remind us of the true essence of plastic surgery: to restore, to heal, and to improve the quality of life. These procedures underscore the vital role that plastic surgeons play in helping individuals overcome physical challenges and lead healthier, more fulfilling lives.

As plastic surgeons, we must always balance the demands of aesthetic enhancements with the ethical responsibilities of our profession. While cosmetic procedures have their place, they should not be pursued recklessly or for superficial reasons alone. Surgeons must take the time to educate patients, manage their expectations, and ensure that they are making informed decisions.

The contrast between body-sculpting surgeries and reconstructive surgeries like cleft repairs highlights the dual nature of plastic surgery: one that can cater to desires for beauty, but also one that can profoundly impact lives by restoring function and dignity. Ultimately, the true value of plastic surgery lies not in its ability to sculpt appearances, but in its capacity to heal, empower, and uplift those who need it most.

Healers of Form and Function: The Plastic Surgeons' Gift

In the realm of medicine, where miracles are spun,

Plastic surgeons work under the sun.

With skilled hands and hearts full of care,

They mend what was marred, to make it fair.

For those denied form at the start of life's race,
Or deprived by fate, they offer grace.
From birth's misfortune to accidents' plight,
They bring back hope with precision and light.

Their tools are gentle, their vision keen,
To restore what was lost, unseen yet serene.
In the theatre of healing, they stand tall,
Repairing form and function for all.

A cleft lip mended, a scar erased,
With each delicate stitch, a life is embraced.
Burns and wounds, no longer just scars,
Under their care, transformed into stars.

They craft new beginnings with every repair,
Turning despair into dreams with utmost care.
In their hands, a canvas of flesh and bone,
Becomes a testament to skills finely honed.

For every child who smiles anew,

For every life they change, both old and few,

Plastic surgeons, silent heroes, rise,

Bringing beauty and function back to eyes.

With dedication deep and artistry rare,

They sculpt with love, beyond compare.

In the journey of healing, they play a part,

Mending bodies and uplifting hearts

8

The Lethal Mix: Pub Culture, Two-Wheelers, and Hormonal Rush Among Bangalore's Youth in Late 1980s and 1990s Bangalore

The 1980s to 1990s in Bangalore marked the beginning of a cultural transformation, especially among the youth. With the rapid rise of pub culture, a surge in the availability of two-wheelers, and a potent hormonal rush fuelled by newfound freedom, students and young professionals began to embrace a lifestyle that was exciting yet dangerously reckless. This period was defined by a heady cocktail of adrenaline, a mix of 'Love Hormones' and alcohol, speed, and a carefree attitude toward life, leading to a spike in road accidents and injuries.

As a plastic surgeon working in this environment, my tryst with facial LeFort fractures, or nasal and zygomatic, mandibular fractures became an unforgettable chapter in my career. These complex fractures, which often resulted from high-velocity accidents involving two-wheelers, required a unique blend of skill and serendipity to treat. The consequences of this youthful recklessness were not just broken bones – they were shattered lives[3].

The Rise of Pub Culture and Two-Wheeler Mania

In the early nineties, Bangalore began to shed its quiet, laid-back image, transforming into a vibrant city buzzing with energy and opportunity.

The rise of pub culture played a significant role in this transformation. Pubs and bars sprang up on Brigade Road, MG Road, and Koramangala, becoming popular hangouts for the city's young crowd. Students, particularly from the city's many colleges and universities, flocked to these establishments, eager to experience the freedom that came with youth and independence.

At the same time, the roads of Bangalore were becoming increasingly congested with two-wheelers. Affordable bikes like the Hero Honda, Ind Suzuki, Rajdoot Yamaha, and Kawasaki Bajaj became a rite of passage for young men and women, symbolising freedom and status. With a bike between their legs and a pub at the end of their journey, many young people felt invincible. However, this sense of invincibility often led to risky behaviours, such as riding under the influence of alcohol, overspeeding, and disregarding traffic rules.

The combination of pub culture and two-wheelers created a lethal mix. It was a time when a pitcher of beer cost a mere ₹50 and came with free French fries, making it accessible even to students with limited means. The intoxicating mix of alcohol and testosterone (or its female equivalents) often led to poor decision-making. Riding a bike at night after a few drinks became an all-too-common occurrence, with the consequences ranging from minor scrapes to fatal crashes.

The Hormonal Rush: Reckless Freedom and Its Aftermath

The hormonal rush of youth played a significant role in driving this reckless behaviour. Adolescence and early adulthood are times of heightened emotions, impulsivity, and a desire to push boundaries. The surge of hormones like adrenaline, dopamine, and testosterone or its female equivalent drove young people to seek out thrills and test their limits. The combination of alcohol, speed, and the heady feeling of freedom created a dangerous environment where caution was often thrown to the wind.

Unfortunately, the price of this recklessness was often paid in blood and broken bones. Hospitals in Bangalore saw a surge in accident cases, many of which involved students and young professionals who had fallen victim to their own impulsive decisions. Head injuries, fractures, and trauma cases became routine for emergency departments across the city.

As a plastic surgeon, I was often called upon to treat the aftermath of these accidents, particularly when they involved facial injuries. The high-velocity impact of a bike crash often led to LeFort fractures—serious facial fractures that affect the midface, including the cheekbones, nose, and upper jaw. These fractures are named after the French surgeon René LeFort, who classified them into three types based on the severity and location of the fracture.

Operating on LeFort Fractures, Zygomatic, and Nasal or Mandibular Fractures: An Exercise in Skill and Serendipity

Treating LeFort fractures or other facial bone fractures is a complex and delicate task, requiring both surgical skill and a touch of serendipity. These fractures involve multiple bones in the face and can result in significant disfigurement if not treated properly. The challenge lies in restoring both the function and appearance of the face, the dental occlusion, vision, and ensuring that the bones heal in their correct positions and that the patient regains normal facial symmetry.

In many cases, treating these fractures required a combination of open reduction and internal fixation, using plates and screws to hold the bones in place. The delicate nature of the facial bones meant that even a slight misalignment could lead to long-term complications, including chronic pain, difficulty chewing, and breathing problems. Precision was key, as was an intimate understanding of facial anatomy.

However, despite the best efforts of surgeons, the outcome of these surgeries often depended on factors beyond our control. The extent of the injury, the timing of the surgery, and the patient's overall health all played a role in determining the final result. This is where serendipity came into play—sometimes, despite our best efforts, the outcome was influenced by luck or unforeseen variables.

One of the most challenging aspects of treating LeFort fractures was dealing with the psychological impact on the patients. Many of these young people had been vibrant and full of life before their accidents, and now they were faced with the reality of a long and painful recovery. The disfigurement caused by facial fractures can be devastating, particularly for individuals in their prime years, when appearance and self-image are so closely tied to identity. Helping these patients heal emotionally was just as important as addressing their physical injuries.

Lessons from a Reckless Era: The lethal mix of pub culture, two-wheelers, and the hormonal rush of youth in 1990s Bangalore left a trail of devastation that was felt not just in hospitals but also in homes and families across the city. The reckless pursuit of freedom and thrills came at a high cost, with many young lives altered forever.

As a surgeon who treated the victims of this era, I learned that even the best surgical skills cannot always guarantee a perfect outcome. Serendipity often played a role in the healing process, reminding me that medicine is as much an art as it is a science. Yet, despite the challenges, every successful surgery—every restored face—was a testament to the resilience of the human spirit.

Today, Bangalore continues to evolve, but the lessons of the 1990s remain relevant. The allure of speed, freedom, and excitement still drives young people to take risks. As a society, we must find ways to balance this desire for adventure with a responsibility for safety and well-being. Only then can we prevent another generation from paying the price for reckless freedom.

When the upper and lower dentition are wired together, the mouth can't be closed for a period of four weeks, more if Arch Bars are used; less if plates and screws are used. Feeding is through a liquidised diet taken through the sides of the teeth, but no swimming or sodas! The fizz comes through the nose. Swimming is not recommended for obvious reasons.

Dance of Love Hormones

In the twilight of dawn, where dreams gently sway,

Whispers of love begin their ballet.

Oxytocin, the cuddle's warm embrace,

Weaves bonds of hearts in a tender space.

Dopamine, the spark in a lover's glance,

Ignites joy's flame, setting hearts to dance.

With each touch and glance, it spirals high,

Painting the world with a jubilant sky.

Serotonin, the calm in love's sweet song,

Steady as the day where lovers belong.

Its rhythm soothes, like a lullaby,

Bringing peace to souls as moments pass by.

Endorphins, the bliss in a shared laugh,

Easing the path, cutting worries in half.

With each smile, they lift the heart's weight.

Making every moment feel just right, not late.

In this symphony of hormones, love finds its way.

A timeless dance in night and day.

Together, they craft a tale so sweet.

In every heartbeat, in every meet.

So, here's to the hormones, love's invisible art,

Painting emotions on the canvas of the heart.

In their dance, we find our story.

A love unending, in all its glory.

Fractured Facial Bones

A sudden crash, a forceful blow,

The fragile bones give way below.

The face once whole, a map of grace,

Now bears the marks of time and place.

Fractures carve their jagged lines,

Across the cheek, the jaw confines.

The brow, the nose, the orbital wall,

Each splintered crack tells of the fall.

The LeFort lines, like rivers, flow,

Through broken planes, that pain will show.

Yet underneath the swelling's mask,

The healing waits, its steady task.

With surgeon's hands, the bones align,

Piece by piece, they intertwine.

Titanium plates, a steady guide,

Restore the face where breaks divide.

But more than bone and bruised skin,

The spirit feels the fracture's spin.

A mirror shows the outer scars,

But hides the deeper battle scars.

Still, time will mend what pain has torn,

And faces cracked will be reborn.

For strength lies not in bone alone,

But in the soul, that's never shown.

Through broken lines, a beauty stays,

In healing's quiet, gentle ways.

And though the fractures fade from sight,

The journey speaks of endless fight.

9

"We Cannot Make Scars Disappear, But We Can Revise Scars and Hide Them"

Every outpatient day at St. John's Medical College Hospital, Bangalore, we had patients come for scar revision at seen and unseen areas of a patient's anatomy! Scars are a reminder of the body's capacity for healing. They are the physical marks left behind after the skin has been damaged and subsequently repaired. Yet, despite the healing process, scars can be a source of psychological distress for many people. Whether they result from surgery, injury, or disease, scars often serve as unwelcome reminders of trauma. Plastic surgery, particularly scar revision, offers a way to diminish the appearance of scars. However, it's important to recognise that while we can revise scars and camouflage them, we cannot make them completely disappear.

Tattoo excision was another challenge as primary excision and closure would not be possible in certain cases, and therefore, we had to either opt for split skin graft, local skin flaps, or tissue expander, which was becoming popular.

The Nature of Scars: To understand the limitations of scar revision, we must first understand the nature of scars themselves. When the skin is injured, the body produces collagen to repair the damage. The new collagen fibres do not replicate the original tissue perfectly; instead, they create a structure that is different from the surrounding skin. This difference is what forms a scar. The type of scar that develops depends on several factors, including the depth and size of the wound, the location on the body, the individual's genetics, and how the wound was treated.

While scars are a natural part of the healing process, they can have profound impacts on a person's self-esteem and quality of life. For some, scars are seen as disfigurements, prompting feelings of embarrassment or self-consciousness. Others may associate scars with painful memories, making it difficult to move on from certain events. The desire to erase these marks is understandable, yet complete scar removal is beyond the realm of current medical possibilities.

The Goal of Scar Revision: Scar revision is a surgical procedure aimed at improving the appearance of scars. It is important to set realistic expectations with patients: the goal is not to make the scar vanish but to revise it in such a way that it becomes less noticeable. The term "revision" reflects the process of revisiting and refining the scar, much like editing a draft to improve its readability, without erasing the original text entirely.

Plastic surgeons employ a variety of techniques to revise scars, depending on the type and location of the scar. These techniques include excision, where the scar tissue is surgically removed and the wound is closed with fine sutures; dermabrasion, which smooths the scarred skin; and laser therapy, which can reduce redness and flatten raised scars. Each of these methods can significantly improve the appearance of a scar, but none can restore the skin to its original state.

We revise and make scars to fall into the lines of facial expression, and dermabrasion of the face in badly scarred post-pimple cases. Smallpox scars are passé.

Hiding Scars: Strategic Camouflage :In many cases, scar revision is as much about camouflage as it is about revision. Plastic surgeons often work to reposition or reshape a scar so that it becomes less visible. For example, scars can be repositioned along natural skin creases or lines, making them blend in with the body's contours. In some cases, the direction of the scar can be changed to align with these natural lines, or it can be hidden in less noticeable areas such as hairlines or folds in the skin. The skill of the surgeon lies not only in their technical ability but in their artistic vision for how to blend a scar into its surroundings.

Another aspect of hiding scars involves managing the colour contrast between the scar and the surrounding skin. Techniques such as laser therapy or steroid injections can reduce the colour difference, helping the scar to blend more seamlessly with the adjacent skin. Additionally, some scars may be treated with pigmentation treatments to even out skin tone.

The Emotional and Psychological Impact: While the physical benefits of scar revision are clear, the emotional and psychological impacts are equally important. For many patients, reducing the visibility of a scar can lead to a significant boost in self-confidence and overall well-being. It can provide a sense of closure, allowing individuals to move beyond their past experiences and focus on the future.

However, it is essential for patients to understand that scar revision is not a miracle cure. It is a procedure that can improve appearance but not completely erase the past. Therefore, patient education and counselling are crucial parts of the process. By setting realistic expectations and emphasising the goal of improvement rather than perfection, surgeons can help patients achieve satisfaction with the outcome.

Scar revision is a powerful tool in the hands of a skilled plastic surgeon. Through various techniques, scars can be revised, reshaped, and hidden to blend more naturally with the surrounding skin. However, it is important to recognise that scars, as a result of the body's healing process, cannot be made to disappear completely. The role of the surgeon is to refine and revise, to camouflage and conceal, but not to erase. Understanding this balance between medical possibility and patient expectation is key to successful outcomes in scar revision surgery. In the end, while we cannot make scars vanish, we can transform them into something less burdensome, allowing individuals to move forward with renewed confidence. Scarred emotions need a healing touch in the figurative and physical sense.

Physical Scars and Emotional Scars – Revisiting and Remembering Them No More

We cannot make the scars disappear,

Though we may wish them gone,

Etched deep in skin, they whisper clearly.

Of battles fought and won.

But still, with steady hands, we guide,

With sutures fine and skill,

We pull the edges close, aligned,

To soften what they will.

We lead the lines through creases, fold.

Them into nature's grace,

Let scars be hidden, smooth and bold,

To blend upon the face.

For though they stay, we shape their tale,
Revising what's been torn,
Not to erase, but to unveil.
A healing once forlorn.

Scars upon the skin remain,
A trace of pain and strife,
But in our hands, they shift, they change,
A softer mark on life.

"With Z and W Plasty's art,"
We turn the rigid line,
We break the form, reshape the part,
And let it realign.

The scar won't vanish, disappear.
But woven with such care,
It hides within the folds, unclear.
As if it's barely there.

Through cuts and sutures deftly placed,

The eye no longer sees,

The remnants of what once were faced.

Are cloaked in subtleties.

10

Body-Sculpting Surgery: Beyond the Surface of Perfection

In today's image-conscious world, body-sculpting surgeries such as liposuction, rhinoplasty, and other cosmetic procedures have become increasingly popular. Often driven by societal pressures, personal insecurities, or the allure of "perfect" appearances, individuals turn to plastic surgeons in hopes of transforming their bodies and lives. While these procedures can offer immense satisfaction when done correctly, they are often overrated, with the consequences sometimes being disastrous.

In stark contrast to these elective cosmetic surgeries, there are reconstructive procedures like cleft lip and palate repairs that serve as a lifeline to individuals born with congenital deformities. These procedures don't just change appearances—they change lives. As a plastic surgeon who has encountered both sides of the spectrum, I can empathise deeply with the unfortunate children and parents who seek out cleft repairs. Their stories remind us of the true essence of plastic surgery, which is often lost in the glamorisation of aesthetic enhancements.

The Allure and Risks of Body-Sculpting Surgery: Body-sculpting surgery, which includes liposuction, tummy tucks, breast augmentations, and buttock lifts, has seen a surge in demand over the past few decades. Social media, celebrity culture, and the relentless pursuit of the "ideal" body have fuelled this trend. People seek these procedures to enhance their appearance, boost their self-esteem, or conform to certain beauty standards. Liposuction, for example, is often marketed as a quick fix for stubborn fat deposits that diet and exercise alone cannot eliminate.

However, the reality of body-sculpting surgery is far more complex than the glossy advertisements suggest. Liposuction, while effective in removing fat, carries risks such as infections, blood clots, contour irregularities, and even death in extreme cases. What is often-overlooked is that liposuction is not a weight-loss surgery, nor is it a substitute for a healthy lifestyle. When performed irresponsibly or excessively, the results can be uneven or unnatural, leaving patients dissatisfied or, worse, with permanent deformities.

Similarly, rhinoplasty, or nose reshaping surgery, is one of the most popular cosmetic procedures globally. It promises to refine one's facial features, creating a more harmonious appearance. Yet, it is also one of the most challenging surgeries in plastic surgery, requiring precision, artistry, and an understanding of facial anatomy. A poorly executed rhinoplasty can lead to functional issues like difficulty breathing, as well as aesthetic problems that are difficult to correct. Revision surgeries, which are more complex and riskier, may be necessary to fix the mistakes of an initial operation.

The consequences of poorly performed body-sculpting surgeries can be disastrous, leaving patients with physical and psychological scars. While some may see these procedures as a path to happiness and confidence, the reality is that they carry significant risks that should not be ignored. Patients should be fully informed of these risks, and surgeons should emphasise the importance of realistic expectations. Cosmetic surgery is not a panacea for all of life's problems, and it should be approached with caution and respect for the body's limitations.

Sculpting the Shell: The Body is Merely the Shell of My Soul - John Denver – in Eagles and Horses – First Told by Plato

We carve the flesh, we shape the form,

With scalpel's edge or Botox needle's norm,

To tighten skin, to lift, reduce.

As youth's illusion we produce.

A tummy tucked, a breast reborn,

A face uplifted, newly worn—

But in this dance with sharpened steel,

The risks are real, the wounds can heal...

Yet time, that patient artist, still,

Will have its way, despite the will.

For every line, each wrinkle's grace,

Is etched with wisdom on the face.

To age, not fight, but walk the years,

Embrace the change, release the fears.

For beauty blooms, not forced by art,

But in the rhythm of the heart.

Why chase the clock, or strive to freeze?

When peace is found in nature's ease?

Let age bestow its quiet charm,

Unsculpted, soft, without alarm.

11

Operating on Celebrities: Stress, Secrecy, Skill, Serendipity, and Scalpel Solace

Operating on a celebrity brings with it a unique blend of emotions and pressures. As a surgeon, the operating room is your domain, a place where precision, skill, and calm are paramount. But when the person lying under the knife is a high-profile celebrity, the dynamics shift dramatically. The convergence of media attention, patient privacy, heightened expectations, and personal reputation can weigh heavily on the surgeon's shoulders. At the core of this experience are five defining elements: stress, secrecy, skill, serendipity, and the solace a surgeon finds in the scalpel.

The Weight of Stress: Stress is an inherent part of any surgical procedure, but the presence of a celebrity patient amplifies it manifold. The stakes are higher because of the public's obsession with famous personalities. Any outcome, whether success or failure, is scrutinised on a much larger stage. A surgeon must contend with the knowledge that a slip of the scalpel, a minor complication, or even an unexpected delay could lead to widespread media coverage, potentially harming their reputation and the celebrity's carefully crafted public image.

The pressure to be perfect in such cases is immense. Even in the most controlled of surgical environments, unpredictability is a given. The surgeon must grapple not only with their own anxiety but also with the emotional state of the patient, who may be more vulnerable than usual due to the heightened sense of privacy and personal investment in the procedure's outcome. The celebrity's concern with their physical appearance or bodily function, especially for those in the entertainment industry, further intensifies the stress. The burden of ensuring a flawless result becomes a mental tightrope walk for the surgeon.

Secrecy as a Sacred Oath: Operating on a celebrity demands a high degree of secrecy, often surpassing the standard expectations of doctor-patient confidentiality. Celebrities' personal and medical information is highly valuable, and any breach of privacy can result in public scandal, lawsuits, and a permanent loss of trust. The operating team, from nurses to anaesthesiologists, must be thoroughly briefed on maintaining discretion, and hospitals often enforce stricter security measures to prevent leaks.

This requirement for secrecy goes beyond protecting the patient's dignity; it also includes shielding the details of their physical vulnerabilities, which could tarnish their public persona. In the age of social media, even the smallest rumour can spiral out of control. Surgeons must not only manage the technical aspects of the procedure but also the logistical challenge of keeping it under wraps. This can mean anonymous entries into operating theatres, confidentiality agreements, or even scheduling surgeries during off-hours to avoid public attention.

For the surgeon, secrecy becomes a second job, an invisible but ever-present aspect of their work. It requires a fine balance between transparency with the patient and absolute discretion in their communication with the outside world.

The Mastery of Skill: Despite the heightened stress and secrecy, the core of the experience remains what it always has been: skill. A surgeon's competence is their most reliable asset, especially when operating on someone of public significance. Whether it is reconstructive surgery, cosmetic enhancement, or a life-saving procedure, the surgeon's expertise must shine through. In the end, the scalpel does not care about fame—it demands the same precision and knowledge as with any other patient.

For many surgeons, their most defining trait is their ability to focus under pressure, compartmentalising external distractions in order to focus on the task at hand. The procedures themselves may not differ in technical complexity from those performed on other patients, but the psychological pressure means that a high level of mastery is required.

Surgeons must rely on years of training, experience, and confidence in their abilities to manage this pressure. When the spotlight is on, only expertise and skill can guide the hand holding the scalpel.

Serendipity: The Unpredictable Element: In surgery, no matter how carefully planned or meticulously executed, serendipity—or luck—can play a role. Human anatomy, despite the best imaging and diagnostic tools, can hold surprises. The unexpected can arise at any point during a procedure. When operating on a celebrity, these surprises carry greater consequences. A minor complication that would ordinarily be routine may become significant because of the patient's status and the increased scrutiny that follows them.

Serendipity also works in more fortunate ways. An unexpected ease in a procedure, a well-timed discovery of a hidden issue, or a body that responds better than anticipated can turn a potentially difficult surgery into a success. These moments of unexpected fortune remind the surgeon of the complex interplay between skill and chance in the operating room.

For surgeons working with celebrities, acknowledging serendipity helps manage expectations—both theirs and the patient's. It serves as a reminder that even in the most controlled environments, outcomes can be influenced by forces outside their control.

Scalpel Solace: The Sanctuary of Surgery: Despite the overwhelming external pressures of operating on a celebrity, the scalpel remains the ultimate source of solace. For the surgeon, it is the tool through which they exert control, precision, and healing. The act of surgery itself can be deeply meditative, a return to the fundamentals of medicine. The focus required during surgery offers a mental escape from the pressures of fame, media, and expectation.

When a surgeon is in the zone, the celebrity status of the patient fades away, leaving behind only the immediate goal: to repair, heal, or enhance. The sterile environment of the operating theatre becomes a sanctuary from the external noise. It is here, with the scalpel in hand, that the surgeon finds peace and purpose, free from distractions and grounded in the craft they have honed over years.

This solace is perhaps the most important coping mechanism for surgeons handling high-profile cases. It serves as a reminder that, at its heart, surgery is a deeply personal, human interaction. Fame and fortune cannot alter the fundamental need for compassion, care, and healing. The surgeon's connection with the patient—celebrity or not—is ultimately what drives them to do their best.

Operating on celebrities is a unique experience that combines heightened stress, the necessity of secrecy, the demand for unparalleled skill, the unpredictability of serendipity, and the solace found in the surgeon's craft. The celebrity status of a patient does not change the fundamental dynamics of surgery, but it adds layers of complexity that test the surgeon's ability to remain calm, focused, and discreet. Through it all, the surgeon must rely on their years of experience, trusting that their skill with the scalpel can bridge the gap between the patient's expectations and the unpredictable nature of surgery.

In the end, operating on a celebrity is not just about technical proficiency; it is a balancing act that requires mastering the human aspects of care—empathy, confidentiality, and unwavering focus. It is in this delicate equilibrium that the surgeon finds both the challenge and the fulfilment of their craft.

Celebrities Surrender to be Sculpted, Surgeons Stress to Succeed

Sculpted and beneath the lights, the world is still.

A famous face, yet human, still.

The weight of names, the press, the crowd,

Yet here, in silence, none are loud.

The scalpel gleams, the cut is precise,

The stakes are high, yet skill sufficed.

No fame, no gold, can ease the strain,

But steady hands, they know the game.

In whispers move, in shadows creep,

The secrets that we vow to keep.

The world may pry, the cameras seek,

But in this room, our lips stay meek.

Serendipity, a hidden guide,

In twists of fate, the heart abides.

What we expect, what we don't see,

The dance of chance, the mystery.

Stress like thunder in the air,

Yet calm descends with every prayer.

For in the craft, the mind is free,

A surgeon's peace, serenity.

The world outside may rage and roar,

But here within, there's something more.

The scalpel cuts, the truth is clear—

It's not their fame, but care we bear

12

My Entry into Regional Cancer Centre, 1995: Triumphing in Promotions, Outwitting Ersatz

Bureaucrats and Unholy Trinities

My entry into the Regional Cancer Centre (RCC) as an Assistant Professor was a defining moment in my career, one marked by resilience, preparation, and an unwavering faith in my abilities. It wasn't just about demonstrating my worth as a surgeon; it was about standing tall before a panel, where one particular member—a pseudo-bureaucrat with delusions of grandeur and a health secretary to boot—was determined to trip me up with obscure questions. His goal was clear: to catch me off guard, score some intellectual brownie points, and put me in a position of discomfort. But he underestimated me. In the end, it was my preparation, general knowledge, and presence of mind that secured my entry into this hallowed institution, while his misguided attempts to thwart me only added to my sense of triumph.

The panel interview had already been a rigorous exercise, but the pivotal moment came when this particular individual, clearly relishing the opportunity, posed a question meant to stump me. With a smug look, he asked, "Can you name the Nobel Laureate in Surgery?" It was a question he raked up from his midnight oil-burning sessions, no doubt, something he believed would prove beyond my knowledge. He was hoping I would falter, giving him the satisfaction of scoring a brownie point. His plan, however, backfired spectacularly.

Without missing a beat, I replied, "Alexis Carrel, the Frenchman, for his pioneering work in vascular surgery." I could see the disappointment flash across his face as I continued, "And before him, Theodore Kocher, the Swiss surgeon, for his groundbreaking work on the thyroid." His disturbed expression was unmistakable. 'I asked you to name only one,' was this guy's reply— he hadn't expected me to know, let alone deliver such a precise answer. The room seemed to shift as I outshone the rest of the candidates, not just with this answer, but with a calm confidence that carried me through the entire process.

That moment was a turning point, and I knew I had secured my place. This paper pusher of a

bureaucrat was a mercenary who delayed the result, and later was informed that I had been selected as an Assistant Professor. It was not just a professional achievement—it felt like a personal victory over those who underestimated me. I had stepped into the hallowed halls of the Regional Cancer Centre, a trusted destination for cancer detection, treatment, palliative care, and research. This state-of-the-art institution was not only a place of healing but also a place where innovation and excellence were expected, and I had proven that I belonged.

Yet, this was just the beginning. Over the next twenty-five years, I dedicated myself to my work, combining my skills as a plastic surgeon in post-ablative reconstructive surgery and surgical oncology.

With a deep commitment to the field of cancer treatment, it was years later that I shifted laterally to become Head of Palliative Medicine, overseeing Oral Morphine production and involved in training in Palliative Care as State, National, and International Faculty once on a UN assignment. My journey was not without its challenges, and as time passed, I once again found myself at the mercy of internal politics. When the time came for my promotion to Professor in Palliative Medicine, I faced a new set of adversaries—an unholy trinity consisting of my institution's Director, a Radiation Oncologist, his rumoured sidekick, the Director of an Institute next to ours, an Anaesthetist, and a third whom I can only describe as the Illegitimate Papa of Palliative Care. Yes, for sure, they were the unholy trinity of the Devil, the false prophet, and the anti-Christ!

These men, driven by their own agendas, made repeated attempts to block my promotion, much as that bureaucrat had tried to derail my entry years before. Three times, they tried to nip my progress in the bud, failed me thrice attempting to stifle my surge in the institution and beyond. Their actions were petty and driven by personal insecurities, but what they did not realise was that, just like before, I was not alone in this battle. God was in control, guiding me through every challenge, ensuring that their efforts would ultimately be in vain. Through an RTI query (Right to Information), I was perplexed how these accidental warts on the faces of their respective institutions could conclude in twenty minutes of a dumb charade, as it was written that 'Dr. Cherian Koshy doesn't have the attitude, aptitude and compassion or commitment to be in Palliative Medicine'. Looking back, I realise that my journey into the RCC and my rise within its ranks were never just about me. They were about perseverance, preparation, and faith in a higher plan. From that initial interview where I outshone the ersatz bureaucrat to the years of hard work that followed, I always believed that no obstacle could stand in the way of true merit. My adversaries could gossip, manipulate and throw every roadblock in my path, but they couldn't change the fact that my work spoke for itself.

In the end, I thwarted their attempts, and my promotion came not because of them, but despite them. I had earned my place, and nothing they did could take that away. If anything, their attempts to hinder.

My progress only served to highlight the pettiness and insecurity that governed their actions, while I continued to focus on what mattered—my patients, my research, and the mission of the RCC. Entering the RCC as an Assistant Professor was one of the proudest moments of my life, not because of the title or position, but because of what it represented. It was a triumph over small-mindedness, over the pseudo-intellectual games of men who tried to assert power where they had none. It was a reminder that preparation, knowledge, and faith in oneself can outshine any attempt to undermine your worth.

Ten years later, following when I faced the unholy trinity who tried to block my promotion, this time as Professor of Palliative Medicine and failed thrice, I drew strength from that initial victory, knowing that I had faced worse before and emerged victorious. God was in control then, as He was now, and in the end, justice prevailed. My journey in the RCC is not just a story of professional achievement; it is a testament to resilience, faith, and the ultimate triumph of merit over mediocrity, good over evil.

In hindsight, I laugh when dhoti-clad, non-matriculate Public Service Commission Members, or ersatz bureaucrats, Institution Directors, or Experts with their flawed diction, pathetic vocabulary, retarded accent, grammar, and articulation, whose fodder was their shenanigans and schadenfreude - all of whose resume could be written on the reverse of a postage stamp - are wallowing in oblivion, not even being a footnote in history. I am putting pen to paper, organising my thoughts into print, remembering the power of forgiveness which I practice 24/7! God is great!

'You can stop the onslaught of an army, but not an idea or a concept whose time had come' – Victor Hugo. Immodestly speaking, maybe I was an idea!

But Knowledge, to their eyes, her ample page.

Rich with the spoils of time did ne›er unroll;

Elegy Written in a Country Churchyard – Thomas Gray (26 December 1716 – 30 July 1771)

'Bureau-crazy'

In lofty rooms where papers pile,

The bureaucrat sits, removed by miles,

Of ink and stamps, and rules entwined,

A world of forms, devoid of mind.

Each document is a rigid task,

Each box to tick, a hollow mask

Of what unfolds beyond the door:

A patient waiting, frail and sore.

The doctor stands with trembling hands,

Where human pain meets healing plans;

Not paper stacks, but beating hearts,

Not memos filed, but vital parts.

For every form that must be signed,

A patient's breath, a fragile mind,

Awaits the care, the tender word,

A touch of hope, a life deferred.

Yet one writes laws, while one writes lives,

Through endless codes, bureaucracy thrives,

But healing needs no ink nor seal,

Just hands that know, and hearts that feel.

So let the paper mountains fall,

For patients' cries outweigh them all,

No bureaucrat can truly see

The depth of human frailty.

In every room where lives are saved,

The doctor knows the price is grave;

No signature can heal the heart,

No paper plays the healer's part.

Where Excellence is Evil, and Accomplishment Anathema

In a land where brilliance dares not shine,

Where merit's light is deemed malign,

Excellence wears a cloak of shame,

And whispers tremble at its name.

Accomplishment, once proud and bold,
Is cast aside, left in the cold,
For here, ambition turns to dust,
And toil is met with muted distrust.

The tallest tree, the brightest flame,
Is struck down low, denied its claim,
For in this place of shadowed halls,
The fear of greatness builds the walls.

Where small minds reign and envy feeds,
On every noble thought and deed,
They chain the hands that craft and build,
And mute the voice of dreams fulfilled.

Yet still, the heart that knows its worth,
Will rise again from the spiteful earth,
For though they scorn what's pure and true,
Excellence will break through the blue.

Life's Transverse Wave

Life is a wave, moving to and fro,
With crests of joy and troughs of woe,
In moments high, we touch the skies,
In moments low, the spirit sighs.

The crests bring light, a radiant glow,
Where laughter and love freely flow,
But in the troughs, when shadows fall,
We learn to rise, to stand tall.

For every wave that pulls us deep,
There's a rise again, a promise to keep,
Through highs and lows, we learn to be brave,
Riding the rhythm of life's transverse wave.

13

Cancer – A Cell Going Berserk, A Rogue Cell's Mischief

Cancer is a disease that begins when a single cell in the body mutates and begins to grow uncontrollably. This rogue cell can proliferate, evade normal regulatory mechanisms, and form tumours that can spread to other parts of the body through a process called metastasis. The alarming aspect of cancer is its ability to affect any part of the body, from the skin to the lungs, bones, brain, or blood. These cancerous cells arise when mutations occur in genes responsible for regulating cell growth and repair, and such changes can be triggered by various factors like environmental toxins, radiation, genetics, or lifestyle choices.

Despite the complexity and aggressiveness of cancer, the good news is that significant advances in medical science offer hope. The tools we have today allow us to combat cancer effectively, often leading to complete cures or long-term disease-free periods while maintaining a good quality of life for many patients.

The Tools at Our Disposal

1. Surgery: For many localised cancers, surgery is the primary curative option. The goal is to remove the tumour and affected tissues before cancer spreads. Advancements in surgical techniques, such as minimally invasive and robotic surgeries, have improved outcomes while reducing recovery time and complications.

2. Radiation Therapy: Radiation uses high-energy waves to kill or damage cancer cells, targeting tumours with precision. Innovations like intensity-modulated radiation therapy (IMRT) allow for better targeting of cancer cells while sparing healthy tissues, thus reducing side effects.

3. Chemotherapy: Chemotherapy involves using powerful drugs to kill rapidly dividing cells, which include cancer cells. While it has side effects due to its effect on healthy cells, modern regimens and supportive care have made chemotherapy more tolerable for patients.

4. Immunotherapy: One of the most promising developments in cancer treatment, immunotherapy works by harnessing the body's own immune system to recognise and attack cancer cells. Drugs like checkpoint inhibitors and CAR T-cell therapy have revolutionised the treatment of certain cancers, especially in advanced stages.

5. Targeted Therapy: Unlike chemotherapy, which can affect both healthy and cancerous cells, targeted therapy focuses specifically on the genetic and molecular changes that drive cancer growth. These treatments are more precise, often leading to fewer side effects.

6. Hormonal Therapy: For cancers like breast and prostate cancer, which are driven by hormonal signals, drugs that block or modify hormone production can effectively control the disease.

7. Advances in Early Detection: The earlier cancer is detected, the more treatable it is. Screening programmes such as mammography, colonoscopy, and HPV testing have contributed to earlier detection and, consequently, better survival rates. Genetic testing can also identify high-risk individuals, enabling preventive measures.

8. Supportive and Palliative Care: Beyond curing cancer, modern medicine focuses on ensuring quality of life for patients. Palliative care addresses symptoms like pain, fatigue, and emotional distress,

helping patients maintain dignity throughout treatment and beyond.

A Holistic Approach to Cancer Treatment

While these medical tools are essential, cancer care is increasingly becoming a multidisciplinary effort. Patients benefit from coordinated care involving oncologists, surgeons, radiologists, pathologists, and other specialists, all working together to tailor treatments to individual needs. This personalised approach not only increases the chances of a cure but also focuses on minimising the impact of treatment on the patient's overall well-being.

The integration of psychological support, nutrition, and rehabilitation services ensures that patients are not only surviving cancer but thriving beyond it. Recovery is about more than just being disease-free; it's about returning to a life of meaning and purpose, where physical and emotional health are prioritised.

Though cancer can start from something as simple as a single cell going berserk, modern medicine offers a powerful arsenal to fight this disease. Complete cures are increasingly achievable, and even in cases where a cure is not possible, many patients can enjoy extended, high-quality lives. As research continues, we may move even closer to a future where cancer is not a scourge but a manageable condition, with hope for all.

14

Tobacco-Related Cancers and the Impact of Surrogate Advertising by Wills - 'Misusing Celebrity Cricketers'

Tobacco-Related Cancers - Portents for the Future, © Health For the Millions, Cherian Koshy, Rachel Cherian Koshy, Sept-Oct 1998, pp. 18-19 Vile, Vicious, Vapid – the Tobacco Smokescreen, Cherian Koshy, Rachel Cherian Koshy, © Kerala Medical Journal Vol. 40, No. 2, pp. 26-29

'For over thirty years and at altitudes of over thirty thousand feet, we were held hostage to second-hand smoke and subjected to pulmonary rape' - This was the opening statement of a previous Chief of Cabin crew who had worked for several International Airlines and is now leading an anti-tobacco campaign worldwide. I felt mesmerised by the play of words with its profound scientific content. For decades on end, smoking was permitted inflight and as this towering personality of a lady stunned the participants at the World Cancer Congress in Washington DC, 2006, which I had the privilege to attend as a special invitee of the American Cancer Society. I had a great feeling shaking hands with celebrities that included the inimitable late Larry King Jr with his baritone voice and trousers with shoulder straps and online interacting with Mary Patricia McAleese, President of Ireland (November 1997- November 2007).

Tobacco remains one of the leading causes of preventable deaths worldwide, and its association with cancer is well-documented. Tobacco-related cancers, particularly lung cancer, head, and neck cancers, and oral cancers account for millions of deaths annually. In India, this crisis is exacerbated by the aggressive marketing strategies employed by tobacco companies, often through surrogate advertisements, and the resulting public health consequences, have been devastating. One such example is Wills, a brand by ITC, which sponsored Indian celebrity cricketers, using their influence to promote smoking subtly, a practice that has since had dire consequences on Indian youth.

Every hour, more than sixty-five patients die in India from tobacco-related cancers, diseases, and pain.

Tobacco-Related Cancers: The Burden of Disease

Tobacco consumption is linked to multiple types of cancer, with lung cancer being the most prevalent. Other cancers associated with tobacco use include those of the mouth, throat, oesophagus, and bladder, pancreas, and stomach. In India, tobacco is consumed in various forms—cigarettes, bidis, and smokeless tobacco, all of which contribute to an enormous health burden. Lung cancer alone is responsible for thousands of deaths each year, cancers of the oral cavity are also particularly high in India, due to the widespread use of smokeless tobacco and betel quid.

Tobacco-related cancers not only affect individuals' physical health but also have a ripple effect on their families and society at large. Treatment costs, loss of productivity, and emotional suffering add to the overall burden on families and healthcare systems.

Surrogate Advertising: The Role of Wills and Cricketer Sponsorship

In the past, Wills, a popular cigarette brand in India, became notorious for its clever use of surrogate advertising. By sponsoring celebrity Indian cricketers, including some of the most iconic sports figures in the country, Wills skirted around advertising restrictions for tobacco products. The celebrity cricketers wore branded merchandise, and major cricket tournaments were titled "Wills Trophy", allowing the brand to enter homes and minds without explicitly promoting smoking.

This form of indirect promotion normalised smoking among young audiences who idolised these cricketers. Smoking became associated with success, masculinity, and sportsmanship, indirectly encouraging young people to take up the habit. The brand association with cricket—India's most beloved sport—created a false image of tobacco consumption being linked to national pride and athletic achievement.

The Devastating Impact on Youth

One of the most tragic aspects of this type of advertising was its impact on school children – in metros. Many youngsters, motivated by the allure of celebrity endorsements and wanting to emulate their cricketing heroes, took up smoking. Tobacco companies were indirectly recruiting a new generation of smokers through this surrogate advertising, and the consequences became evident over time. Cigarette sales countrywide skyrocketed in most Indian cities. Fifteen years after these aggressive marketing campaigns, an NGO followed up on thousands of schoolchildren. The results were heartbreaking. A significant number of those who had been influenced by these campaigns, they had developed chronic lung diseases, such as Chronic Obstructive Pulmonary Disease (COPD), which is often caused by long-term smoking. Some have progressed to more serious illnesses like lung cancer, and others faced early mortality or incapacitation due to smoking-related diseases.

Many of these individuals had never been able to rise in life, both due to their health challenges and the social stigma attached to tobacco-related illnesses. Instead of thriving, these young people, once full of potential, they were held back by the very habit they had innocently been drawn into. The use of cricketers as endorsers had a particularly insidious effect, as these celebrities represented aspirations, hope and success for the youth further blur the dangers of smoking.

Public Health Response and the Need for Stronger Regulations

Although significant strides have been made in controlling tobacco advertising in India, the damage done by earlier campaigns like those by Wills cannot be undone. Public health initiatives now focus on education, awareness, and anti-tobacco campaigns to counter the decades of misleading advertisements. India has implemented The Cigarettes and Other Tobacco Products Act (COTPA) to curb tobacco consumption, but the legacy of such surrogate advertising still looms large.

More robust regulations are required to close loopholes that allow surrogate advertising to thrive. In addition, cricketing bodies and other sports associations must reject tobacco sponsorships entirely and promote healthier, life-affirming brands to prevent future generations from being lured into smoking.

A Need for Accountability

The role of celebrity endorsements in promoting harmful behaviours, like smoking or online rummy must be recognised and addressed. The use of cricketers to indirectly marketing cigarettes to impressionable young people was not only unethical but also resulted in long- term harm to the health of thousands. Today, palliative care teams are witnessing the consequences of these campaigns in the form of lung cancer, COPD, and other tobacco-related diseases. The human cost of these unethical advertising strategies cannot be overstated. And many online gaming apps may be banned, and woe unto you celebrities if you indulge in promotions!

As a society, there is a moral responsibility to protect the youth from harmful influences, particularly those disguised under the banner of sportsmanship and national pride. Tobacco-related cancers can be prevented, and it starts with eliminating all forms of tobacco promotion, ensuring that future generations are not misled into addiction and disease.

It is time to prioritise health over profit and ensure that no more lives are lost to the subtle allure of surrogate tobacco advertisements.

The carcinogen nicotine in tobacco is named after Jean Nicot, French Ambassador to Portugal,

(1559–1571) who popularised it in France, Europe, and their colonies.

A Fool and His Fire

"A cigarette," Shaw said with wit

Is fire and fool, that's the gist of it,

With paper and tobacco tight,

It burns away both health and light.

The hazards come with every puff,

A deadly game, it's never enough,

Disastrous fumes, lungs take their toll,

As fire consumes both breath and soul.

The body coughs; the spirit wanes;

Yet still the fool ignites the flames

For what? A moment's fleeting peace,

While life and strength begin to cease.

The fire burns until none remain,

Leaving death, disaster, and bitter stains,

So, heed the words; let wisdom speak,

For in that smoke, the future's bleak.

15

Social Media Gossip on Cancer Aetiology and the Wellness Cult, Merchants of Misinformation: A Modern Day Hazard

In the age of social media, information is readily accessible, often democratised, and at times, dangerously misleading. Nowhere is this more concerning than in the realm of cancer aetiology—where the origins and causes of cancer are distorted by myths, pseudoscience, and wellness propaganda. Unfortunately, misinformation often masquerades as truth, with influencers, self-proclaimed health gurus, and various online personalities spreading unverified or blatantly false claims. These claims are frequently couched in appealing narratives, such as "living healthy" or following a natural lifestyle, which, more often than not, amount to little more than pseudoscience. Far from enlightening the public, these discourses fuel confusion and create cult-like followings, misdirecting people away from legitimate medical advice.

The Pervasiveness of Misinformation

Social media platforms like Facebook, Instagram, YouTube, and TikTok have become hotbeds for false claims about cancer's causes, prevention, and treatment. While these platforms can be powerful tools for spreading awareness, they have also enabled a parallel rise in pseudoscientific content. The algorithms that govern these platforms prioritise content that garners engagement—meaning, sensational or fear-based posts tend to gain more visibility. Misinformation about cancer aetiology, whether in the form of miracle cures or simplistic explanations about diet and lifestyle changes, thrives in such an environment.

For instance, there are widespread claims that specific diets, like alkaline diets, can "cure" or "prevent" cancer by altering the body's pH levels. This is scientifically baseless, yet it continues to be promoted widely by so-called wellness influencers. Similarly, myths that certain everyday products, like deodorants, microwave ovens, or non-organic foods, are primary causes of cancer have permeated public discourse. These unverified claims are often stated with an air of authority, obscuring the reality that cancer is a complex, multifactorial disease whose causes range from genetic predispositions to environmental factors and lifestyle choices—but not in the simplistic manner these influencers suggest.

The Cult of Wellness

Much of the misinformation about cancer aetiology on social media is spread under the guise of the "wellness" movement. While wellness in itself is not inherently problematic, it has been co-opted by influencers and marketers who commodify health as a product. The result is a cult-like following where the principles of evidence-based medicine are sidelined in favour of vague, unproven, and sometimes dangerous recommendations. These promoters of "natural living" often sell supplements, detox kits, or personalised health regimes with promises that they can prevent or even cure cancer.

Wellness influencers often equate "natural" with "good," implying that medical treatments like chemotherapy or radiation are toxic or harmful, whereas natural remedies are benign and healing. This false dichotomy oversimplifies the reality of cancer treatment, where the benefits and risks of any intervention must be carefully weighed. The very notion that a disease as complex as cancer can be prevented or treated with juice cleanses, yoga, or essential oils is a dangerous form of denialism that can lead to people foregoing life-saving medical treatments.

The Warning Signs of Pseudoscience

The discourse surrounding cancer aetiology on social media is more of a warning than an example of how public health information should be shared. First, it is dispassionate, lacking the critical empathy and understanding required to deal with the intricacies of such a life-threatening illness. Promoters of pseudoscience are often more focused on self-promotion and financial gain than on truly educating or helping individuals who are suffering. They present a misleadingly simplistic and often monetised version of healthcare, which preys on the vulnerable.

Second, pseudoscience thrives on the illusion of authority. It uses scientific jargon out of context to give credence to false claims. Terms like "toxins," "immune boosters," or "cell regeneration" are frequently thrown around without any real scientific basis. This form of discourse creates a dangerous veneer of credibility that can mislead those unfamiliar with legitimate scientific studies. The fact that these influencers operate without oversight allows them to make bold claims that have little or no grounding in real science.

The Need for Critical Discouragement

There is a growing recognition that social media platforms need to take responsibility for the spread of misinformation about cancer and other health-related issues. The sheer volume of pseudoscientific content makes it critical that such information is actively discouraged. Educational campaigns that teach people how to discern credible sources from false ones, along with stricter regulations around health misinformation, are essential.

The public must also be encouraged to approach cancer information with a critical eye. If a piece of advice sounds too good to be true—like a miracle cure or a simple lifestyle change that promises to prevent cancer—it likely is. Reliable information on cancer aetiology comes from peer-reviewed research, trusted healthcare organisations, and expert clinicians, not from influencers or wellness bloggers.

It's crucial to emphasise that cancer is a multifaceted disease, influenced by genetic, environmental, and behavioural factors. Scientific understanding of cancer is constantly evolving, and credible sources will acknowledge this complexity. In contrast, pseudoscience offers simplistic, black-and-white answers that may appeal to our desire for easy solutions but ultimately mislead and harm.

Social media can be a double-edged sword when it comes to public health information. While it has the power to disseminate useful and life-saving knowledge, it also amplifies pseudoscience and misinformation. When it comes to cancer aetiology, the rise of wellness influencers and misinformation peddlers is more of a warning than a healthy example. The allure of simple solutions and natural cures may attract large followings, but they often do more harm than good by diverting people from evidence-based medical advice. It is vital to discourage the spread of such information and promote critical thinking, helping individuals seek out scientifically validated knowledge about cancer. Social media, while influential, must not become a breeding ground for false hope and dangerous misinformation.

16

Cancer Surgery: An Unrelenting Battlefield

Cancer surgery stands as one of the most demanding fields in medicine. No part of the anatomy is spared from the ravages of this unforgiving disease, which manifests not only as physical affliction but also as a complex web of psychological, social, and emotional impacts on both patients and caregivers. The task of a cancer surgeon is formidable. Unlike most surgical fields where tissue preservation is often a primary goal, cancer surgery calls for a merciless and uncompromising approach to tumour excision. The surgeon cannot afford the luxury of leaving behind any malignant cells, for even the smallest remnant can signal a resurgence of the disease. This requirement for wide, clear margins results in significant tissue loss, which must be addressed through reconstructive techniques—thus, the role of a cancer surgeon merges with that of a reconstructive artist.

In head and neck surgery, for instance, the removal of tumours often necessitates the excision of vital structures, leaving disfiguring gaps in places central to identity, speech, and basic function. Similarly, in breast cancer surgery, the surgeon must sometimes be ruthless in the removal of breast tissue to ensure complete tumour resection. Yet, the implications of such extensive surgeries extend far beyond the operating table. Patients are left grappling with deformity, disability, and a lingering sense of decay. Society, often unforgiving in its reaction to physical disfigurement, can further isolate these individuals, leaving them feeling disenfranchised and detached from their previous lives.

Reconstruction in such scenarios often involves complex procedures such as osteomyocutaneous, or myocutaneous, skin flaps, or free flaps. These reconstructive methods are designed to restore some semblance of normalcy, but the road to recovery remains arduous. Surgeons must be meticulous in planning and executing these flaps to ensure that blood supply is adequate and that the tissues integrate well with the remaining anatomy.

In visceral malignancies, the situation is equally grim. For instance, colorectal cancers may necessitate a colostomy, while bladder cancers might require a urinary diversion. These diversion procedures impose a lifetime of adjustments for patients, altering their daily routines, self-image, and interactions with others. The psychological burden of living with a permanent stoma, for example, can be immense, adding another layer of suffering to the physical pain and exhaustion of battling cancer.

For the surgeon, the challenges are not only technical but also deeply emotional. The weight of responsibility is immense. Every decision made in the operating room has far-reaching consequences for the patient's quality of life. Surgeons are often as stressed as the patients and their families, their minds besieged by uncertainties about outcomes, potential complications, and the adequacy of tumour resection. The fear of recurrence haunts both patient and surgeon alike, an ever-present shadow that lingers long after the initial surgery is over.

The relationship between the surgeon and the patient is also unique. It is one of intense dependency and trust. The patient places their life in the surgeon's hands, hoping for the best but aware of the profound uncertainties that lie ahead. The surgeon, in turn, must navigate these expectations while balancing the clinical realities of cancer surgery. This bond is forged in the crucible of shared vulnerability, where both parties are acutely aware of the stakes involved.

Tumour boards exist in major Tertiary Care Cancer Centres, involving surgeons, radiation oncologists, and medical oncologists. Risk versus reward, benefit versus burden are considered for a consensus and discussed with the family.

Cancer surgery, therefore, is not just a battle against a biological enemy but a struggle against the multifaceted impact of the disease. The deformity, disability, and social isolation it brings are just as challenging as the tumour itself. And while the surgeon can excise cancerous tissue, they cannot always remove the emotional scars left behind. In this relentless field, success is often measured in survival, but survival alone does not always equate to victory. The true challenge is in restoring a sense of wholeness to patients, both physically and emotionally, as they navigate life after cancer.

Breast Cancer Globally: Early Detection and Treatment Options

Breast cancer is the most common cancer among women worldwide, with more than 2.3 million cases diagnosed annually. As the incidence of breast cancer continues to rise globally, early detection and effective treatment options remain critical to improving outcomes and survival rates. Although advances in medical technology and awareness have made early diagnosis more common in many regions, significant disparities exist in access to both detection and treatment.

Early Detection: A Key to Survival

Early detection of breast cancer dramatically increases the chances of successful treatment and long-term survival. Methods of early detection include:

Mammography: This remains the gold standard for early detection, allowing doctors to identify abnormalities in the breast tissue before symptoms appear. Regular mammography screenings have been shown to reduce breast cancer mortality by detecting cancer at earlier, more treatable stages. In high-income countries, mammography is widely available, but access is limited in low- and middle-income countries.

Clinical Breast Exams and Self-Examination: While mammography is crucial, clinical breast exams and breast self-examinations also play important roles in detection, especially in regions where screening programmes are not widely available. Education about self-examination empowers women to recognise early signs of cancer and seek medical attention promptly.

Ultrasound and MRI: For women with dense breast tissue or at high risk of breast cancer, ultrasound and magnetic resonance imaging (MRI) are used alongside mammography to provide a more detailed view of breast tissue and detect tumours that might not be visible on mammograms.

Global Disparities in Early Detection

While early detection is a powerful tool, significant disparities exist between high-income and low-income countries. In high-income countries like the United States, Canada, and those in Europe, routine screening programmes are common, and women are diagnosed at earlier stages, improving their chances of survival. In contrast, women in low- and middle-income countries often face late-stage diagnoses due to limited access to healthcare, lack of awareness, and social stigmas surrounding breast cancer. As a result, mortality rates in these regions are higher despite lower incidence rates.

Treatment Options for Breast Cancer

Breast cancer treatment has evolved considerably, offering a range of options depending on the stage and type of cancer. The main treatment modalities include:

Surgery: Surgery is often the first line of treatment for breast cancer. It includes lumpectomy (removal of the tumour and a small margin of surrounding tissue) or mastectomy (removal of the entire breast). Sentinel lymph node biopsy is often performed to determine if cancer has spread to the lymph nodes.

Radiation Therapy: After surgery, radiation therapy is commonly used to kill any remaining cancer cells in the breast, chest wall, or lymph nodes. This treatment reduces the risk of recurrence, especially after a lumpectomy.

Chemotherapy: Chemotherapy, the use of drugs to destroy cancer cells, is often recommended for more advanced stages or aggressive forms of breast cancer. It can be used before surgery (neoadjuvant chemotherapy) to shrink tumours or after surgery (adjuvant chemotherapy) to eliminate any remaining cancer cells.

Hormonal Therapy: For hormone receptor-positive breast cancer, drugs that block oestrogen or progesterone (such as tamoxifen or aromatase inhibitors) can be effective in preventing cancer recurrence. Hormonal therapy is often prescribed for several years after surgery.

Targeted Therapy: Targeted drugs, such as trastuzumab (Herceptin) for HER2-positive breast cancer, specifically attack cancer cells with certain characteristics, sparing healthy cells. This form of therapy has revolutionised treatment for specific breast cancer subtypes and reduced the side effects typically associated with chemotherapy.

Immunotherapy: A newer treatment option, immunotherapy boosts the body's immune system to fight cancer. It is used primarily for patients with advanced or metastatic breast cancer, showing promise in improving survival rates.

Challenges and the Way Forward

While significant strides have been made in breast cancer treatment and early detection, challenges remain. In many developing countries, access to screening and treatment is limited by economic, infrastructural, and educational barriers. The cost of advanced treatments, such as targeted therapy and immunotherapy, can be prohibitive, leaving many patients in low-income regions without access to life-saving care.

To address these challenges, there is a need for greater global collaboration to increase awareness, expand access to screening programmes, and ensure that effective treatments are affordable and widely available. Public health campaigns emphasising early detection, combined with efforts to make advanced treatments more accessible, will be crucial in reducing the global burden of breast cancer.

Breast cancer remains a significant global health challenge, but early detection and a broad range of treatment options offer hope for better outcomes. While high-income countries have made remarkable progress in survival rates, the focus must now shift to ensuring that women in low- and middle-income countries have the same access to early detection and effective treatments. Through a combination of education, policy changes, and international cooperation, breast cancer outcomes can be improved worldwide.

Breast Cancer in Rhyme

Breast Cancer in Rhyme, Cherian M. Koshy, © Kerala Medical Journal, Vol. 38, No. 2, p. 27

Additional Professor, Surgical Oncology,

Regional Cancer Centre.

(Written while sipping iced lemon tea at Honolulu Airport Departure Lounge, awaiting flight.)

Disclaimer: Twenty years old – Treatment modalities have changed

It is any woman's fear,

That an organ to her and lover so dear,

Be afflicted by such a disease,

Making all ill at ease.

From hormones to heredity, as ethologists claim,

Even high calories, a factor they blame,

But incidence remains much the same.

This fact, so distressing to any dame.

Sometimes so unrelenting is its scourge,

Nevertheless, to combat the physician's urge,

Disease-free period is the result,

To a patient's cancerous insult.

"A disease of the breast," so we believed,

But later, it was revealed.

That breast cancer is a systemic disease, not so kind,

Hence, different treatment modalities combined.

Staging, at best, is a management guide.
And also, an indicator for prognosis beside;
Shouldn't there be a parameter for emotional state?
Otherwise, where do feelings relate to her fate?

Surgery still helps in loco-regional control.
Lumpectomy, mastectomy, modified, or conservation, same the goal.
Axilla may be sampled, axilla may be dissected.
Thus, lymph node status detected.

Radiotherapy, a must where the choice is right,
Although surgeons underestimate its might,
As physicians, it should be our fight,
To make our patients' future bright.

Chemotherapy benefits premenopausal women with a positive node.
And those 'inoperable,' an initial load.
Hormone manipulation has similar to offer.
Where discussions are open and decisions are proper.

To pathologists, breast cancer may be 'invasive' or 'non-invasive.'

But sure, it is the nightmare of every 'Eve'.

Screening permits early detection.

And hence, better patient selection.

Sentinel node biopsy, the trend,

To patient and surgeon, its value is lent.

Its concept is godsent.

Creating in our understanding a dent!

Breast cancer scars a woman's image.

This is what I've been able to gauge.

To my patients, past, present, and future,

I dedicate these lines to His nurture!

Thyroid Cancers

Thyroid cancers are a diverse group of malignancies, each with distinct characteristics and prognoses. Among them, Papillary Thyroid Carcinoma (PTC) stands out as the most common and, fortunately, one of the least aggressive. Representing approximately 80% of all thyroid cancers, PTC is often described as having a "good prognosis," a statement that, in the world of oncology, is a profound relief for both doctors and patients alike.

Papillary thyroid cancer arises from the follicular cells of the thyroid, and its hallmark feature is the presence of papillary structures in its pathology. The tumour typically presents as a slow-growing nodule in the thyroid gland, and in many cases, it is discovered incidentally. The majority of patients diagnosed with PTC are younger women, although it can affect both genders and people of all ages.

What makes PTC remarkable, especially when compared to other forms of cancer, is its excellent prognosis. The survival rates for papillary thyroid cancer are impressively high, with more than 90% of patients living beyond ten years after diagnosis. This is largely due to the slow growth of the tumour, its relative sensitivity to treatment, and the early detection of the disease in most cases.

Surgical intervention, typically involving a thyroidectomy, is the primary treatment for PTC. This is often followed by radioactive iodine therapy to eliminate any remaining thyroid tissue and potential metastases. Patients may also require lifelong thyroid hormone replacement therapy to maintain normal metabolic function. Though the treatment is comprehensive, it is effective, and recurrence rates remain low.

As a surgeon specialising in both cancer and reconstructive procedures, my experiences with thyroid cancer, particularly the papillary variety, have often been marked by optimism. My patients frequently recover well, and the long-term outlook is positive. These outcomes stand in contrast to the more challenging and heart-breaking cases I have encountered in my career.

I recall one particularly reflective moment while sipping iced lemon tea at Charles de Gaulle Airport in Paris. I was en route to Washington, D.C., to attend the World Cancer Congress as a special invitee of the American Cancer Society. In that liminal space, between the demanding duties of my profession and the excitement of international recognition, I felt a deep sense of gratitude for the progress we have made in treating thyroid cancers. It was a moment of quiet celebration for the lives saved and the futures restored.

In that serene moment, I penned a poem that encapsulated my thoughts:

A Sip of Gratitude

(Written at Charles de Gaulle Airport, Paris.)

Beneath the sky of wanderers, I pause,

Sipping iced tea, tasting the tang of a pause.

From scalpel's edge to healing light,

We fight the shadows, chase the night.

In the thyroid's fold, where cells once strayed,

Papillary whispers a hope well-laid.

With steady hands, we carve the path,

Defying fate, outpacing wrath.

And though the journey's long and wide,

We stand with strength, with grace beside.

For every soul, a chance renewed,

In life's great gift, we are imbued.

From Paris to Washington, the miles stretch far,

But in each heart, we plant a star.

For every patient, every tear,

We press on forward, without fear.

Silent sentinel, shaped like a butterfly,

You perch so quietly beneath the skin,

A small, soft gland, but with a high purpose,

Master of the body's ceaseless spin.

You whisper thyroxine through the veins,

A symphony of energy you compose,

From dawn to dusk, in life's busy lanes,

You fuel the fire, the warmth that flows.

With every heartbeat, with every breath,

You balance moods, from joy to sorrow.

In your rhythm lies the dance of health,

A steady beat that shapes tomorrow.

But when you falter, oh tiny friend,

The body stumbles, unsure, confused.

Too fast, too slow, extremes can bend.

The fragile balance you've carefully fused.

Yet with your power comes healing too,

As medicine guides you back to grace,

The world's smallest engine, pure and true,

In your quiet strength, we find our pace.

In these quiet moments of reflection, it becomes clear that while the work of a surgeon is often physically and emotionally demanding, the rewards are immense. Being able to witness the resilience of my patients and see them move forward with their lives is a reminder of why I chose this path. The journey from curing to healing continues, and in the treatment of papillary thyroid cancers, we are fortunate to witness a success story that gives hope to countless individuals worldwide.

The Thyroid in Rhyme

© Cherian Koshy, MS, M.Ch The Thyroid in Rhyme - (Invited Paper), Cherian Koshy, Kerala Surgical Journal, 1997, Vol. 4, No. 2, p. 95, published twenty years ago

Nearly twenty-five grams of endocrine tissue,
Could result in a small or big issue.
Has an 'isthmus' overlying the third and fourth tracheal rings,
Oh, what havoc the two lobes and this brings!

Developmentally starts at the foramen cecum.
Descends but in some,
Prefers the tongue over the pre-tracheal position
Confusing the physician when forming a decision.

Elaborates on hormones abbreviated as T3 and T4,
As if two are not enough, there is one more,
Calcitonin from the parafollicular or 'C' cells,
Opposite to parathormone is where its function dwells.

What a role these thyroxines play!
Its level is high or low, and treatment you delay,
Cold-intolerant, thick-skinned, sluggish victim you see,
Or thin sweating exophthalmic cardiac wreck as the case may be.

'Goitre' is the general term for thyroid swellings.
To iodine deficiency, inflammatory, or neoplastic reasons fall,
Clinical examinations, FNACs, blood tests, and uptake studies,
Categorise patients as 'medical' or 'surgical' after sharing of fees!

Simple goitre may be nodular or diffuse.
For diffuse type, iodine as a treatment has been in use.
For the 'nodular' variety, the knife you need,
Always with the blade, you do a better deed!

Solitary nodule, an enigma to say the least,
Could make the difference between beauty and beast.
Uptake differentiates as 'warm', 'hot', or 'cold'.
'Cold' it is a neoplasm we are told.

Thyroid neoplasia: a world of its own,
Papillary cancer prefers lymph nodes for seeds to be sown,
Whereas follicular cancer metastasises to bone,
'Anaplastic' feared most, infiltrates to make trachea groan!

Medullary cancer has a tale of its own,

Prefers company as 'MEN II' as its incidence is known,

Whatever the histology, surgery is the answer.

May be followed by adjuvant treatment like any other cancer.

During surgery, it is any surgeon's fear,

Those recurrent laryngeal nerves, which are so near,

Injury or insult, and a patient's hoarse voice you hear,

May necessitate a tracheostomy or cost a life so dear.

Surgery in toxic goitre, at ease one can never be.

Though uncontrolled and of toxicity, patient is free,

The unwelcome 'storm' sets in without any notice,

Where is the surgeon's ease when the patient's life is on lease?

The thyroid has more potential for rhyme,

If only I had the time,

My prayer is that all patients be euthyroid,

And be free of other problems one may see.

Author

© Dr. Cherian Koshy MS, M.Ch (Plastic Surgery)

Retd, HOD, Additional Prof, Regional Cancer Centre

Trivandrum

(My Work of 30 minutes written waiting at a check-in counter at Charles de Gaulle Airport, Paris)

17

Composite Reactions in Cancer Surgery: The 'Commando Operation'

In the aftermath of the Second World War, a revolutionary surgical procedure emerged in the realm of cancer surgery, known as the "Commando Operation." This highly complex and daring surgery, typically performed on patients with head and neck cancers, required an exceptional combination of skill, speed, precision, 'sniping', and the willingness to take significant risks. It was named after the specialised military units that carried out high-risk, high-impact missions during the war, reflecting the operation's bold and aggressive nature.

The Commando Operation involved a composite resection, where surgeons would remove not only the primary tumour but also a large portion of surrounding tissues, including parts of the jaw, tongue, and lymph nodes, to ensure complete cancer eradication. The surgery was extensive, often necessitating reconstructions to restore form and function. The multidisciplinary nature of this surgery meant that it involved plastic surgeons, oncologists, and otolaryngologists working together in a highly coordinated effort.

Speed was crucial because patients could deteriorate quickly during the operation due to blood loss or complications, making meticulous planning and swift execution vital. Surgeons had to make rapid, life-altering decisions on the operating table, often without knowing the exact extent of the cancer until the surgery was underway.

Skill, particularly in terms of surgical finesse and anatomical knowledge, was indispensable. Precise snipping of tissues to remove cancerous cells while preserving as much normal tissue as possible required years of training and experience. Surgeons had to balance aggressiveness in tumour removal with the ability to reconstruct vital structures immediately. In those early days, the lack of advanced technology meant that the surgeon's expertise was the most critical tool.

Risk-taking was inherent in the Commando Operation, with a high possibility of complications such as infection, significant blood loss, and post-operative disfigurement. However, the potential reward—saving a life and offering a chance of cure—often outweighed these risks.

In many ways, the 'Commando' operations in cancer surgery marked the beginning of an era of aggressive, multidisciplinary approaches to complex cancers, with surgeons pushing the boundaries of what was considered possible. The legacy of these operations still influences modern surgical oncology, where skill, speed, and risk-taking continue to play pivotal roles in patient survival.

Commando Surgery

Born in the shadow of war's grim face,

A term emerged from battle's grace,

Commandos in white, with scalpels keen,

Charging through flesh, where life is seen.

With a sniper's eye and a surgeon's hand,
They strike where cancer takes its stand,
A composite war, respect and save,
Rebuild what's lost, from brink to brave.

Risk runs high, like soldiers' creed,
Each pulse a drumbeat, lives in need,
Aspiring residents, hearts aflame,
Fatigue their foe in this deadly game.

The clock ticks loudly, exhaustion weighs,
But in their minds, resolve stays.
Limbs, life, and hope are the prize,
In victory's light, success will rise.

Lives reclaimed, futures restored,
From chaos of flesh, order is scored.
A commando's mission, sharp and bright,
Saving lives, in the darkest fight

18

Cancer is Limited

Cancer is so limited…
It cannot cripple love.
It cannot shatter hope.
It cannot corrode faith.
It cannot eat away peace.
It cannot destroy confidence.
It cannot kill friendship.

I cannot metastasise to the soul.
It cannot shut out memories.
It cannot silence courage.
It cannot reduce eternal life.
It cannot quench the Spirit.

Credited to Anonymity.

"Cancer is Limited," is a powerful reminder of the resilience of the human spirit in the face of one of life's most terrifying adversaries. Cancer, despite its pervasive and destructive nature, remains limited in what it can do to a person's essence. While it ravages the body, it cannot reach the most profound parts of who we are.

Cancer cannot cripple love. The bonds we form with others, the deep emotional connections, and the love we give and receive, stand unshaken by the disease. Love transcends the physical, touching the spiritual, emotional, and intellectual realms where cancer has no power. Relationships often deepen in the face of adversity, with love becoming a force of healing and comfort.

It cannot shatter hope. Hope is a beacon of light, a source of strength that cancer cannot dim. Whether hope lies in a cure, in quality of life, or in the afterlife, it sustains individuals through their darkest hours. Hope is deeply personal, often connected to faith, beliefs, and a person's inner resolve to keep going.

Cancer cannot corrode faith. Faith, whether in a higher power, the goodness of life, or simply the possibility of better days, is immune to cancer's reach. For many, faith provides the foundation for endurance, courage, and even joy in the midst of suffering. It is a wellspring from which strength is drawn when all else feels lost.

It cannot eat away peace. Inner peace, cultivated through mindfulness, spirituality, or acceptance, remains untouched by cancer. The peace that resides within the soul can be a sanctuary, offering calm in the storm. This peace, often born from deep introspection or spiritual practices, becomes a shield against the turmoil cancer may cause.

Cancer cannot destroy confidence. Even when the body weakens, a person's sense of self-worth, their achievements, and the knowledge of their abilities remain. Confidence, grounded in a lifetime of experiences, cannot be erased by illness. It lives in memories of successes and in the dignity with which one faces challenges.

It cannot kill friendship. True friendships are immune to the destructive forces of cancer. Friends stand by each other, providing support, laughter, and understanding. Cancer may change the dynamics of a friendship, but it cannot sever the ties that bind people together. In fact, adversity often strengthens these connections.

Cancer cannot shut out memories. Our memories are the treasure troves of our lives. The joyful, the bittersweet, the significant—they are ours to keep. Cancer cannot erase these moments, nor can it tarnish the legacy of a life well-lived. Memories continue to provide comfort, especially when the future feels uncertain.

It cannot silence courage. Courage, the quiet determination to face what must be faced, flourishes in the midst of adversity. Whether it's the courage to undergo treatment, to face the unknown, or to live life fully despite the circumstances, cancer cannot take away this inner strength.

Cancer cannot invade the soul. The soul, the very essence of who we are, remains untouchable. The body may suffer, but the soul, with all its dreams, beliefs, and desires, stays intact. It is the soul that often leads the fight against cancer, fuelling the will to endure and find meaning in the journey.

It cannot reduce eternal life. For those who believe in the afterlife, cancer has no power over eternal existence. The promise of something beyond this life offers solace, reinforcing that cancer's reach is confined to the temporal world. The concept of eternal life provides hope that transcends physical suffering.

Cancer cannot quench the spirit. The human spirit, vibrant and resilient, cannot be extinguished. Even in the face of immense suffering, the spirit often shines brightly, manifesting in acts of kindness, moments of joy, and an unyielding will to persevere. The spirit continues to soar, unaffected by cancer's grasp.

Lastly, cancer cannot lessen the power of the resurrection. For those with Christian faith, the resurrection symbolises the ultimate victory over death. This belief in resurrection instils a sense of peace and assurance that cancer, though powerful, does not have the final word. The promise of resurrection means that life triumphs over death, hope conquers despair, and love prevails over all.

In conclusion, cancer, despite its ferocity, is limited. It can touch the body, but it cannot reach the essence of who we are. Love, hope, faith, peace, confidence, friendship, memories, courage, the soul, eternal life, the spirit, and the power of the resurrection—these are all realms where cancer has no dominion. The human experience, rich and multidimensional, remains triumphant in the face of the disease.

Cancer Is So Limited

It cannot touch the heart's embrace,

Nor dim the glow of hope's bright face.

It cannot break a bond so strong,

Or steal the notes from love's sweet song.

It cannot corrode faith's steady hand,

Nor wash away peace like shifting sand.

It cannot claim the strength of soul,

Or shatter dreams that make us whole.

It cannot silence courage's cry,

Or stop the friendship we hold high.

It cannot dim the light of days,

Or tear apart what memory saves.

Though it may try with ruthless strife,

It cannot dim eternal life.

For in the Spirit, love burns bright,

A flame that cancer cannot fight.

19

A Choice and not Chance: Transitioning into Palliative Care

My lateral shift to becoming the Head of Palliative Medicine at the Regional Cancer Centre (RCC) was not a spontaneous decision, but rather a thoughtful and visionary proposal made by Dr. M. Krishnan Nair, the founder Director of the RCC. Dr. Nair, a man of great intellect and foresight, saw potential in me that I had not yet fully considered. It was his belief in the importance of palliative medicine, and in my ability to elevate its role within the institution, that led to one of the most significant transitions of my career.

I still vividly remember the day Dr Nair called me to his office. He looked at me with the quiet confidence that he was known for and said, "Cherian, you can make a difference and lead by example. You can improve the visibility of the Regional Cancer Centre on the international landscape. Please consider shifting laterally to Palliative Medicine." His words struck a chord with me. He saw in me not just a surgeon, but a leader capable of taking on a challenge that was still in its infancy in India. I felt like I was on cloud nine, being praised not for my surgical skills, but for my strumming on the guitar, writing, oratorial, or teaching skills by this legend of a man we fondly call MKN, honoured by the Government of India with the Padma Shri. I wept when I heard of his death.

Dr. Nair's belief in my abilities went beyond the technical skills I had honed as a General and Plastic Surgeon. He recognised my ability to communicate, both in writing and speaking, and saw how these skills could be harnessed to advocate for Palliative Care, a field that was just beginning to gain recognition in India. His confidence in me was palpable when he said, "I'm impressed with you. Besides, you have a brilliant academic background with your general surgical and plastic surgery skills and have proved your worth in cancer surgery."

This was a pivotal moment for me. Dr. Nair was not just offering me a new role; he was presenting me with an opportunity to contribute to something greater, something that could transform patient care at the RCC and beyond. His vision was clear: this career switch would benefit the institution and me equally. He saw Palliative Medicine as a specialty that needed strong leadership, someone who could champion its cause and ensure that the RCC became a leader in this emerging field on the global stage.

Dr. Nair's parting words during that conversation have stayed with me ever since: "You will know and become known." They carried a profound meaning. By embracing this lateral shift, I would be stepping into a new realm of knowledge, gaining insights into the holistic care of patients facing life-limiting illnesses. At the same time, this transition would allow me to gain recognition for pioneering work in a field that was still finding its footing in India.

Making the switch from a well-established career in surgery to a relatively nascent field like Palliative Medicine was not without its challenges. Yet, Dr. Nair's encouragement and belief in the importance of this work made the decision easier. He understood that Palliative Medicine was not just about managing symptoms; it was about enhancing the quality of life for patients in their most vulnerable moments. His vision for the RCC was one where Palliative Care would be as integral to cancer treatment as surgery, chemotherapy, or radiation.

In hindsight, this lateral shift was one of the most rewarding decisions of my life. It allowed me to blend my surgical expertise with compassionate care, offering a holistic approach to treatment that I had not fully explored before. Under Dr. Nair's guidance, I was able to build a department that not only provided exceptional care to patients but also became a model for other institutions both nationally and internationally.

Dr Nair's vision for me, and for the RCC, was one of growth, leadership, and making a difference. His belief in my ability to take on this challenge was the catalyst that led me to embrace Palliative Medicine with the same dedication and passion that I had brought to my surgical career. His words continue to inspire me, reminding me that true leadership is about recognising potential, fostering growth, and creating a legacy that benefits not just individuals, but entire communities.

I took the plunge, a watershed moment in my life. After all, I had operated and created smiles on literally hundreds of patients and trained several talented junior surgeons, obviously far better than me.

Chance versus Choice

We walk the line of chance and choice,

Two forces with a silent voice.

One throws the dice, a random call,

The other shapes what we become, after all.

Chance is the wind that bends the trees,

The storm that brings us to our knees.

It's fate's wild card, the luck we find,

Or the cruel twist that blinds the mind.

But choice, it whispers in the night,
A quiet flame, a guiding light.
It's in our hands, the paths we take,
The steps we choose, the moves we make.

Chance sets the stage, but choice decides.
Which way we turn, where courage hides.
In moments small, in seconds brief,
We choose our joy, or choose our grief.

Chance may bring the stormy skies,
But choice will teach us how to rise.
Though fate may spin the wheel at will,
Our choices shape the journey still.

So let the winds of chance blow free,
For in our hearts, we hold the key.
With every choice, we chart the course.
Of life's great journey, its quiet force.

20

Defining Experience Under the Founder of Modern Hospice, Dame Cicely My Time and Training at St. Christopher's Hospice: A Career Saunders

In my journey from plastic surgery to palliative care, the time I spent at St. Christopher's Hospice in Sydenham, East London, under the guidance of Dame Cicely Saunders, marked a pivotal moment. Selected from nearly a thousand applicants for the Multi-professional Training Programme in Palliative Care, I, along with a Romanian colleague and a healthcare professional from Africa, embarked on an experience that was not only physically and intellectually enriching but profoundly spiritual. Training with individuals from almost every continent—Balkan states, Eastern Europe, Africa, the USA, Oceania, and even the Isle of Man—was a unique opportunity to learn from a diverse group of healthcare professionals and from none other than the founder of the modern hospice movement.

Three selected from perhaps a thousand applicants – Bubbling with joy, free air tickets and a daily allowance far above my needs, and free accommodation. Unworthy me, God's gift - His doing, God - the unlimited absolute inhabitant of eternity and time, is only a vestibule to eternity!

The Selection Process: An Unforgettable Moment

The journey to St. Christopher's began with a surprise—an unexpected telephone interview. When I applied, the number of candidates was overwhelming, and being shortlisted to three (Romania, Zambia, and India) was itself a significant achievement. The day of the interview is etched in my memory. The phone rang, and on the other end was a representative from the hospice who, in a matter of minutes, would assess my suitability for this prestigious programme. I recall answering with conviction, drawing on my years of experience in surgery and my emerging passion for palliative care, hoping that my words conveyed the dedication and deep sense of purpose I felt.

Shortly after, I received the news: I had been selected. The excitement and honour of being chosen for training at the hospice founded by Dame Cicely Saunders—the woman who revolutionised the care of the terminally ill—was indescribable. It was a game-changer in my career, a turning point that would transition me from my successful career in plastic surgery to the noble field of palliative care.

Learning from the Global Community

What made the experience at St. Christopher's so extraordinary was the diversity of the participants. My fellow trainees came from nearly every corner of the world—Balkan states, Eastern Europe, Africa, Oceania, and even places as distant as the Isle of Man. Each participant brought with them not only their professional expertise but also their unique cultural perspectives on illness, death, and healing. This global tapestry of caregivers created an atmosphere of rich dialogue and exchange, where we learned from each other as much as from our instructors.

Dame Cicely Saunders, the towering figure behind the modern hospice movement, was the epitome of grace, wisdom, and compassion. Her vision was not limited to clinical treatment but extended to addressing the emotional, spiritual, and social needs of patients and their families. The exposure to such a multidisciplinary, holistic model of care was eye-opening for many of us. We witnessed how much healing could be achieved, even when curing was no longer possible.

The Avant-Garde Practice of Palliative Medicine

St. Christopher's was not merely a hospice; it was a beacon of avant-garde practice in palliative medicine. What I experienced there went far beyond medical textbooks or surgical precision. It was an immersion into the art of truly caring for patients—not just their bodies but their minds and spirits as well.

Dame Cicely Saunders taught us that palliative care was not about giving up but about shifting the focus from cure to comfort, from aggressive treatments to alleviating suffering, from prolonging life at any cost to enhancing the quality of the time that remained. This philosophy resonated deeply with me. In my previous career as a plastic surgeon, I had always been driven by the desire to heal, to restore, to fix. But palliative care demanded a different kind of healing—the kind that came from acceptance, dignity, and compassion.

The practical training was, of course, invaluable. We learned to manage complex symptoms—pain, breathlessness, and agitation—with a combination of medications, psychological support, and a deep understanding of the patient's individual needs. But beyond the clinical, we were trained in the art of listening. We learned to sit beside patients and simply be present, offering them the comfort of knowing they were not alone.

A Spiritual and Emotional Transformation: The experience was not just an intellectual or professional enrichment; it was a spiritual journey. St. Christopher's taught us the power of empathy and human connection. I learned that palliative care, at its core, is about bearing witness to the suffering of others without turning away. It is about walking with patients and their families during the most vulnerable and challenging times of their lives.

This holistic approach changed how I viewed medicine and healing. I realised that while surgery had given me the tools to fix broken bodies, palliative care gave me the tools to soothe broken spirits. It allowed me to connect with patients on a deeper, more human level, offering comfort, peace, and dignity even when the disease could not be cured.

The spiritual aspect of the training was equally profound. Palliative care often confronts questions about the meaning of life, death, and what comes after. St. Christopher's Hospice fostered an environment where we could explore these questions, both for our patients and ourselves. The emphasis on compassionate care and on respecting each patient's unique spiritual and emotional needs was a revelation.

A Career Reborn: My time at St. Christopher's was a watershed moment in my career, transitioning me from a high-performing plastic surgeon to a compassionate palliative care physician. The experience shifted my focus from curing to healing, from fixing to listening, and from doing to being present. It was here that I understood that true medicine is not just about eradicating disease but about adding life to days when days cannot be added to life.

Dame Cicely Saunders' teachings and the enriching global community of caregivers I met at St. Christopher's have continued to inspire me throughout my career. The lessons I learned there are deeply embedded in my practice today, guiding every patient interaction and reminding me that healthcare is at its best when it is delivered with empathy, humility, and respect for the human spirit.

In the end, my time at St. Christopher's was not just about learning a new medical specialty—it was about redefining what it means to care, to heal, and to walk alongside those who need it the most. It was an experience that shaped the course of my professional life and, more importantly, deepened my understanding of what it means to be human.

Shortlisting and Selection in Palliative Care at St. Christopher's London, 2003

A ring through the wire, across the seas,

The voice on the line, a moment of peace.

Chosen, I was, for a path unforeseen,

To tread where the healers, the givers, had been.

St. Christopher's doors, the Mecca, they called,

A place where suffering's silence was stalled.

Dame Cicely's wisdom, her voice like a prayer,

Guided me gently beyond all despair.

With moist eyes, I marvelled, humbled, and blessed,

For this journey of learning, a chance to invest.

Among souls from the corners of every wide land,

Together we stood, hearts held in hand.

The world became smaller, but purpose grew large.

As we followed her lead, her compassionate charge.

That moment in time, with gratitude rife,

Changed my direction and gave shape to my life.

21

Battles of the Mind and Cries of the Heart: Addressing Total Pain in Patients - Preventing an Ache Becoming an Agony

In the realm of medicine, especially in the care of those with chronic illnesses, there is a profound need to understand that pain extends far beyond the physical body. Dame Cicely Saunders, the founder of the modern palliative care movement, introduced the concept of Total Pain, a multidimensional experience that encapsulates the physical, emotional, social, and spiritual suffering a patient endures. For many patients, their aches—the physical manifestations of disease—intensify into agony not just because of biological factors but through the battles of the mind and the cries of the heart. Understanding and addressing this complexity is crucial to easing the journey through illness.

The Nature of Total Pain

Total Pain transcends the mere physical sensation that can be treated with medication. It involves the mind's capacity to magnify suffering, the heart's cries for connection, and the spirit's yearning for meaning and resolution. Each element of pain feeds into the others. Physical pain might trigger anxiety and depression, while unresolved emotional conflicts or existential dread may exacerbate the perception of physical discomfort.

Social isolation or the strain of family relationships adds another layer, compounding the suffering a patient experiences.

For a clinician, understanding Total Pain requires not only medical expertise but an attunement to the invisible battles a patient fights daily. It means recognising that pain is often worsened by fear, loneliness, guilt, or the distress of facing one's mortality. For instance, a patient nearing the end of life may not only struggle with the pain of cancer but also the existential terror of ceasing to exist, or the guilt of feeling like a burden to their loved ones. The cries of the heart—whether for companionship, understanding, or forgiveness—are often left unheard in the sterile environment of hospitals focused on treating physical disease.

The Mind as Amplifier: Battles and Fears

Patients with chronic or terminal conditions often wrestle with mental anguish, which can intensify their physical pain. The uncertainty of the future, the loss of independence, and the potential for prolonged suffering feed into a psychological battle. This mental struggle, marked by anxiety and depression, plays a crucial role in how pain is perceived and processed. When left unaddressed, these emotional battles can turn physical discomfort into unbearable agony.

For example, a patient who fears dying alone or whose relationship with a loved one is fractured may experience worsening pain due to the mental burden of unresolved emotional issues. In this case, pain cannot be effectively treated with medication alone. The battle of the mind—the swirl of fears, regrets, and unspoken concerns—requires compassionate engagement. Clinicians must learn to ask not just about where it hurts physically but also where it hurts emotionally and spiritually. This holistic approach acknowledges that many patients experience profound suffering when they feel they lack control over their lives or fear what lies ahead.

The Cries of the Heart: Emotional and Spiritual Dimensions

The heart, often symbolising emotional and spiritual well-being, plays a pivotal role in Total Pain. For some patients, the heart cries out for meaning, for forgiveness, or for the resolution of inner conflict. Facing death, many patients are consumed by questions of legacy, purpose, and unresolved relational issues. The emotional burden of these concerns frequently overshadows even the most severe physical symptoms.

When these cries are ignored, patients may feel abandoned and unseen, which exacerbates their suffering. In palliative care, emotional and spiritual pain are as real as physical pain. A woman dying of cancer might not only ache from her disease but also from the unresolved tension between her and her estranged children. A man battling heart disease may be haunted by regrets of past decisions or spiritual doubts that have plagued him for years. These emotional cries, left unheard, often deepen their physical pain.

The process of addressing these emotional wounds is deeply personal and requires a unique sensitivity. Offering a space for patients to share their inner struggles—whether through conversation, counselling, or simply the compassionate presence of a caregiver—can help soothe the cries of the heart. This approach acknowledges that patients are not just bodies needing repair, but whole beings with emotional, social, and spiritual dimensions that demand attention.

Resolving Total Pain: Beyond Medical Interventions

Treating Total Pain involves a multidisciplinary approach, encompassing not just medical interventions but also emotional and spiritual support. The resolution of such pain often requires addressing the complex interplay between mind, body, and soul. Medical professionals, counsellors, social workers, and chaplains each play a vital role in this process.

For example, managing the physical component of pain with medication is just the first step. Understanding the emotional landscape of the patient—acknowledging their fears, grief, and hopes—helps to alleviate mental distress. Social support systems, including family and community networks, are also essential in addressing the sense of isolation and abandonment many patients feel. Lastly, addressing spiritual pain—whether it involves questions of faith, forgiveness, or the search for meaning in suffering—often requires engagement with chaplains or spiritual counsellors who can guide patients through the existential questions that arise near the end of life.

In practice, the resolution of Total Pain is not a one-size-fits-all approach. Each patient's pain is unique, shaped by their history, relationships, and worldview. A truly holistic care plan should reflect this individuality. For instance, music therapy has been shown to ease both emotional and physical pain by providing a sense of calm and connection, as illustrated by a story I recall about a young girl gifting a terminal patient with a Discman. The music provided more solace than medication could, bridging the gap between the patient's physical agony and their mental anguish.

Easing the Agony: The journey through illness is fraught with battles of the mind and cries of the heart, all of which can magnify physical pain into something more unbearable. Understanding and addressing Total Pain is essential for any clinician working with patients who suffer from chronic or terminal illness. It demands an approach that acknowledges the deep interconnectedness of body, mind, and spirit.

By addressing not just the physical but also the emotional and spiritual aspects of pain, we offer patients the opportunity to find peace and comfort, even in the face of incurable disease. The relief of suffering is as much about hearing the unspoken fears and heartaches as it is about treating the physical symptoms. Only by responding to the whole person—mind, body, and soul—can we truly alleviate the agony that arises when aches are amplified by the battles of the mind and the cries of the heart.

Total Pain

More than the body aches alone,

The mind and heart, in whispers, groan.

Not just the flesh, but the soul and thought,

In pain, a deeper truth is caught.

The wound that bleeds is easily seen,

But silent battles rage between.

The chambers of a restless mind,

Where fears and sorrows twist and bind.

A heart that cries for love, release,

Seeks comfort, yearns for quiet peace.

The spirit's search for something more,

To understand what lies in store.

Total Pain speaks in layers.

Beyond the body, in quiet prayers.

It's not just bones and nerves that break,

But every fear and past mistake.

The mind questions all it knows,
As memories and doubt encroach.
The spirit trembles, seeks a hand.
To guide it through this shadowed land.

So treat the pain, but not just the skin,
Look deeper where the wounds begin.
In mind, in heart, in soul's unrest,
The fullness of this pain is addressed.

For healing comes when all are heard—
Not just through drugs or soothing words.
But through a presence that will stay,
To hear the cries, to light the way.

In body, mind, and spirit, see.
The intertwined complexity.
Total Pain, a call so vast,
For care that holds until the last.

22

Palliative Care - A Misunderstood and Maligned Word

The term "palliative care" is often used both in context and out of context in medical and everyday conversations. Despite the increasing awareness of the specialty, it remains somewhat misunderstood. Many people associate it solely with end-of-life care, failing to grasp its broader and deeper meaning. The word "palliative" itself derives from the Greek word pallium, meaning a cloak or cover, and this origin provides an essential insight into the philosophy of palliative medicine. The core idea is that palliative care offers a "cloak" to patients—a protective covering that seeks to alleviate suffering and ensure comfort, irrespective of the underlying disease.

Today, the principles of Palliative Care juxtapose with the treatment trajectory from day one of diagnosis of any life-limiting or life-threatening illness.

In palliative medicine, the focus is on managing symptoms and improving the quality of life, rather than aggressively treating the disease itself.

The race for quality doesn't have a finishing line.

In countries with extreme cold, where I have friends, Eastern Europe, Russia, and the Balkans, one needs several layers of clothing, some causing discomfiture – these are 'cloaks' to make oneself comfortable and warm! But for ease and comfort once inside a conference venue, there are

'Cloak Rooms' where the thick furry coats are deposited – albeit nearer home, 'cloak rooms' at Railway Stations connote spaces to unburden yourself of your heavy baggage while on a short visit elsewhere!

In 'Palliative Care', symptoms are 'cloaked' by a treatment plan whose primary aim is patient comfort, adding 'life' to years, not necessarily 'years to life'.

Palliative Care in Rhyme

© Mary Ann Libert, Inc, USA

© Dr Cherian Koshy, Regional Cancer Centre, Trivandrum, India

(Translated into Amharic)

A care so whole for body and soul,
When pain and suffering take their toll,
Can we underestimate the team's role?
Making the patient's comfort their sole goal.

With limits for cure but nil for care.
We are called to love and share.
We give and take, bless and bear.
'We have limits.' Can we speak and dare?

Pain and suffering, misery and sorrow,
The lot of those who live in time they borrow!
With a life-limiting illness, this is their plight.
It behoves us to help them with all our might.

Morphine and syringe drivers - are they all?
For those for whom pain may befall,
Shouldn't we understand 'Total Pain'?
To uplift many as they go on Memory's Lane.

'To live with hope and in dignity, to die.'
Is what we give before the patient's last sigh!
Giving all a 'good death' they deserve,
Is our calling to those whom we serve!

'When pain is inevitable, but suffering is optional.'
Shouldn't we give our best before the knell?
Yes, these are humankind's cardinal events,
Yells, Bells, and Knells

To ease pain with the ethos of care,

Is our vocation with our time to share?

With us, it is better to endure the suffering.

Topping our efforts with a,

Silent Prayer

Help to the Dying, to the bereaved, the Strength,

To the larger community, through breadth and length,

The Message of Healing and Hope we Proclaim,

Through 'Passions of Touch' Aflame.

Yes, it is 'Low-tech but high-touch,' so we say.

When distress is common during any day,

We say, 'We say we are with you as always.'

'And will help you reach Mercy's Shore.'

Death is a leveller from the young to the old,

Our message to all is to be bold,

Because, as in a war, we can loudly sing,

'Where is Graves' Victory and Death its Sting?'

Author, Dr. Cherian Koshy, MS, M.Ch (Plastic Surgery).

Additional Professor Palliative Medicine

This took me 30 minutes to compose, standing at a check-in counter... in Narita Airport, Tokyo.

Palliative Care

Palliative care, a gentle hand,

In moments when the shadows stand,

It does not seek to cure or mend.

But walks beside us, like a friend.

It whispers softly when hope seems thin,

And helps the quiet strength begin,

To ease the pain, to soothe the fear,

To let each breath feel calm, feel clear.

It's not the battle but the peace,

Where burdens carried may release,

A tender space, where love holds sway,

And life is honoured day by day.

For in its care, there's more to see—
The dignity of being free,
To find our way, to let things be,
And face the end with dignity.

Palliative care, a sacred art,
That tends the soul and heals the heart,
It seeks not years, but days made bright,
To fill the dark with tender light.

It's not the measure of the time,
But how each moment feels sublime,
With comfort, grace, and love's embrace,
To meet the end with a peaceful face.

For dignity in death, we find,
When life's still cherished, kind to kind,
And in those final breaths we share,
There's honour in the quiet care.

Quality of life, the goal we seek,

Not strength of body, but of will,

Held close with warmth, without regret—

A life fulfilled, remembered yet.

23

Echoes of Mercy, Whispers of Love: The Sacred Chemistry Between Physicians and Patients

The relationship between a physician and a patient is an intricate and delicate one, layered with trust, vulnerability, and profound responsibility. It is more than a mere transaction of care; it is a bond formed in the crucible of suffering, hope, and healing. The phrase "Echoes of Mercy, Whispers of Love" perfectly encapsulates the essence of this relationship, where every interaction resonates with compassion, and every word is imbued with care. This relationship, when treated as sacrosanct, transcends the limitations of clinical practice and touches the realm of the sacred.

The Sanctity of the Physician-Patient Relationship

At the heart of the physician-patient relationship lies an unwritten covenant: a promise of care, respect, and non-judgemental support. Physicians are entrusted with the most intimate details of a patient's life, their fears, anxieties, and pain. In return, patients expect not just medical treatment, but an acknowledgement of their humanity. This dynamic creates a unique chemistry—one that requires both scientific rigour and emotional intelligence.

Mercy and love in medicine go beyond clinical competence; they are about seeing the patient as a whole person, not just as a diagnosis. Echoes of mercy in this context refer to the physician's ability to alleviate suffering with empathy. It's about listening to the unspoken pain, the subtle cues of discomfort, and the quiet cries for help that often go unnoticed in the hustle of medical routines. Whispers of love, on the other hand, are the gentle reassurances, the kind words, and the moments of presence that remind patients that they are not alone in their journey.

Compassion is a cornerstone of the physician-patient relationship. It is through compassionate care that physicians practice the art of healing, not just the science of curing. This is especially true in fields like palliative medicine, where the goal is not always to cure but to comfort. In these moments, mercy and love take centre stage as the physician becomes a guide through the most difficult aspects of a patient's journey—illness, pain, and, sometimes, death.

Physicians who practice with compassion create an environment where patients feel heard, valued, and understood. This chemistry fosters trust, which is crucial for effective medical treatment. When patients trust their physicians, they are more likely to follow treatment plans, share concerns, and engage in their own care. This trust is not built on clinical knowledge alone but on the echoes of mercy and whispers of love that permeate every interaction.

The Ethical Dimensions of Care

The practice of mercy and love in medicine is not just a moral choice; it is an ethical imperative. Physicians hold power in the relationship, and with that power comes the responsibility to do no harm—physically, emotionally, or psychologically. The sacrosanct nature of the physician-patient relationship means that every action, word, and decision must be guided by principles of beneficence, non-maleficence, autonomy, and justice.

In upholding these ethical principles, physicians must recognise the inherent dignity of each patient. Mercy and love become the ethical foundation upon which decisions are made. Whether it's choosing the right words to break bad news, offering a comforting presence during a difficult procedure, or ensuring that a patient's wishes are respected at the end of life, these values guide the physician's actions. In this way, the chemistry of the relationship is preserved, and the sacred trust between physician and patient remains intact.

Despite the ideal of practising with mercy and love, modern medicine often presents challenges that can strain the physician-patient relationship. The increasing pressures of healthcare systems—time constraints, administrative burdens, and the demands of technology—can erode the human connection that is so vital to healing. Physicians may find themselves struggling to balance the demands of their profession with the need to offer compassionate care.

In such an environment, it becomes even more important to remember the sacredness of the physician-patient relationship. Physicians must actively cultivate their capacity for mercy and love, even in the face of these challenges. This may involve taking moments of reflection, seeking support from colleagues, or finding ways to reconnect with the core values that drew them to medicine in the first place.

A Sacred Bond: The relationship between physicians and patients is, at its core, a sacred bond—a covenant forged in trust, compassion, and care. "Echoes of Mercy, Whispers of Love" are not just poetic ideals but practical principles that can transform the practice of medicine. When the chemistry between physicians and patients is treated as sacrosanct, the healing process becomes more than a clinical exercise; it becomes a profound expression of humanity.

Physicians who practice with mercy and love honour the dignity of their patients, create a foundation of trust, and offer comfort in times of great vulnerability. In doing so, they not only fulfil their ethical and professional responsibilities but also contribute to a deeper sense of healing—one that transcends the physical and touches the soul.

Echoes of mercy, whispers of love.

Echoes of mercy, whispers of love,
A sacred bond from skies above,
Between the hands that heal and mend,
And hearts that break but slowly bend.

In every touch, a silent plea,
A doctor's care, a soul set free,
Where science meets the human art,
And healing flows from heart to heart.

The patient's trust, a fragile thread,
The family's hope, though filled with dread,
Together in this sacred space,
A dance of grace, a gift of faith.

For there's a chemistry unseen,
A bond that lies in what has been,
A bridge between the hands that guide.
And those who stand so close beside.

Metaphysical, this gentle tie,

That lets the spirit soar and fly,

In echoes soft and whispers clear,

Where love and mercy draw so near.

24

The Role of Music in Pain Control

More Than the Force of Gravity or the Power of the Google is the Strength of Gracious Giving - © Dr. Cherian Koshy

The power of music transcends science. It is often said that where words fail, music speaks. For a patient suffering from excruciating pain, this statement takes on a profound and literal meaning. In the sterile environment of hospitals, surrounded by the hum of machines and the cold efficiency of modern medicine, the unexpected gift of a Discman with headphones from a tenth-standard schoolgirl changed everything for one of my patients. Despite all my technological skills and medical expertise, I could only partially alleviate his agony. Yet, this simple act of kindness provided a level of relief that science could not.

Pain is a complex and multifaceted experience, particularly in cases of chronic or terminal illness. While medication can dull the sensation, it rarely touches the emotional and psychological components of pain. For this patient, each dose of pain medication was just another step in a long, exhausting battle. Yet, when it was time for his next round of medication, I often found him sleeping, headphones in place, listening to music. The melody had become his respite, soothing his pain in ways that medicine could not.

This experience highlights an often-overlooked aspect of pain management: the role of music in pain control. Music therapy has long been recognised as a complementary treatment for pain. Studies have shown that music can reduce the perception of pain by diverting attention, altering mood, and creating a sense of comfort and control. It engages the brain in a way that diminishes the awareness of pain, replacing it with rhythm, melody, and, importantly, emotion. David, who killed Goliath and became King of Israel and Judah, was requested to play the lyre to soothe King Saul's troubled heart (1 Samuel 16:14–16).

When we are happy, we tend to focus on the tune—the uplifting notes and the beat that make our hearts dance. But in moments of pain or anxiety, we focus on the lyrics. The words become a mirror for our emotions, allowing us to process our feelings in a way that feels safe and familiar. Music can validate our suffering, giving voice to the emotions we may not be able to articulate. For my patient, the lyrics likely became a lifeline, grounding him in a reality outside of his pain.

The success of this simple, gracious gift where science failed is a humbling reminder that healing often transcends the boundaries of medicine. Despite advances in technology and pharmacology, the human experience of pain is not something that can be entirely captured or controlled by science alone. Pain exists not just in the body but in the mind and soul, and it is in these realms that music finds its greatest power.

This experience also highlights the importance of compassion and human connection in healthcare. The girl who gifted her Discman to my patient may not have understood the science of pain, but she understood the power of kindness. Her small act of generosity provided a level of comfort that my medical interventions could not. It is a reminder that healing is not always about curing; sometimes, it is about offering comfort, presence, and a way to endure.

In many ways, the strength of gracious giving is greater than the force of gravity or the power of Google. It taps into something deeper and more intrinsic to our humanity—the ability to connect with one another on an emotional level, to share in each other's suffering, and to offer solace in whatever way we can. This is a strength that cannot be measured or quantified, but it is one of the most powerful forces in the world.

In conclusion, the role of music in pain control is a testament to the complexity of the human experience. While science and technology offer powerful tools for managing physical pain, they cannot address the emotional and psychological dimensions of suffering. Music, on the other hand, has the unique ability to reach into those hidden places, offering relief and comfort where medicine falls short. And sometimes, as this experience taught me, the simplest acts of kindness—those that come from the heart—are the most powerful interventions of all.

Loneliness and Aloneness

In my loneliness, I found a way,

Through strings and keys, I'd softly play,

A melody to soothe the soul,

To fill the emptiness, make me whole.

The hum of tunes, the chords I'd strum,

Became my solace when words were numb,

A quiet balm for unseen pain,

In music's arms, I'd breathe again.

But one day came a patient's cry,

Of agonising pain, pain no skill could pacify,

Despite my art, despite my care,

I felt my hands were empty, bare.

And then she came, a girl so sweet,

With kindness rare, her heart complete,

A schoolgirl of a group of ten, with a Discman in hand,

And headphones, like a gentle strand.

She placed it near the patient's side,

And with a gift, the pain had died—

No medication could compare.

To the healing that she shared.

For more than science, more than might,

Is the power of a heart's pure light,

A legacy of giving true,

That healed where I could not break through.

Her gift was more than just a song,
It carried grace, both soft and strong—
The strength of giving, selfless, free.
A force beyond what we can see.

So let it be a truth we find,
That in the simple, love-aligned,
There's healing in a gift of care.
A legacy beyond compare.

St. Thomas School, with pride, we tell,
Of minds that soared, of hearts that swelled,
Accomplished souls from halls of grace,
Who've risen high to claim their place.

But amid the stars, one shines more brightly,
A gesture pure, a humble light—
A girl, with all her youthful charm,
Who healed with kindness in her palm.

Where science faltered, cold and bare,
And technology couldn't ease the care,
Her simple gift, a Discman, small,
Did what we couldn't do at all.

The music flowed, the pain erased.
A miracle of love embraced—
And in that moment, doctors stood,
In awe of what true giving could.

For all the knowledge, all the skill,
We learned that day a greater thrill—
That from the heart, in silence deep,
A gift of music made pain sleep.

St. Thomas School, its legacy proud,
Has seen success in voices loud.
But this one girl, with grace untold,
Gave more than silver, more than gold.

Her gift outshone the brightest name,

And put professionals to shame,

For in her giving, pure and true,

She taught us all what love can do.

25

Death of a Prince

It was well past midnight, and I found myself waiting in the departure lounge of Mumbai's International Airport. The flight to Addis Ababa, the capital of Ethiopia, was scheduled for 6:30 AM. I was part of a three-member team invited to conduct a Palliative Care Workshop for doctors and nurses in Addis. In the early hours of the morning, one often hopes for a peaceful greeting and good news, but my phone rang. The call was from the father of a patient I had recently discharged from my ward at the Regional Cancer Centre in Trivandrum. His twelve-year-old son, who had battled Ewing's sarcoma of the hip bone for three years, had passed away the previous night. The father said, "I didn't want to disturb you, doctor."

I had given the boy the nickname "Rajkumar," which means prince. He was on the cusp of becoming a teenager, with a prominent Adam's apple and a voice that was beginning to crack. The repeated hospital admissions and gruelling treatment protocols had made him wise beyond his years. Rajkumar could converse easily about spiritual and existential issues—so much so that he could have put many chaplains and counsellors to shame.

Rajkumar's father spoke calmly, but I found myself choking up when he thanked me for "what I did." He went on to say, "We made it home safely. Raj slept well on the train, and his friends greeted him at the railway station. That evening, he even played cricket. The stumps were crafted by the local timber merchant. Raj insisted on batting, and he reached his half-century with a sixer, which, as always, landed in the neighbour's yard. His friends made sure he was never out."

Rajkumar's illness had progressed, and his family, from Palghat—a ten-hour train ride from Trivandrum—was not eager to pursue further treatments that offered no guarantee of a cure and might even do more harm than good. I wanted to support them in their decision. After all, what had I really done? I used to smile at Rajkumar and run my fingers through his Elvis Presley-style puff of hair. The family had come to terms with his impending death, but I wanted him to die well, in the place where he belonged. After all, death is the ultimate form of healing.

Despite the concerns of some senior colleagues, the family placed their trust in me. My conscience urged me to ensure that Rajkumar made it home to Palghat while he was still able to travel by train, with a reserved berth to sleep on. I even told them about an Indian Railways reservation extension counter a kilometre away in Patton near the Regional Cancer Centre. I made sure their tickets were ready, and I personally typed up his discharge summary, prescribing only medications to enhance his quality of life in the time he had left: painkillers, sedatives, vitamins, and the like.

Rajkumar's face radiated a zest for life. For him, chemotherapy no longer mattered. He knew he had already outlived many others with the same diagnosis. Rajkumar didn't want to count the days; he wanted the days to count. "After all," he used to remind me, "we all have to die—some young, some old. Between birth and death, we have the enterprise of life." His words still echo within me. "And remember," he once added, "life is a pilgrimage."

Death of a Prince

In Mumbai Airport's Departure lounge, with morning bright,

A greeting came, soft and light,

A father's voice, a gentle sound,

That spun my world and turned it around.

He spoke of his teenaged son, a warrior who fought bone cancer.

A battle fought, and he was not alone.

Yet in those final hours of recurrence and need,

A doctor's hand had planted a seed.

I remembered well that tender face.

The fight for comfort, slow with grace,

His pain, once fierce, had found release,

And in my care, he knew some peace.

I knew he had to reach his home.

Where friends and loved ones freely roam,

For there, in warmth, he'd take his rest,

Surrounded by the ones who knew him best.

And so I hurried, heart and mind,

To ease their way, not to confine.

This precious time to sterile walls—

He needed a life beyond those halls.

The train was set, their journey clear.

And though his end was drawing near,

The prince returned to where he belonged.

To say goodbye in love's sweet song.

I wept to hear that he had died.

But in my tears, there was no pride—

Just gratitude, that I could be.

A part of his last legacy.

The father's thanks, a gentle breeze,

That brought me to my knees with ease,

For all I did was let him go,

To meet his end with peace aglow.

And in that lounge, a quiet day,

I held those words in tender sway,

Grateful for the chance to serve,

A moment where all hearts converge.

26

My Journey to Maui, Hawaii: A Life-Changing Experience in Leadership Training

Bureaucrats and politicians are a toxic mix. We need to avail government sanction to leave the country and all that these paper pushers at the Secretariat need to check was if there are any financial commitments the government would incur on my trip. The usual story, sanction delayed for two months, and on a personal query these blokes wanted to know the mode of selection! I said 'it is for a person who deals with patients and not paper, I will leave the country even without a prior sanction, files don't hatch if you sit on them'! A day before my departure it was ready, I was told, but I never bothered to collect it and there was no 'Look Out Notice at the Immigration'!

My trip to Maui, Hawaii, was a journey for a month's leadership training of both geographical and personal transformation, one that took me through five different airports and across cultures, ideas, and personal revelations. From the moment I left Trivandrum, my path was set on a course that would not only expand my professional horizons but also enrich my understanding of life in meaningful ways.

The first leg of the journey began with a flight from Trivandrum to Chennai, a routine I had grown accustomed to over the years. From Chennai, I boarded a flight to Bangkok, where the transition into a more international atmosphere began. The airport, bustling with travellers from all walks of life, reminded me that I was now embarking on something much bigger. My next stop was Tokyo, a city with its own unique energy and culture, though I barely had time to experience it during my layover. Finally, I crossed the International Date Line on my flight to Honolulu, marking not just a new time zone but also a new phase in my journey. From there, a short flight brought me to Maui, where I would be staying in a luxurious five-star setting for the next month.

The training I attended in Maui was advanced leadership training, drawing participants from over fifty nations. This was a unique opportunity to meet and interact with credentialed friends and professionals from all corners of the globe. The environment, enriched by diverse perspectives, was nothing short of a catapult that propelled me to an acme of learning and personal growth.

One of the most impactful lessons I took away from this experience was around the art of setting goals. I learned that a GOAL is an acronym: Good, Objective, Ambitious, and Life-Enhancing. This redefined my approach to both personal and professional aspirations, emphasising that a goal must not only be challenging but also enriching to one's life. The concept of SMART goals—Specific, Measurable, Attainable, Realistic, and Time-Framed—was another crucial takeaway. For the first time, I grasped that goals are not just vague aspirations; they must be carefully crafted and pursued with precision.

Among my peers, I had the pleasure of making friends with a group of Brazilians who, in a casual conversation, introduced me to something I had never fully understood before—the soccer offside rule. Their diagrammatic explanation demystified this enigmatic aspect of the game for me. It was a revelation that symbolised much more than just soccer; it represented the power of clear communication and the breaking down of barriers between complex ideas and simple understanding.

The training sessions also introduced me to powerful tools like SWOT analysis, a method for assessing strengths, weaknesses, opportunities, and threats. This framework became a key part of my analytical toolbox, helping me approach both personal and professional challenges with greater clarity and strategic thinking. Additionally, Maslow's hierarchy of needs was added to my repository of knowledge, reminding me that leadership is not just about ambition or success but about fulfilling basic human needs before striving for self-actualisation.

Maui itself, with its natural beauty and serene environment, provided the perfect backdrop for such profound learning. The beaches, mountains, and lush greenery created a space where reflection and growth seemed almost effortless. In-between training sessions, I found time to explore the island, its rich culture, and its warm, welcoming people. These moments of connection with the land and its people further reinforced the importance of balance in life—between work and rest, between ambition and contentment.

By the end of the month, I returned home not just with new knowledge but with a fresh perspective on leadership, life, and the power of goals. The experience had been a game-changer, one that expanded my horizons in ways I had never anticipated. I realised that leadership is not merely about managing others but about continuous self-improvement, understanding diverse perspectives, and setting goals that are not only ambitious but also life-enhancing.

The journey to Maui, the people I met, and the knowledge I gained have left an indelible mark on my life. It was more than just a trip; it was a journey towards becoming a better leader and, ultimately, a better person.

Time in Maui, Hawaii

Reaching Maui was a wondrous feat,

A month in paradise, a rare retreat.

The journey was long, both exhausting and grand,

Yet excitement surged as I touched the land.

Across the dateline, I soared in flight,

The captain's voice, soft yet bright,

"Look down below, Pearl Harbor's in view,"

Oh dear, it was peaceful, the skies so blue.

Hula dancers swayed in vibrant delight,

Their 'Mudras' akin to Bharatanatyam's light,

A dance of grace, a cultural blend,

Where East and West seemed to transcend.

In a church, the conch's ancient call,

Echoed in harmony, embracing all.

Spiritual whispers filled the air.

A sense of peace beyond compare.

Visiting the volcano high atop, its rumble, fierce and wild.

Terrifying as nature's untamed child,

Yet whale watching on serene shores,

Filled my heart with joy, and nothing more.

Maui's essence, a symphony grand,

A blend of nature, sea, and sand,

Geography, culture, beauty, and grace,

A tranquil, sacred, breathtaking place

27

The Lord's Nelson

After I transitioned full-time to Palliative Medicine and End-of-Life Care at the Regional Cancer Centre in Trivandrum, my daily encounters were filled with pain and suffering. Yet, I was often touched by the composure of the dying and their families. One such patient was named Nelson. I promised him and his family that if I ever organised my thoughts into a book, his name and story would be included, just as he would always remain in my heart.

Nelson had a severe tumour of the upper lip, which had eroded into his maxillary space, orbit, and nasal cavity. He endured excruciating pain, and his fungating wound left us all numb with helplessness. Losing vision in his left eye only compounded his tragedy.

While Nelson's external wounds were horrifying, it was the inner pain that struck me most. His suffering brought these words to mind: "May we perceive your inner sore—the burning pain, the aching void, the haunting fears of disability, decay, and death. May your suffering make us deeply human, so that we do not let you fade in agony, pain, and loneliness."

Nelson's pain was eventually controlled, and he became calm and composed. One day, he confided that he was preparing to meet his Maker, the Lord. It was then that I began to think of him as the Lord's Nelson.

Whenever I walk around Trafalgar Square and see the statue of Lord Nelson, the famed naval commander who defeated Napoleon, I am reminded of my patient Nelson, who is no longer with us. Lord Nelson of Trafalgar had only one functional eye and was knighted for his service, becoming "Lord Nelson." Similarly, my Nelson had lost vision in one eye, but he remained the Lord's Nelson in his own right. Horatio Nelson was knighted and became Lord Nelson in 1797.

Cancer may have ravaged Nelson's body, but it could not invade his soul. It could not steal his eternal life or crush his indomitable spirit.

The Lord's Nelson and Lord Nelson

Two Nelsons stand, two battles fought,

Both brave in ways that can't be taught.

One on the seas with cannons' roar,

The other, on a different shore.

Lord Nelson sailed through storm and fire,

At Trafalgar, his fate conspired.

With every ship, with every wave,

He knew the sea would be his grave.

Yet he triumphed, made history's page,

A hero crowned, a naval sage.

But another Nelson fought a fight—

In silence, yet with equal might.

'My Patient the Lord's Nelson worn and frail'
His body struck by cancer's gale.
His face, once whole, now marred with pain,
One eye closed by fate's cruel reign.

He didn't seek a battle's fame,
But wished to rest, to end the flame.
"I want to meet my Lord," he said,
"After my last breath, when I am dead."

His war was waged with chemo's burn,
With surgery and the hope to learn
If life could yet be held once more—
But suffering showed another door.

Where Nelson of the Navy stood,
And fought for England's noble good,
My Nelson fought for every day,
A fight for breath, a fight to stay.

Two Nelsons, each with battles great

One with ships, the other fate.

Both prefixed and suffixed Lord in different ways,

Both heroes in their final days.

For though the seas may take their toll,

And cancer strips away the soul,

Both men found peace beyond the fight.

Their battles end in the limelight

Both had a loss of eyesight

A cruel fate's toss

But it's not for us to ask why?

It's for His Glory to fight and die!

28

A Plastic Surgeon's Journey, Navigating Palliative Care: From Guitar Strings to Global Stages

My journey with music began in my teenage years, when I first picked up a guitar. What started as a casual interest quickly became a passion, one that I honed with dedication and hard work guided by my maestro classmate. As I worked through chords, rhythms, and scales, little did I know that this instrument would one day accompany me through life's travels, across oceans and time zones, and onto stages around the world. During my medical college days, I played for a band 'The Cor-Puzzles' (The Heart Puzzles), and this was before colour photography, smartphones, computers, keyboards, rhythm pads, MIDI cords, synthesisers, in the early seventies.

As a Plastic Surgeon and Palliative Care Physician, I have crisscrossed the globe, attending conferences, sharing knowledge, and, along the way, finding moments to connect through music. My guitar became more than just an instrument—it became a bridge between my professional life and a world of creative expression. From Colombo to Antalya, London to Seoul, my skills as a guitarist found a place in various bands, often making me the cynosure of my colleagues.

It's an unexpected image, perhaps—a surgeon on stage, fingers dancing across guitar strings, playing alongside musicians from different cultures. Yet, in these moments, the boundaries of profession, nationality, and expectation fall away, leaving only the music. The lead, the drums, the singing, the accompaniment—it all comes together in a way that is electric, eclectic, and surreal.

One of my most memorable experiences was in London, at St. Christopher's, a place steeped in history and significance for me as a Palliative Care Physician. After the soirée, I found myself on stage, guitar in hand, performing in front of an audience that perhaps never expected to see an Indian doctor in such a role. The question echoed silently in the room: "Can Indian doctors outshine in music as well?" For me, the answer was already clear.

In these moments, the accolades I've received in my medical career—best paper, best debater awards—seem to pale in comparison. Music, after all, reaches into a different part of the soul, one that no surgical skill or medical knowledge can touch. It connects us in ways that transcend language, culture, and profession.

Music has been a constant companion on my journey, a thread that weaves through the different chapters of my life. It has allowed me to express what words often cannot, to share joy and emotion in ways that are universal. On stage, under the lights, with the sound of the guitar resonating through the air, I am not just a surgeon, not just a physician—I am a musician, part of a larger, more profound rhythm.

This watershed moment in my life, where music and medicine intersect, has shown me that we are never defined by just one role. Whether in the operating room or on stage, we bring our whole selves to the task, blending skills and passions in ways that can surprise even ourselves. In these experiences, I have found that the boundaries between my professional identity and my creative expression are not as rigid as they seem. The question, "Can Indian doctors outshine in music as well?"—to me, it's not just about outshining.

Life is Like Playing a Guitar - Strings are Still Attached

Life is like playing a guitar, they say,

A melody crafted, then swept away.

Each note we pluck, each chord we find,

Leaves echoes of music, a trace behind.

Even when the song fades to air,

The strings remain, still lingering there.

Tied to the wood, to memory's thread,

Their silent hum, though the song is dead.

I've strummed my way through many a night,

In Dublin, Colombo, with pure delight.

In Antalya, London, with friends so dear,

Our music is flowing, without a fear.

But twice in Ireland, with wonder, I stared,

At the harp and the lyre, so finely prepared.

Their notes are like whispers, their tones so pure,

I watched, enraptured, their beauty, sure.

Though my hands itched for familiar strings,

I marvelled at what such magic brings.

For life, like music, must move along—

But the heart stays tuned to every song.

The melodies end, but the strings hold tight,

Bound to the soul, to the endless night.

And though I've played and walked away,

The music in me will always stay.

29

Disenfranchised Grief: The Unacknowledged Mourning

Disenfranchised grief occurs when individuals experience a significant loss but are denied the opportunity to openly mourn, receive social support, or express their grief publicly. Unlike conventional bereavement, where society acknowledges the loss and provides a space for mourning, disenfranchised grief leaves the griever isolated, often silenced, and struggling to navigate their emotions without validation.

This form of grief can arise in several situations. For example, the death of a pet, while deeply painful for the owner, may not be considered significant by society, leaving the individual to grieve without acknowledgement. Similarly, the loss of a close friend, rather than a family member, can be sidelined, with sympathy primarily directed toward immediate family. In cases of miscarriage or stillbirth, parents often face a profound sense of loss, yet the societal response may be muted or even dismissive, leaving them to grieve privately.

Another common scenario is the loss of a relationship that lacks formal recognition, such as the death of a former spouse or a romantic partner in a non-heteronormative relationship. In such cases, societal norms may not offer the same mourning rituals or support systems available to more publicly recognised relationships. Those grieving may feel marginalised, as if their grief is less valid or unworthy of the empathy extended to others.

The consequences of disenfranchised grief can be severe. Without the social support that accompanies acknowledged loss, individuals may struggle with prolonged sorrow, isolation, and emotional suppression. The inability to share their grief openly can lead to feelings of guilt or shame, further complicating the healing process.

In essence, disenfranchised grief underscores the importance of recognising and validating all forms of loss, regardless of societal conventions. Every individual's grief deserves acknowledgement, and creating space for those experiencing unrecognised sorrow can be a vital step toward emotional healing and inclusion.

Presentation at Limerick: Disenfranchised Grief in Cancer at the Palliative Care Congress.

Travelling 350 kilometres west of Dublin to Limerick for the Palliative Care Congress was a significant moment in my career. The congress, a gathering of experts, caregivers, and clinicians in the field of palliative medicine, was a unique platform for sharing ideas, discussing patient care, and exploring new dimensions of suffering and healing. It was here that I presented my findings on the existence of disenfranchised grief in cancer patients and their families, and to my great satisfaction, the concept was met with wide acceptance and interest.

Disenfranchised grief is a form of grief that is not openly acknowledged, socially supported, or publicly mourned. While grief is often associated with the death of a loved one, my presentation shed light on the many overlooked forms of grief that cancer patients and their families experience. Cancer, especially in its terminal stages, causes not only physical decline but emotional and psychological loss. Patients may experience grief over the loss of their independence, identity, or future dreams. Caregivers, similarly, can experience anticipatory grief as they witness the gradual decline of their loved ones, often without societal recognition of their sorrow.

I emphasised that in the context of cancer, these less visible forms of grief can be just as profound as the grief that follows death. Yet, they are often ignored by healthcare systems and social circles alike. Many patients mourn the loss of their autonomy or physical abilities long before their disease takes its final toll. Meanwhile, caregivers and loved ones begin to mourn in silence, long before the actual bereavement period begins. The absence of societal acknowledgement for this kind of grief means that those affected do not receive the emotional or social support they need.

The Palliative Care Congress in Limerick provided the perfect audience for this discussion. The congress is known for attracting forward-thinking clinicians and researchers who aim to improve the quality of life for terminally ill patients. During my presentation, I outlined several case studies and real-world scenarios where disenfranchised grief manifested in cancer patients. The emotional burdens they carried were often invisible, as neither their families nor healthcare providers fully understood the depth of their internal suffering.

I convinced at the Palliative Care Congress in Limerick, on the banks of the beautiful River Shannon, Ireland, that my study proved that there was an element of disenfranchised grief in cancer. People still harbour needless fears that cancer is contagious, houses with cancer patients may have a uriniferous odour. To add insult to injury, a death from tobacco-related cancers, the onus was unfortunately on the deceased!

30

Politicians Versus Physicians: Moral Cancers and the Merit Divide

In the clash between politicians and physicians, an uncomfortable truth emerges: a moral divide that separates those who serve the public from those who serve themselves. While physicians dedicate their lives to healing and saving others, politicians often find themselves embroiled in power struggles, public image contests, and the pursuit of credit at any cost. This divide becomes most visible in moments of crisis, where the ethical and professional integrity of healthcare workers is placed in stark contrast to the opportunistic behaviours of politicians. Why did they go gung-ho and gaga?

The story of Dr Anoop Kumar, a critical care specialist from Kozhikode, Kerala, who identified the deadly Nipah virus in 2018 in north Kerala, exemplifies the kind of quiet heroism that defines the medical profession. Alongside him, nurse Lini Puthussery, who tragically succumbed to the virus while treating an infected patient, stands as a symbol of selflessness. Her sacrifice was posthumously honoured with the National Florence Nightingale Award, a small gesture to recognise the magnitude of her contribution. Yet, while these brave souls were battling a deadly virus, politicians seemed more focused on scrambling for credit and digital space. It was, and remains, a sickening display of opportunism that highlights the growing moral cancer within politics.

The pandemic response, whether to the Nipah virus in Kerala or COVID-19 globally, has shown us that the merit divide between politicians and physicians is more pronounced than ever. Physicians, with their rigorous training and deep sense of responsibility, are expected to act with utmost precision and compassion. Their role demands not only intellectual merit but also a moral compass grounded in the well-being of others. Every decision a physician makes can mean the difference between life and death, and this weight of responsibility is carried with quiet dignity. The lives of people are placed in their hands, and for physicians, there is no room for ego, only action.

Politicians, on the other hand, seem to operate in a different sphere entirely. The pursuit of power often overshadows any genuine desire to serve. In the scramble to be seen as effective leaders, many politicians resort to shallow displays of competence, using crises as platforms for self-promotion rather than opportunities for genuine service. This is the moral cancer that has infected politics: a disregard for the people they are supposed to represent, replaced by a fixation on optics and personal gain. While physicians work tirelessly to solve real problems, politicians often appear more interested in protecting the image of leadership than actually leading.

In the case of the Nipah virus, this moral cancer became all too visible. While doctors like Dr. Kumar were identifying and responding to a deadly virus with speed and precision, politicians were quick to capitalise on the situation. Instead of supporting the efforts of the medical community, many sought to claim credit, distorting the narrative for their own political gain. In the process, they overshadowed the real heroes, those who had risked and lost their lives to protect the public.

The response to this type of behaviour should be one of deep moral outrage. It is reprehensible when the selfless work of physicians is reduced to a backdrop for political theatre. Nurse Lini Puthussery's death was not a stepping stone for political gain; it was a tragedy that should have united the country in a shared commitment to protecting healthcare workers and ensuring that such sacrifices would never be in vain. Instead, the focus was misplaced, and the true story of courage and dedication was lost amidst the noise of political posturing.

This merit divide between politicians and physicians is not new, but it has become more glaring in recent times. The increasing complexity of global health crises demands leaders who can rise above the fray of politics and support those on the front lines. However, when politicians prioritise their own image over the well-being of their constituents, they undermine the very fabric of the society they are supposed to serve.

What is needed is a realignment of values, where merit and service are recognised and rewarded, not distorted by political agendas. Politicians should take a cue from the medical community: serve with integrity, prioritise the well-being of others, and recognise that real leadership is about action, not image. Only then can we begin to address the moral cancers that threaten to erode public trust and diminish the sacrifices made by those who truly serve.

In conclusion, the divide between politicians and physicians reflects a larger issue within society. The merit of a nation lies in its ability to honour those who serve selflessly, rather than those who seek only to serve themselves. Dr. Anoop Kumar and Nurse Lini Puthussery represent the best of humanity, while the politicians who sought to exploit their efforts represent the worst. We must bridge this merit divide by holding our leaders accountable and ensuring that true merit, not political manoeuvring, is what we honour as a society.

When a Clown Enters a Palace, He Doesn't Become a King - the Secretariat Becomes a Circus

When bureaucrats strut with a politician's gait,

And when politicians play with the people's fate.

Donning the robes meant for healers of fate,

The halls of governance echo with jest.

A carnival rising where wisdom once resided.

They claim the throne, with pomp and sway,

But knowledge slips further with each passing day.

For a clown in a palace is not crowned by gold,

Yet turns the palace into a circus uncontrolled.

The scalpel they grasp, but not with a hand,

That knows the pulse of a suffering land.

They juggle with rules while patients await,

Trapped in the chaos they legislate.

In the end, it's the people who sigh.

As laughter rings hollow and hope passes by.

For when jesters rule where healers should reign,

A circus is born, but it's the people who bear the pain.

31

The Team Approach in Healthcare: Transforming Illness into Wellness by Repositioning "We" over "I"

Healthcare today increasingly recognises the importance of a team approach, where the patient is not just a recipient of care but the central figure in a collaborative effort. The concept that "Illness becomes Wellness" when the "We" is repositioned to where "I" is reflects a fundamental shift in thinking. It underscores the idea that patient welfare is maximised when care is a collective, multidisciplinary effort, rather than an isolated, individual pursuit. By examining the essence of teamwork in healthcare, we can better understand how it enhances patient outcomes and leads to true healing.

At the heart of the team approach is the patient-centred model. Traditionally, healthcare has often been hierarchical, with the physician at the top and the patient at the bottom, passively receiving treatment. This model fails to consider the holistic needs of the patient — not just their physical symptoms but also their emotional, psychological, and social dimensions.

The patient-centred approach repositions the patient as an active participant in their care. It promotes a dialogue between patients and caregivers, where the patient's voice is valued in decision-making processes. This shift from a physician-led model to a team-based, patient-centric one fosters a deeper sense of trust, empathy, and understanding.

The Role of the Multidisciplinary Team: (TEAM = Together We Achieve More) No single healthcare provider can meet all the complex needs of a patient. Illness affects not just the body, but also the mind, spirit, and overall well-being. This is where the strength of the multidisciplinary team comes into play. A team typically consists of physicians, nurses, physical therapists, social workers, nutritionists, pharmacists, and sometimes spiritual care providers, all collaborating to address the patient's needs from multiple perspectives.

Each member of the team brings a unique skill set, contributing to a more comprehensive care plan. For example, while a surgeon may address a patient's physical needs, a palliative care specialist can address pain and symptom management, and a social worker may help with the emotional and logistical challenges of illness. By working together, the team ensures that all aspects of a patient's condition are treated, not just the immediate symptoms.

TEAM = Together, We Achieve More

In quiet rooms where whispers dwell,

Where stories shared no words can tell,

A hand extended, soft and near,

To calm the weight of pain and fear.

Together, every heart and hand,

Lifts up the soul that cannot stand.

The push of wheels, the quiet grace,

Of walking steadily, keeping pace.

From fetching meds to holding tight,

A steady shoulder through the night.

We ease the load that love must bear,

Relieving those who give their care.

For when one falters, we are there,

A team with strength and love to share.

No task too small, no role too slight,

We stand as one to spread the light.

Repositioning "We" Over "I"

The phrase "Illness becomes Wellness if 'We' is repositioned where 'I' is" beautifully encapsulates the transformation that occurs when healthcare is delivered as a collective endeavour. The word "illness" itself begins with an "I," symbolising the isolation and burden that often accompanies sickness. When the focus shifts from "I" to "We,", the burden is shared, and the patient is supported by a network of caregivers who work in unison towards the same goal: wellness.

This repositioning requires a mindset change in both healthcare providers and patients. Providers must move away from a culture of autonomy and control to one of collaboration and humility, where they recognise that their role is part of a larger whole. Likewise, patients must feel empowered to voice their concerns, participate in decision-making, and trust that their care team is there to support them.

Enhancing Communication and Coordination

Central to the success of a team approach is communication. In an environment where multiple professionals are involved in a patient's care, seamless communication becomes vital. A breakdown in communication can lead to fragmented care, where important information is lost or not shared promptly, potentially jeopardising the patient's outcome.

To avoid this, teams must employ efficient coordination strategies, such as regular interdisciplinary meetings, shared electronic health records, and open channels of communication with the patient and their family. Effective communication ensures that all team members are aligned with the patient's care plan and goals, thereby improving outcomes and patient satisfaction.

Fostering Empathy and Compassion

A team approach also emphasises the need for empathy and compassion in patient care. When multiple healthcare providers come together, each has the opportunity to see the patient through a different lens. This holistic view promotes a deeper understanding of the patient as a person, not just as a medical case.

Empathy is often fostered in the dialogue between team members as they share their insights about the patient's condition and how it impacts different aspects of their life. Compassionate care stems from this shared understanding and is more likely to lead to patient satisfaction and improved well-being.

Empowering Patients Through Shared Decision-Making

One of the most empowering aspects of the team approach is its encouragement of shared decision-making. Rather than being passive recipients of care, patients are invited to actively participate in the choices surrounding their treatment. When patients feel heard, respected, and involved in the decision-making process, their sense of control and agency over their own health increases.

This participatory role can be particularly transformative in fields like palliative care, where the patient's values, wishes, and quality of life take precedence over purely clinical objectives. Patients who are empowered in this way often experience greater satisfaction with their care and a stronger sense of wellness, even in the face of serious illness.

Toward Wellness Through Unity. The team approach, with the patient as the centre of focus, represents the future of healthcare. It repositions "We" where "I" used to be, transforming illness into wellness through collaboration, empathy, and shared responsibility. By embracing this model, healthcare providers can offer more comprehensive, compassionate, and effective care, ensuring that patients are not just treated but truly cared for. In this collective effort, wellness becomes not just the absence of disease, but the presence of a balanced, meaningful life.

'We' Replacing 'I'

In the dance of letters, a subtle shift,

A world transforms with just a twist,

From "I" to "We," a magic spell,

Illness becomes wellness, and all is well.

An "I" stands lonely, frail, and weak,

A single soul, too tired to speak.

But add a "We" and hearts align,

Strength in numbers, a brighter sign.

We stand together, hand in hand.

Through trials and storms, we make our stand,

For in this transposition, a truth we find,

Wellness blooms when hearts are kind.

From solitary pain to shared delight,

We lift each other, day and night,

In the garden of support, we grow,

Where "I" was alone, "We" now glow.

So, let us cherish this simple change.

Embrace the power within our range,

For in the alphabet's gentle dance,

Illness turns to wellness, given a chance.

32

A Patient I Shall Call Babu - The Emotional Role of Perfumes in My Career

In the realm of medicine, some patients leave an indelible mark on your soul, their lives intertwined with your own in ways that go beyond the clinical. Babu was one such patient. He was in his early thirties when I first met him—a young man grappling with the harsh reality of cancer. His diagnosis was a base tongue cancer, which had spread down his throat, requiring an extensive and gruelling surgery. I performed a bilateral neck dissection and a total laryngectomy. The procedure saved his life, but it left him without a voice, forcing him to rely on an electro-larynx to speak.

Babu, however, was not one to be easily defeated. He fought valiantly through the challenges that followed, embracing life with a resilience that was truly inspiring. He became more than just a patient; he became my "man Friday," someone who was always there, dependable and steadfast. For seven years, Babu lived with the aftermath of his surgery, using his electro-larynx to communicate and maintaining a positive outlook despite the odds stacked against him. His strength and perseverance were a testament to the human spirit's capacity to endure.

Unfortunately, as with many cancer patients, Babu's story took a tragic turn. He developed an aggressive recurrence in his neck, a recurrence that was swift and devastating. His face became swollen, his eyelids bloated, and eventually, he lost his sight. The cancer, which we had fought so hard to control, had returned with a vengeance, leaving him in a state of profound suffering. Babu was kept in a secluded cubicle, surrounded by curtains, as his family members came to bid him their final farewells.

I knew that Babu's time was drawing near, but I also knew that I had to see him one last time. As I entered his cubicle, the sight of him, so changed by the disease, was heart-breaking. Yet, in that moment, something extraordinary happened. Despite his blindness, Babu recognised me. His face, swollen and distorted by the cancer, suddenly radiated with a smile—a smile of recognition, gratitude, and, ultimately, farewell.

It was one of the institution's best-kept secrets: Babu, though he could not see, was familiar with the scent of the white musk perfume I often wore, or perhaps the Old Spice aftershave lotion. That scent, a small and seemingly insignificant detail, was enough to trigger a memory, a connection, between us. In that instant, Babu knew I was there. His smile was not just a reaction to my presence; it was a final gesture of acknowledgement, a way of saying goodbye.

I cannot fully describe the emotions I felt in that moment. There was sadness, of course, knowing that this would be the last time I would see Babu alive. But there was also a profound sense of peace. Babu had found a way to communicate something powerful with that smile—a sense of closure, of acceptance. He died shortly after, still smiling, and I like to think that in those final moments, he found a measure of comfort, not just from me, but from the life he had lived and the people who had loved him.

Babu's story is one that will stay with me forever. It reminds me that in medicine, we are not just treating diseases; we are caring for people—people with memories, emotions, and relationships. The bonds we form with our patients can transcend the physical, reaching into the realms of the emotional and even the spiritual. Babu's smile, his final gesture of recognition, was a powerful reminder of the human connection that lies at the heart of medicine.

In the end, Babu taught me something invaluable. Medicine is not just about curing; it's about caring. It's about being present in the moments that matter, about offering comfort when a cure is no longer possible. And sometimes, it's about recognising that even the smallest gestures—a familiar scent, a comforting touch—can make

The Last Smile, Scent, and Sense

His face was ravaged, his body worn,

By cancer's grip, so cruel, so torn.

His eyelids swelled, his vision gone,

Yet still, his spirit lingered on.

He could not see me by his side,

The man I knew had slipped inside.

But scent, that fragile thread of time,

Brought us back to one last climb.

White Musk, my favourite, filled the air.

A bond between us, rich and rare.

Though sight had faded from his eyes,

He knew me there, through soft goodbyes.

His final breath, so soft, so still,
A smile appeared, against death's will.
He knew that scent, he knew it well—
And in that moment, words couldn't tell.

I choked, my throat a knot of pain,
Tears welled up, like summer rain.
For in his smile, I saw the past,
A fleeting moment, held so fast.

His sigh, his peace, his quiet grace,
Though cancer had consumed his face.
He found his rest, I found my tear,
In that last smile, he felt me near.

And as he left, with silent grace,
I'll never forget that gentle face.
Blind to the world, yet still he knew,
That love remains when life is through.

33

My Time on the Ventilator

Ten years ago, I found myself grappling with a diagnosis that could change the trajectory of my life. It wasn't the sharp, intense chest pain that many associate with heart disease, but something far subtler—an insidious exhaustion that slowly chipped away at my energy, my confidence, and my ability to function with the same vitality that once came effortlessly. This creeping fatigue was like an unwelcome shadow, casting doubt over my ability to manage daily routines. Even something as routine as passing through security checks at the airport became an ordeal, where a sudden queasiness made me contemplate turning back.

This undercurrent of fear led me to Prof. Mathew, a cardiologist of repute. The treadmill test was supposed to give clarity, but in those few seconds on the machine, I could feel the weight of something going wrong. Prof. Mathew's focused attention on the monitor made my anxiety palpable, and it wasn't long before he stopped the test, confirming what I had feared. A coronary angiogram followed, and the results were incontrovertible—multiple coronary blocks that required immediate attention.

Facing heart surgery is a humbling experience, even for a physician. The clinical detachment I had honed over years in the medical field began to crumble as I now stood on the other side of the diagnosis. I was fortunate to have access to the best, and my choice for surgery was clear—Dr. Velayudhan Bashi, a surgeon renowned for his skill in performing beating heart coronary bypass surgery. If anyone could navigate the delicate dance of restoring life to my failing heart, it was him.

The surgery itself felt distant, like a complex puzzle being solved far beyond my conscious mind. The real challenge, for me, came afterward, in the intensive care unit, where I experienced what can only be described as a surreal and nightmarish state of being. I was intubated, hooked up to a ventilator to breathe for me while my body was kept paralysed. This paralysis was not just physical; it felt deeply existential. My mind was awake, acutely aware of every sound, every beep of the machines, and yet, I was trapped within my body, unable to respond or interact with the world around me.

It's difficult to articulate the disorientation that comes with this state. The ventilator, meant to be a lifeline, felt like an anchor pulling me down into a strange, disconnected realm. The paralysis was necessary for my recovery, but in that moment, it felt like the ultimate betrayal of my body. My mind was alert, but my limbs were unresponsive, as though I had become a spectator in my own life, powerless and silent.

There's a word that comes to mind—zombie. That's what I felt like, alive yet not fully living, suspended in a state of unnatural stillness. The experience was distasteful in its intensity, a profound disconnection between mind and body that lingered in my memory long after the tubes were removed and the paralysis lifted. It's one thing to read about such experiences in textbooks, to understand them from a clinical perspective, but to live through it is to glimpse a fragility we often ignore.

That time on the ventilator changed me in ways that I am still unravelling. It made me more aware of the fine line we walk between life and its cessation, of the delicate balance that modern medicine can sustain, but not always explain. It brought me face to face with the reality of helplessness, a state I had spent my entire career trying to alleviate in others.

In hindsight, I realise that this experience also gave me a renewed sense of empathy. To be on the receiving end of care, to feel the vulnerability of being utterly dependent on the expertise and compassion of others, deepened my understanding of what it means to be a patient. It reminded me that, while medicine can work miracles, the human experience of illness and recovery is far more complex than any procedure or protocol can encapsulate.

This Day 27th April, 9 years back with a drilled sternum, I was on the Ventilator in Chennai, following a beating heart bypass surgery. (My friend Dr Velayudhan Bashi, easily the best in the world, operated on me. I was a House Surgeon at Trivandrum, and this great man was a final MS student in the same unit.)

I was pain-free, but awareness was dawning on me, paralysed for the sake of the ventilator.

These lines came to my mind lying in the intensive care unit with a drilled sternum. Awareness was present, but I couldn't move as I was paralysed for the sake of the ventilator.

When God wants to drill a man,

And thrill a man,

And skill a man

When God wants to mould a man,

To play the noblest part;

When He yearns with all His heart.

To create such a great and bold man

That all the world shall be amazed,

Watch His methods, watch His ways!

How He ruthlessly perfects

Whom He royally elects

How He hammers him and hurts him,

And with mighty blows converts him.

Into trial shapes of clay, which

Only God understands;

While his tortured heart is crying,

And he lifts beseeching hands!

How He bends but never breaks,

When He does good, He undertakes;

How He uses whom He chooses,

And with every purpose fuses him;

By every act induces him.

To try His splendour out.

God knows what He's about.

Credited to anonymity.

34

The PEPSI Model of Care: Celebrating the Enterprise of Life Through Holistic Healing

In healthcare, particularly in fields like palliative care, we often find ourselves focused solely on the physical aspects of illness, neglecting the intricate web of emotions, relationships, and spiritual needs that accompany a person's journey through suffering and healing. The PEPSI model of care—Physical, Emotional, Psychological/Psychosocial, Spiritual, and Interpersonal—challenges this narrow focus by providing a holistic approach to patient care. This model reminds us that true healing is not merely the absence of disease but an intricate balance of physical well-being, emotional stability, psychological resilience, spiritual fulfilment, and harmonious interpersonal relationships.

Whenever I encounter the acronym PEPSI, it is not the soft drink that springs to mind, but rather the patients who have taught me to celebrate life in its full spectrum. To me, the patient is the real celebrity—the star of the show, not a cricketing icon or a Bollywood star. Every patient is at the centre of their unique "Enterprise of Life," and the PEPSI model provides a framework to support them through this challenging but profound journey.

Physical Issues: Relieving Pain and Healing Wounds

The most immediate concern for many patients is often physical—pain, wounds, and the symptoms of illness that dominate their day-to-day experience. In my years as a plastic surgeon and palliative care specialist, I have witnessed first-hand the power of addressing physical pain. Pain management is the cornerstone of compassionate care, and it requires more than just prescribing medications. It involves understanding the patient's pain, its intensity, its triggers, and, most importantly, how it affects their quality of life.

I once treated a patient who suffered from excruciating pain due to cancer. Despite my best surgical efforts, it was not the intricate procedures or cutting-edge technology that brought him the most relief, but rather something as simple as listening to music. His story taught me that physical pain, while critical to address, often intertwines with emotional and psychological states. Treating the body is only one part of the healing process; the spirit and mind must also be cared for.

Emotional Issues: The Heart's Silent Battles

Illness often comes with a whirlwind of emotions—fear, anxiety, anger, and sometimes even guilt. These emotions are as real as any physical symptom, yet they are often harder to diagnose and treat. The emotional well-being of a patient plays a crucial role in their overall health and recovery.

In palliative care, I have seen patients grappling with the emotional weight of terminal illness, facing their mortality with a mix of courage and fear. As caregivers, we must offer a safe space where these emotions can be expressed without judgement. Acknowledging a patient's emotional state is not a sign of weakness but of deep respect for their humanity.

Psychological and Psychosocial Issues: The Mind and Its Complexities

The psychological or psychosocial aspect of care acknowledges the complex interaction between a patient's mental health and their social environment. This includes their sense of identity, purpose, and the roles they play within their family or community. Illness can strip away these roles, leaving a patient feeling lost or disconnected from who they once were.

Addressing psychological issues is not just about managing mental illness; it's about supporting a person's entire sense of self. Psychosocial care involves fostering resilience, providing counselling, and ensuring that patients feel supported not just medically, but as whole persons.

Spiritual Issues: Transcendence Beyond the Physical

The spiritual dimension of care is often-overlooked in traditional medical practice, but it is essential, especially in palliative care. Spirituality does not necessarily mean religion – it is about a person's search for meaning, connection, and peace, particularly in the face of life-threatening illness.

Many patients, when confronted with their mortality, begin to ask profound questions: What is the purpose of my suffering? What will happen to me after death? How can I find peace? The role of the caregiver here is not to provide answers but to accompany the patient on this deeply personal journey. Spiritual care is about helping patients find a sense of transcendence, whether through religious beliefs, nature, art, or relationships.

Interpersonal Issues: The Dynamics of Caregiving and Family

Finally, the interpersonal aspect of the PEPSI model recognises the importance of relationships between the patient, their caregivers, and their family. Illness can strain these relationships, often leading to conflicts, misunderstandings, or feelings of isolation. Caregivers themselves can become emotionally and physically exhausted, struggling to balance their own needs with those of the patient.

Effective interpersonal care involves fostering communication, ensuring that caregivers feel supported, and addressing any tensions that may arise within the family unit. In my practice, I have seen how strong, supportive relationships can become a powerful source of healing for patients. Conversely, unresolved interpersonal conflicts can hinder a patient's ability to cope with their illness.

The True Celebrity: Celebrating the Patient

In a world that often idolises cricketers and Bollywood stars, I find my true heroes in the patients I care for. They are the ones who teach me resilience, courage, and the value of life itself. The PEPSI model is not just a framework for care; it is a celebration of the patient as the central figure in their own story—a story that is often filled with pain but also with profound moments of grace and strength.

As caregivers, our role is not to be the stars of the show but to support the patient in their journey, to be their co-stars, directors, and crew members, helping them navigate the complexities of illness. The PEPSI model allows us to see the patient in all their dimensions—physical, emotional, psychological, spiritual, and interpersonal—and to honour them as the true celebrities in this enterprise of life.

Through the PEPSI model, we acknowledge that healing is not just about curing; it is about caring for the whole person, celebrating their journey, and walking alongside them, wherever that path may lead.

Not the cola with its flashing lights,

But a model of care in deeper sight.

P for the body, where healing begins,

Easing the aches, the bruises, the sins.

The E stands for emotions we tend.

Where tears and laughter can start to mend.

Once more, for the mind's fragile thread,

We lift up the psyche, where fears have bled.

**S* for the spirit, a beacon of grace,*

Guiding through trials to a sacred place.

I yearn for relationships, bonds we hold tight,

In love and connection, we find our light.

For PEPSI is more than just thirst's shallow thrill,

It's care that quenches the soul, heart, and will.

My true celebrity, in life's sacred fight,

Is the patient who shines with quiet light.

Never a celebrity endorsement of the cola under a klieg light.

Together we celebrate, through joy and through strife,

Not fame, but the gift of shared, cherished life.

35

Theodicy

Theodicy is the philosophical and theological attempt to reconcile the existence of evil, suffering, and injustice in the world with the belief in a benevolent, omnipotent, and omniscient God. The term itself comes from the Greek words "theos" (God) and "dike" (justice), essentially meaning the "justice of God." At its core, theodicy seeks to answer one of humanity's most enduring questions: If God is both all-powerful and all-good, why does evil exist?

This question has challenged thinkers across religious traditions and philosophical schools for centuries. The tension between belief in a good and just God and the undeniable presence of suffering and injustice in the world has given rise to a variety of theodicies, each attempting to offer an explanation that preserves faith in divine goodness while accounting for the harsh realities of life.

The Problem of Evil

At the heart of theodicy is the "problem of evil," which can be broken down into two main types: moral evil and natural evil. Moral evil refers to the suffering caused by human actions—war, murder, theft, cruelty, and so on. Natural evil refers to the suffering caused by natural events—earthquakes, floods, disease, and other forces of nature that cause harm without human agency.

The existence of evil presents a challenge to the traditional conception of God. If God is omnipotent (all-powerful), He should be able to prevent evil. If God is omniscient (all-knowing), He should be aware of all the suffering that occurs. And if God is omnibenevolent (all-good), He should want to prevent evil. Yet, evil exists. This apparent contradiction is known as the "logical problem of evil."

Free Will Theodicy

One of the most common theodicies is the Free Will Defence. This argument suggests that God created human beings with free will, and that the existence of free will necessarily entails the possibility of moral evil. In other words, in order for humans to have genuine freedom, they must be able to choose between good and evil. God does not cause moral evil, but He allows it because free will is a greater good that justifies the risk of evil. Without free will, humans would be mere automatons, incapable of true love, moral responsibility, or personal growth.

While the Free Will Defence explains moral evil, it is less effective in addressing natural evil. Why would an omnipotent and benevolent God allow earthquakes, diseases, and other forms of natural suffering that seem to have no connection to human choice?

Soul-Making Theodicy

Another influential theodicy is the "soul-making" theodicy, articulated by thinkers like John Hick. This approach argues that suffering and evil are necessary for human development. According to this view, the world is not a paradise, but a "vale of soul-making" where individuals are tested and refined through their experiences of suffering. Moral and natural evils provide opportunities for people to develop virtues such as courage, compassion, and resilience. Without challenges and hardships, there would be no need for these virtues to emerge.

In this framework, God allows suffering because it serves a higher purpose: the development of moral and spiritual maturity. Life's struggles are seen as necessary for personal growth, and in the grander scheme, the existence of evil is justified by the greater good it produces.

The Greater Good Theodicy

The "greater good" theodicy posits that every instance of evil or suffering ultimately contributes to a greater good that justifies its existence. This view is often rooted in the belief that God's wisdom and perspective are infinitely greater than human understanding, and what we perceive as evil or unnecessary suffering may actually be part of a divine plan that we cannot fully comprehend.

In this theodicy, the presence of evil is seen as a temporary condition that will ultimately be resolved in the fulfilment of God's purpose. Even though we may not see the reasons behind specific instances of suffering, we can trust that they serve a higher purpose that will ultimately lead to a greater good, whether in this life or in the afterlife.

Theodicy in Religious Traditions

Different religious traditions offer their own approaches to theodicy. In Christianity, the suffering of Jesus on the cross is often seen as the ultimate example of how God can bring good out of evil. The crucifixion, an act of profound moral evil, becomes the means of humanity's redemption and the path to eternal life. In this sense, Christian theodicy emphasises the idea that God shares in human suffering and works through it to bring about salvation.

In certain other religious persuasions theodicy is explained in 'karmic language' or the undergoing of suffering as a desktop shortcut to paradise. Suffering is seen as a test of faith, with the promise that those who remain patient and steadfast in the face of adversity will be rewarded in the afterlife. The idea of life as a test is central to Islamic teachings on theodicy, as it emphasises trust in God's wisdom and justice, even when the reasons for suffering are not immediately apparent.

The Limits of Theodicy

While theodicies offer explanations for the existence of evil, they are not without their critics. Some argue that no explanation can truly justify the immense suffering in the world, particularly in cases of extreme or gratuitous evil, such as the suffering of innocent children or the horrors of genocide. The existence of such evils, they contend, challenges the coherence of traditional theistic beliefs.

Additionally, some theologians caution against overly rationalising or intellectualising the problem of evil. Suffering is not just a philosophical problem to be solved, but a lived reality that affects individuals in deeply personal ways. Theodicies, while providing intellectual frameworks, may not always address the emotional and existential dimensions of suffering.

Theodicy remains one of the most challenging and enduring questions in philosophy and theology. The existence of evil and suffering in a world governed by an all-powerful, all-knowing, and all-good God is a mystery that has yet to be fully resolved. While various theodicies offer explanations—whether through the lens of free will, soul-making, greater goods, or divine testing—none of them completely eliminate the tension between faith and the reality of suffering.

Ultimately, theodicy may not provide definitive answers to the problem of evil, but it invites us to grapple with profound questions about the nature of God, the purpose of life, and the meaning of suffering. In doing so, it challenges us to find ways to live with compassion, hope, and trust, even in the face of life's most difficult and painful experiences, with health adored.

In shadows deep, where sorrows lie,
We ask of heaven, "Why, oh why?"
In pain, in grief, in tear-streaked night,
We seek the justice in God's light.

Yet through the veil of suffering's shroud,
A mystique lingers, soft but loud.
For in the depths of human ache,
Is there a mystery to partake?

Theodicy whispers, not to explain,
But to marvel at grace in pain.
A tapestry woven in threads unseen,
With majesty guiding the in-between.

The hand of God, in trials we face,
Is neither absent nor displaced.
For every tear, a purpose grows,
In ways that only heaven knows.

In suffering's furnace, faith refines.

And through the storm, His mercy shines.

Though minds may bend and hearts may break,

His justice moves for love's own sake.

In mystique, in mystery, we find,

A trust that soars, though eyes are blind.

And marvel we, though small we are,

At God's grand majesty in eternity.

36

It's Nice to be Important, But More Important is to be Nice

In a world where success is often measured by power, influence, and prestige, the notion of kindness can seem almost antiquated. Yet, when we strip away the superficial layers of achievement and status, what remains is a simple truth: while it is indeed nice to be important, it is far more important to be nice. Kindness, humility, and compassion leave a lasting impact that goes beyond the accolades and recognition one may receive from external success.

The Nature of Importance

To be important means to wield influence, make decisions that affect others, and have a voice that is heard in significant circles. Importance, in many ways, equates to a form of power. Politicians, CEOs, doctors, and educators, among others, often find themselves in positions where their choices shape the lives of many. In these roles, importance can bring positive change, foster innovation, and inspire growth. Yet, it also carries the risk of detachment, of losing sight of the very people such power is meant to serve.

Importance, when pursued for its own sake, can easily morph into arrogance. When a person becomes consumed by their status, they may start to see themselves as separate from or superior to others. The human connection is sacrificed in the name of efficiency, and empathy gives way to ambition. This is when the distinction between being important and being nice becomes crucial. A person who is only important might achieve great things, but they may not be remembered fondly, nor will they inspire lasting loyalty or love.

The Power of Kindness

Being nice, on the other hand, is a quality that transcends titles, positions, and power. Kindness is not tied to social status or wealth; it is an inherent human quality that is accessible to everyone. To be kind is to recognise the dignity and worth of others, irrespective of their position in life. It is to treat people with respect, understanding, and patience.

In personal and professional interactions, kindness fosters trust and builds lasting relationships. While someone may forget what an important person did or said, they will always remember how that person made them feel. Kindness creates an environment where people feel valued and supported, which can be transformative in workplaces, homes, and communities.

Consider the role of a leader. A leader who is both important and kind is one who inspires not through fear or authority, but through empathy and understanding. Their followers are motivated not just by respect for their position, but by the personal connection they feel to them. Such leaders build not just teams, but communities that are bound by shared values of care and mutual respect.

Importance Without Kindness: A Hollow Pursuit

History is replete with examples of individuals who achieved great importance but lacked kindness. Their legacies, while marked by success, often bear the stains of broken relationships, unmet human needs, and a lack of compassion. Importance without kindness is a hollow pursuit; it leaves a trail of disillusionment and disconnection.

In contrast, individuals who may not have achieved widespread fame or success, but who have lived with kindness, often leave behind a legacy that is deeply felt by those who knew them. They are remembered for the small acts of generosity, the moments of understanding, and the genuine care they showed to others. Such legacies are not built on titles or achievements but on the quiet, consistent effort to make the world a better place for those around them.

A Balanced Approach

This is not to say that importance and kindness are mutually exclusive. In fact, the most impactful individuals are often those who manage to balance both. They use their influence and power not to elevate themselves, but to serve others. Importance gives them the platform, but kindness gives them the purpose.

Doctors who approach their patients with compassion, leaders who listen to their employees, and politicians who prioritise the well-being of their constituents over their own careers demonstrate that it is possible to be both important and kind. Their impact is magnified because their actions are rooted in a deep understanding of human needs and a desire to make a positive difference.

The Ripple Effect of Kindness.

One of the most beautiful aspects of kindness is its ability to create ripples. A single act of kindness can inspire others to act similarly, creating a chain of positive interactions that spread far beyond the original act. In this way, kindness is contagious. It elevates not only the person who receives it but also the person who gives it.

In professional settings, this ripple effect can lead to greater collaboration, increased morale, and a stronger sense of community. In personal relationships, kindness fosters deeper connections and greater understanding. In every context, kindness acts as a bridge, bringing people together in ways that power and importance alone cannot.

While it is natural to seek success and recognition, it is essential to remember that our true worth lies not in how important we are, but in how we treat others. Importance is transient; titles, positions, and power can all fade. But kindness endures. It is what defines us as human beings and what allows us to connect with one another on a deeper, more meaningful level.

To be important is to be acknowledged, but to be kind is to be remembered. In a world that often values power and prestige, it is kindness that truly transforms lives. And in the end, it is kindness that leaves a legacy worth cherishing.

The Greater Grace

In a world that prizes status and fame,

Where many chase after a well-known name,

It's easy to forget in the grand race,

The power of kindness, the gentler grace.

It's nice to be important, to stand tall,

To be recognised and admired by all.

Yet in the shadows where few may glance,

Lies a deeper truth, a second chance.

For more important than titles or gold,
Is a heart that's gentle, a spirit bold.
To be nice is to give without a thought,
To offer kindness where it's least sought.

A smile can mend where words may fail,
A touch of compassion can right the trail.
In being nice, we find a way,
To bring light to the darkest day.

The impact of kindness, though quiet and small,
Is the greatest gift we can give to all.
In each act of goodness, a seed is sown,
A legacy of love, where kindness is shown.

So, remember, in all you strive to be,
The greatest value is in humility; anyone can see.
It's nice to be important, but hear this advice.
More important is to be nice.

37

Palliative Care – A Paradigm Shift

Palliative care represents a paradigm shift in the medical world, moving away from a disease-centred approach to one that places the patient at the core. This shift is most evident in how we handle complex, life-threatening illnesses where the disease is often only one part of a much larger narrative. Instead of focusing solely on the pathology and the treatments it demands, palliative care is deeply rooted in the human experience of illness, prioritising the physical, emotional, social, and spiritual well-being of the patient.

The contrast between these two approaches can be starkly illustrated through the example of a patient—let's call her A—who was treated for breast cancer five years ago. She underwent surgery, followed by chemotherapy and radiation, only to now present with back pain due to spinal metastasis. In the traditional disease-centred model, the focus would be on her cancer recurrence, and her treatment options would revolve around managing the metastasis—whether through additional chemotherapy, surgery, or radiation.

However, in palliative care, the story shifts. We no longer just talk about the disease but about the person behind it. A is not just a breast cancer patient with metastasis to the spine. She is a single mother from rural Trivandrum with two young children who depend on her for survival. The critical question here isn't just about how to manage her pain or slow the progression of her disease. Instead, it's about how to address her worries about her children's future, how to provide her with the support she needs to continue being present for her family, and how to improve her quality of life despite the prognosis.

This patient-centred approach requires us to step beyond the walls of the hospital or the confines of medical treatments and look at the broader social context in which the patient lives. What does it mean for A to be a mother in a rural setting with limited income? How does her illness affect her ability to provide for her children, and what will happen to them if she is no longer there? These are the kinds of questions that palliative care encourages us to ask, and they underscore the importance of seeing the patient as a whole person rather than just a collection of symptoms or a diagnosis.

This approach also demands a more profound engagement with civil society. In cases like A's, medical professionals alone cannot address all of her needs. While healthcare teams can manage her symptoms and provide her with medical support, addressing her social concerns—such as the future of her children—requires the involvement of broader societal structures. Civil society organisations, NGOs, and community groups can play a vital role in providing financial assistance, emotional support, and educational resources for her children. The integration of these resources into her care plan is essential in truly addressing her needs, not just as a patient but as a mother and a human being.

Palliative care, therefore, challenges us to think beyond the confines of clinical care and to engage with the social and emotional realities of patients' lives. In doing so, it reminds us that healthcare is not just about curing diseases but about healing lives. Healing, in this context, is not the absence of disease but the presence of dignity, comfort, and peace—something that can only be achieved when we treat patients as people first and foremost, recognising the complex web of their lives beyond their medical condition.

Civil society's involvement is critical in ensuring that this patient-centred approach is truly comprehensive. Healthcare systems, particularly in resource-limited settings, are often ill-equipped to handle the broader social determinants of health that significantly impact patients' well-being. Civil society can bridge this gap by providing the support networks, financial aid, and advocacy necessary to ensure that patients like A are not left to navigate these challenges alone.

Palliative Care in Rhyme

© Mary Ann Libert, Inc., USA Journal of Palliative Medicine - Dr. Cherian Koshy, Regional Cancer Centre, Trivandrum, India

(Translated into Amharic, my work of Twenty Minutes, sipping Freshly Brewed Coffee at Narita Airport, Tokyo)

A care so whole for body and soul,

When pain and suffering take their toll,

Can we underestimate the team's role?

Making the patient's comfort their sole goal.

With limits for cure but nil for care.

We are called to love and share.

We give and take, bless and bear.

'We have limits.' Can we speak and dare?

Pain and suffering, misery and sorrow,

The lot of those who live in time they borrow!

With a life-limiting illness, this is their plight.

It behoves us to help them with all our might.

Morphine and syringe drivers - are they all?

For those for whom pain may befall,

Shouldn't we understand 'Total Pain'?

To uplift many as they go on Memory's Lane.

'To live with hope and in dignity, to die.'

Is what we give before the patient's last sigh!

Giving all a 'good death' they deserve,

Is our calling to those whom we serve!

'When pain is inevitable, but suffering is optional.'

Shouldn't we give our best before the knell?

Yes, these are humankind's cardinal events,

Yells, Bells, and Knells

To ease pain with the ethos of care,

Is our vocation with our time to share?

With us, it is better to endure the suffering.

Topping our efforts with a Silent Prayer.

Help to the Dying, to the bereaved, the Strength,

To the larger community, through breadth and length,

The Message of Healing and Hope we Proclaim,

Through 'Passions of Touch' Aflame.

Yes, it is 'Low-tech but high-touch', so we say.

When distress is common during any day,

We say, 'We say we are with you as always.'

'And will help you reach Mercy's Shore.'

Death is a leveller from the young to the old,

Our message to all is to be bold,

Because, as in a war, we can loudly sing,

'Where is Grave's Victory and Death its Sting.'

38

Paradigm Paralysis: The Challenge of Complacency in Professional Growth

---

'Paradigm Shift' and 'Benchmarks' are default words amongst motivational speakers and corporate honchos. Joel Barker, renowned for his exploration of "paradigm shifts," introduced the concept of "paradigm paralysis" to describe a situation where individuals or organisations become stagnant due to an unwillingness or inability to adapt to new ideas or changes. Paradigm paralysis occurs when a lack of motivation or fear of change prevents growth, leading to a state of mediocrity. In the context of professional fields, including medicine, this phenomenon can be particularly detrimental, stifling innovation and impeding progress. Understanding and overcoming paradigm paralysis is crucial for advancing our practices and achieving excellence.

Understanding Paradigm Paralysis

Paradigm paralysis manifests as a resistance to change despite the presence of new information or evolving conditions. This resistance can be driven by several factors, including comfort with the status quo, fear of the unknown, or a lack of motivation to improve. In many cases, paradigm paralysis stems from the belief that existing methods or practices are sufficient, rendering any potential improvements unnecessary.

Joel Barker's concept highlights how entrenched paradigms—the established frameworks through which we interpret and understand the world—can become barriers to progress. When individuals or organisations are bound by outdated paradigms, they may fail to recognise emerging opportunities or respond to shifting demands. Instead of adapting and innovating, they revert to familiar, often inadequate practices, resulting in stagnation and mediocrity.

Paradigm Paralysis in the Medical Profession

In the medical field, paradigm paralysis can manifest in various ways, from resistance to adopting new technologies to reluctance in updating clinical practices. The healthcare profession is continually evolving with advances in research, technology, and patient care strategies. However, when practitioners cling to outdated methods or resist new approaches, they may inadvertently hinder progress and compromise patient outcomes.

Resistance to Technological Advances: Medical technology has advanced significantly in recent decades, introducing new diagnostic tools, treatment options, and electronic health records systems. Resistance to these innovations, whether due to comfort with traditional methods or scepticism about their efficacy, can prevent healthcare professionals from leveraging these advancements to improve patient care.

Adherence to Outdated Practices: Medical knowledge and best practices evolve over time based on research and clinical experience. Paradigm paralysis can occur when practitioners continue to rely on outdated guidelines or techniques despite evidence supporting newer, more effective approaches. This adherence to outdated practices can limit the potential for improved patient outcomes and clinical efficiency.

Reluctance to Embrace Interdisciplinary Collaboration: Modern healthcare often requires collaboration across various specialties and disciplines. Paradigm paralysis may manifest as a reluctance to engage in interdisciplinary teamwork, resulting in fragmented care and missed opportunities for comprehensive patient management.

The Impact of Paradigm Paralysis

The consequences of paradigm paralysis extend beyond individual practices to affect the broader healthcare system. When medical professionals and institutions resist change, they contribute to systemic inefficiencies, reduced quality of care, and slower adoption of beneficial innovations. This stagnation not only impacts patient outcomes but also undermines the profession's ability to adapt to evolving healthcare needs.

Compromised Patient Outcomes: Failure to adopt new treatments, technologies, or evidence-based practices can lead to suboptimal patient outcomes. Patients may receive care that is less effective or outdated, affecting their overall health and recovery.

Reduced Professional Growth: Paradigm paralysis limits opportunities for professional development and growth. When practitioners do not engage with new knowledge or approaches, they miss out on the chance to enhance their skills, stay current in their field, and contribute to advancements in medicine.

Systemic Inefficiencies: Inertia within medical practices can contribute to inefficiencies in healthcare delivery, including prolonged wait times, increased costs, and suboptimal resource utilisation. Overcoming paradigm paralysis is essential for streamlining processes and improving the overall efficiency of the healthcare system.

Overcoming Paradigm Paralysis

To combat paradigm paralysis, healthcare professionals and institutions must embrace a culture of continuous improvement and adaptability. This requires a proactive approach to change, a willingness to challenge existing paradigms, and a commitment to ongoing learning and innovation.

Fostering a Growth Mindset: Encouraging a growth mindset—where individuals view challenges and changes as opportunities for learning and development—can help overcome resistance to new ideas. By cultivating an environment that values curiosity and adaptability, professionals are more likely to embrace change and seek out innovative solutions.

Promoting Lifelong Learning: Continuous education and professional development are crucial for staying current with advancements in medicine. Engaging in lifelong learning helps practitioners remain informed about new research, technologies, and best practices, reducing the likelihood of stagnation.

Encouraging Open Dialogue: Creating a culture of open dialogue and collaboration within healthcare teams fosters the exchange of ideas and perspectives. By encouraging discussions about new approaches and evidence-based practices, teams can collectively identify and address areas where paradigm paralysis may exist.

Implementing Evidence-Based Practices: Emphasising the use of evidence-based practices ensures that care decisions are grounded in the latest research and clinical guidelines. Regularly reviewing and updating protocols based on current evidence helps mitigate the risk of adhering to outdated practices.

Embracing Change for Excellence: Paradigm paralysis represents a significant challenge in the medical profession, where the drive for progress and improvement is essential for delivering high-quality care. By understanding the nature of paradigm paralysis and actively working to overcome it, healthcare professionals can break free from the constraints of outdated paradigms and embrace a culture of continuous improvement.

The pursuit of excellence in medicine requires not only technical skill and knowledge but also an openness to change and innovation. By fostering a proactive approach to change, encouraging lifelong learning, and embracing evidence-based practices, the medical fraternity can move beyond the trappings of paradigm paralysis and achieve greater heights in patient care and professional development.

Paradigm Paralysis

We stand, unmoved, beneath the weight.

Of yesterday's achievements, great.

No thirst to grow, no drive to see.

The world beyond complacency.

Comfort's chains bind thought and soul,

A stagnant mind, the price of toll,

For in the quiet void, we fall.

To mediocrity's soft call.

What once was sharp, now dulls with time,

A slowing rhythm, stalling climb,

And innovation turns to rust,

As vision fades to brittle dust.

Without the spark, the hunger deep,

We drift through life, half awake, asleep.

Until we find, too late, too blind,

That progress left us far behind.

So break the glass of settled ways,

Ignite the flame, reclaim the days,

For when we fail to push the line,

We lose the chance to truly shine.

39

Suicide Tourism: Ethical Dilemmas and Global Perspectives

In the opening lines of the soliloquy, Hamlet asks whether it is better to 'be or not to be', meaning to live or to die. On its face, this might sound like a simple question: most people would say that it is better, or 'nobler in the mind', to live. William Shakespeare

I heard about this strange form of tourism in 2003 while in London. The premium offers were a circuit at casinos at Monte Carlo, a 24-kilometre drive to enjoy the Cannes Film Festival, experience the Alps, and then die. The price tag would be two thousand to three thousand pounds. Suicide tourism, also known as "assisted suicide tourism" or "euthanasia tourism," refers to the practice of individuals travelling to another country where assisted suicide or euthanasia is legally permitted. Typically, these individuals seek to end their lives in a dignified manner because of terminal illness, chronic pain, or unbearable suffering. While this concept highlights the disparity in global laws surrounding assisted dying, it also raises complex ethical, legal, and societal questions.

Origins and Destinations

Switzerland, particularly through organisations like Dignitas and Exit, is the most well-known destination for suicide tourism. Since the early 2000s, individuals from around the world, particularly from countries where assisted suicide is illegal, have travelled to Switzerland to end their lives. The Swiss legal framework permits assisted suicide under specific conditions, and the involvement of non-Swiss citizens is neither prohibited nor actively encouraged, leading to a steady influx of "suicide tourists."

Other countries, like Belgium, Luxembourg, Canada, and the Netherlands, also allow assisted dying under certain circumstances, but Switzerland remains the most prominent destination for non-residents.

The Appeal of Suicide Tourism

For many, the option of suicide tourism represents the ultimate assertion of autonomy over their lives. Terminally ill patients who face prolonged suffering or poor quality of life often seek a dignified death, free from the constraints of unbearable pain. For them, suicide tourism offers a legal and medically supervised way to end their lives on their own terms.

Furthermore, some individuals travel abroad because they lack access to appropriate palliative care in their home countries. While palliative care aims to relieve suffering and improve the quality of life for those with serious illnesses, it is not always available, affordable, or effective in alleviating all forms of suffering. As a result, some patients view assisted suicide as their only option for relief.

The fact of the matter is that there is an 'intent to kill' in assisted suicide or euthanasia, but letting die is another matter altogether in patients with metastatic cancer spread to the lung, liver, bone, or brain.

Sadly, those who opt for such a mode of death are not those in agonising pain or terminal illness, but those who have lost the purpose of living and continued existence in a post-truth or metamodern world.

Ethical and Legal Dilemmas

The concept of suicide tourism presents a host of ethical dilemmas. Supporters argue that people should have the right to choose how and when they die, particularly if they are enduring immense suffering. They contend that denying individuals this option forces them to endure unnecessary pain and strips them of their autonomy.

Opponents, however, raise several concerns. Firstly, they argue that allowing people to travel abroad for assisted suicide could lead to a "slippery slope" where the value of human life is diminished, and vulnerable individuals, such as those with disabilities or mental health conditions, may feel pressured to end their lives prematurely. The fear is that societal acceptance of assisted suicide could normalise death as a solution to suffering rather than focusing on improving care and support systems.

There are also concerns about the potential for coercion or exploitation. Patients may be influenced by family members, caregivers, or financial circumstances to pursue assisted suicide, even if they are not fully committed to the decision. Safeguards are essential to ensure that individuals are making autonomous and informed choices, free from external pressures.

From a legal perspective, suicide tourism highlights the disparity between different countries' approaches to assisted dying. In many countries, assisted suicide remains illegal, and those who assist in the act may face criminal charges. However, when individuals travel to another country to end their lives, they effectively bypass the laws of their home nation, raising questions about jurisdiction and the international regulation of assisted suicide.

The Role of Medical Professionals

The involvement of medical professionals in suicide tourism also presents ethical challenges. Physicians are typically bound by the Hippocratic

Oath, which emphasises the duty to do no harm. The act of assisting in a patient's death can be seen as conflicting with this duty, and many medical professionals struggle with the moral implications of participating in assisted suicide, even in jurisdictions where it is legal.

In euthanasia or assisted dying, there is an 'intent to kill', but in a cancer patient with metastasis to lung, liver, bone, or brain, letting die is different. Moreover, a majority of the world's population believes in the existence of a slice of divinity in us, and only He has the right to take life if He has given us the gift of life.

In Switzerland, for example, assisted suicide is permitted under certain conditions, but euthanasia (where the physician actively administers a life-ending drug) is illegal. The patient must administer the lethal medication themselves, and physicians are responsible for ensuring that all legal and medical requirements are met. This delicate balance between providing compassionate care and adhering to ethical guidelines can be difficult to navigate for healthcare providers.

Suicide tourism does not only affect the individuals who choose to end their lives but also has profound implications for their families and society as a whole. Family members may struggle with the decision of their loved ones to pursue assisted suicide, and the act itself can leave lasting emotional scars. While some families support the decision as an act of mercy and autonomy, others may feel guilt, grief, or even anger at the choice.

On a societal level, the practice of suicide tourism raises questions about how we care for our most vulnerable populations. The fact that individuals feel the need to travel abroad to access assisted dying points to gaps in healthcare systems, particularly in the areas of palliative care and mental health support. Addressing these gaps should be a priority to ensure that patients have access to a full range of options for end-of-life care.

The future of suicide tourism will likely depend on how countries navigate the evolving debates surrounding assisted suicide and euthanasia. Some countries may choose to liberalise their laws in response to public demand, while others may tighten restrictions to prevent the practice. International discussions on the ethics and legality of assisted dying could lead to more standardised regulations or even global agreements on the issue.

As suicide tourism continues to provoke debate, it is crucial to ensure that the rights and dignity of individuals are respected while also safeguarding vulnerable populations from harm. The focus should not only be on the legality of assisted dying but also on improving the overall quality of life for those facing terminal illness or chronic suffering, ensuring that death is not seen as the only option for relief.

Suicide tourism is a complex phenomenon that sits at the intersection of ethics, law, medicine, and human rights. While it offers a solution for individuals seeking to end their lives with dignity, it also challenges society to confront difficult questions about the value of life, autonomy, and the responsibilities we hold toward those who suffer. Addressing these challenges will require thoughtful dialogue, compassion, and a commitment to improving care for all, regardless of the choices they ultimately make. My take on this demeaning tourism was that 'A patient who doesn't suffer would not want to undertake this journey and type of tourism.' The antidote for suicide tourism was

In gilded planes, they fly away,

Where sorrow meets the grand display—

Monte Carlo's glittering nights,

The Alps aglow with frozen heights.

They wander Cannes, in a velvet throng,

Yet feel no joy, no place belongs.

A final trip, the tour's last thread,

To places where the lost are led.

The ache, the void, a hollow cry,

No meaning left beneath the sky,

Where purpose fades like fleeting light,

And life no longer feels so bright.

For those who tread this darkened way,

Promoters find their games to play—

A toast to life, a dance, a cheer,

But death looms quietly near.

In Europe's arms, a legal sigh,

Where laws permit the last goodbye,

They make their peace, their ticket torn,

And bid farewell to life, forlorn.

What sadness this, that life's grand tour.

Ends not in hope, but in a door.

That opens wide to nothing more—

A flight to silence, evermore.

40

Starting Tele-clinics, Connecting the Regional Cancer Centre and Adimali and Munnar - Award from HE Tony Tan, the President of Singapore

Kerala is a state known for its scenic landscapes and excellent human development indicators. However, the state's infrastructural development has often been uneven, and two of its districts, Idukki and Wayanad, stand as glaring examples. Despite their picturesque beauty and ecological significance, these districts are conspicuously absent from Kerala's rail map. The absence of rail connectivity has a profound impact on the people residing in these regions, particularly when it comes to healthcare access, which for some can be a matter of life and death.

The Struggles of Patients from Idukki

Working at the Regional Cancer Centre (RCC), I became acutely aware of the logistical and financial burdens placed on patients from Idukki who needed specialised care. Travelling to Trivandrum for treatment involved significant expenses and time, adding stress to an already taxing journey. A taxi ride to the RCC would cost patients around ₹5,000, while a train journey after reaching Kochi or Alwaye would still amount to at least ₹3,000, excluding the taxi fares to the railway stations. For people battling cancer, such costs were often unaffordable, especially when combined with the physical toll of long-distance travel. The difficulties were compounded by the time-sensitive nature of cancer treatment, where delays could be detrimental.

The Birth of a Solution: The Tele-clinic

It was in this context that an idea began to take shape—one that could bridge the gap between the unconnected districts and the specialised care available at the RCC. Why not start a dedicated Tele Clinic on a weekly basis? At the time, satellite technology was unpredictable, but a breakthrough came when Bharat Sanchar Nigam Limited (BSNL) leased their last ISDN (Integrated Service Digital Network) line for a hospice at Adimali, near the picturesque Munnar in Idukki district. This provided the crucial connectivity needed for the tele-clinic to function effectively.

We had ten beds ready at Karuna Bhavan, a facility run by the Sisters of Destitute, and we ensured that oral morphine was made available for patients requiring palliative care. The facility, modest in its size and scope, offered much-needed respite for cancer patients who could not afford frequent travel to Trivandrum.

Technology as a Bridge

With the help of a UK-based charity, Help the Hospice, we secured funding to purchase a telecamera and a large monitor. These simple yet powerful tools enabled me to see, hear, and emotionally connect with patients and their families from afar. Through the ISDN network, we could conduct consultations that provided not just medical advice but also a sense of reassurance to patients who were often battling not just their illness, but the isolation and helplessness that came with it.

For many, this weekly Tele Clinic became a lifeline. The clinic allowed us to manage symptoms, adjust medications, and offer emotional support—all without the patient having to leave the comfort of their home. The savings in terms of both money and physical strain were significant, and the emotional relief that patients and their families felt was immeasurable.

Recognition Beyond Borders

Despite the importance of this initiative, it largely went unrecognised in my own country. However, I was deeply honoured when my work caught the attention of the global medical community. In Singapore, HE Tony Tan, then President of Singapore and an MIT alumnus, presented me with an award recognising the innovation and impact of the Tele Clinic. It was a moment of validation, not just for me but for all those who believed in the power of technology to bring healthcare to the most underserved populations.

The Road Ahead: Although the Tele Clinic was a success, it underscored the broader need for better infrastructure in districts like Idukki and Wayanad. Rail connectivity is not just about convenience; it is about ensuring that people have access to essential services like healthcare. Until these districts are fully integrated into Kerala's transport network, initiatives like the Tele Clinic will continue to play a crucial role. But they are, at best, temporary solutions to what is ultimately a systemic issue.

In the meantime, the dedication of healthcare workers and organisations that seek to bridge these gaps must be supported. They are the ones ensuring that, even in the face of infrastructural deficiencies, no one is left behind.

HELP for the Hills- Hear, Ease, Link, Palliate

High in the hills, where silence reigns,

A surgeon's heart felt others' pains,

Beyond the scalpel, beyond the cure,

He sought a way to heal for sure.

Through winding roads and misted air,

Where Adimali and Munnar's peaks rise rare,

He forged a link, a lifeline clear,

A gift of hope, to bring them near.

Technology met compassion's gaze,

A tele-clinic's quiet blaze,

Through cables stretched and hearts aligned,

He reached the suffering left behind.

295 kilometres far,

Through valleys deep, beneath the star,

A voice, a face, a guiding hand,

Brought healing from that distant land.

HELP for the Hills, they named it right,

Hear Ease Link Palliate, a guiding light,

Through whispered wires, relief was found,

In every patient, hope unbound.

Leading by example, bold and true,

A plastic surgeon's heart that grew,

From scalpels sharp to screens, solace that gleam,

He made the mountains part of his dream.

And from those heights, lives would renew,

A healer's touch, in every view.

Where once was pain, now comfort spill

A legacy, in the heart of the hills

41

The Need for Truth, Transparency, and Trust in the Doctor-Patient Relationship

The doctor-patient relationship is one of the most profound human connections, deeply rooted in trust, nurtured by hope, and often tested by the uncertainties of illness and treatment. At its best, this relationship can lead to healing, comfort, and a shared journey toward wellness. However, when marred by deceit or a lack of transparency, it can deteriorate into suspicion, fear, and a sense of betrayal. Trust is the foundation upon which this relationship is built, and without it, the connection becomes as hollow and useless as a smartphone without a service provider—a tool that looks functional but is ultimately good for little more than playing games.

The Cornerstone of Trust

Trust is the lifeblood of the doctor-patient relationship. Patients often come to their doctors in moments of vulnerability, entrusting them with their health, well-being, and, in some cases, their very lives. This trust is not easily earned but can be quickly shattered by dishonesty, arrogance, or indifference. A patient places their faith in the doctor's expertise and judgement, believing that their physician will act in their best interest, communicate openly, and provide the most appropriate care.

For the doctor, this trust carries a significant responsibility. The oath to "do no harm" extends beyond physical care to include emotional and psychological support. It involves being truthful, transparent, and honest in every interaction. When a patient feels that their doctor is not being forthright, a subtle poison seeps into the relationship, corroding the bond of trust that is so essential for effective care.

The Role of Truth in Building Trust

Truth is the foundation of trust. Without truth, trust cannot exist. In the context of the doctor-patient relationship, truth encompasses not only accurate diagnoses and treatment plans but also clear communication about the uncertainties and risks that accompany medical care. Patients deserve to know the reality of their situation, even if it is difficult to hear.

Yet, truth-telling in medicine can be a delicate balancing act. While patients need honesty, they also need hope. Too much brutal truth delivered without compassion can lead to despair, while too little can foster false hope and erode trust when the reality becomes apparent. A doctor must navigate this terrain with sensitivity, ensuring that the truth is shared in a way that empowers the patient rather than overwhelms them.

Truth also involves being honest about limitations—both of the doctor and of medicine itself. It is easy for patients to place doctors on a pedestal, viewing them as all-knowing and infallible. But medicine is as much art as it is science, filled with uncertainties and unknowns. A doctor who acknowledges these limitations, who admits when they do not have all the answers, often earns more trust than one who pretends to know it all.

Transparency: The Pathway to Trust

Transparency goes hand in hand with truth. It is the practice of making information accessible and understandable, ensuring that patients are fully informed about their health, treatment options, and the reasoning behind medical decisions. A transparent relationship between doctor and patient fosters collaboration and shared decision-making, where the patient feels like an active participant in their care rather than a passive recipient.

Transparency is particularly crucial in situations involving complex treatments, life-threatening illnesses, or end-of-life care. Patients need to understand the potential outcomes, the benefits and risks of different treatment options, and the reasoning behind recommendations. This requires clear communication, free from medical jargon, and a willingness to engage in difficult conversations.

However, transparency is not just about sharing information; it is also about managing expectations. Patients often come with hopes for a quick fix or a miraculous cure. Being transparent means helping them understand the realistic outcomes, the timeframes involved, and the potential complications. When expectations are aligned with reality, trust flourishes.

Deceit: The Poison in the Doctor-Patient Relationship

Deceit, whether intentional or unintentional, is the antithesis of trust. It can take many forms, from withholding information to sugar-coating a diagnosis to avoiding difficult conversations. While some doctors may believe that sparing patients from harsh realities is a form of kindness, in truth, it is a disservice that can lead to confusion, mistrust, and feelings of betrayal.

I recall a story shared by a colleague about a patient diagnosed with terminal cancer. The oncologist, wanting to preserve the patient's hope, never explicitly told her that her condition was incurable. The patient continued with aggressive treatments, believing that she still had a chance at a cure. When she eventually realised the truth, she felt cheated, not only by the disease but by the very people she had trusted to care for her. Deceit, even born of good intentions, can poison the doctor-patient relationship, leading to disillusionment and a profound sense of loss.

The Importance of Hope in Building Trust

While truth and transparency are essential, so too is hope. Patients need hope to endure the challenges of illness and to persevere through difficult treatments. Hope is not just about believing in a cure; it is about finding meaning and purpose, even in the face of uncertainty. It is about believing that, no matter the outcome, their doctor is with them every step of the way, providing support, care, and understanding.

Hope, however, must be grounded in reality. False hope, built on deceit or half-truths, can be as damaging as no hope at all. A doctor's role is to nurture hope in a way that is honest and compassionate, helping patients find their own sources of strength while preparing them for whatever lies ahead.

Trust as the Foundation of Healing

In many ways, trust is the foundation of healing. A patient who trusts their doctor is more likely to follow medical advice, adhere to treatment plans, and engage actively in their own care. Conversely, when trust is broken, the patient may become disengaged, sceptical, or even resistant to care, leading to poorer outcomes.

Trust also has a profound impact on the emotional and psychological well-being of the patient. Knowing that their doctor is truthful, transparent, and trustworthy allows patients to feel safe and supported, even in the midst of uncertainty. This sense of security can be a powerful force in the healing process, providing patients with the confidence they need to face their illness.

Trust, the Bedrock of the Doctor-Patient Relationship. The doctor-patient relationship is built on trust, nurtured by hope, and poisoned by deceit. Without trust, the relationship becomes like a smartphone without a service provider—a tool that looks promising but lacks the capability to fulfil its potential. For a doctor, trust is both a privilege and a responsibility, requiring a commitment to truth, transparency, and compassion.

In this relationship, the patient is not just a case or a diagnosis; they are a person with hopes, fears, and dreams. They come to their doctor seeking not just medical expertise but also human connection, empathy, and understanding. By fostering trust, doctors can create a space where true healing—physical, emotional, and spiritual—can occur. This, after all, is the essence of medicine: not just to cure, but to care.

Losing Trust in a Relationship: A Smartphone Without a Service Provider

Trust is the bedrock of any meaningful relationship, be it between friends, family members, or romantic partners. Without trust, a relationship loses its essence and becomes an empty shell, much like a smartphone without a service provider—appearing functional on the surface but utterly useless for its primary purpose of connecting with others. In such situations, relationships often devolve into playing games rather than fostering genuine connection and understanding.

Trust: The Invisible Connection

Trust is the invisible yet powerful force that binds people together. It enables individuals to be vulnerable, to open up, and to share their true selves with another. When we trust someone, we believe in their honesty, reliability, and intentions. This trust creates a space where intimacy and emotional connection can flourish. Just as a smartphone relies on its connection to a network to enable communication, a relationship relies on trust to facilitate meaningful interaction.

Without trust, however, the channels of communication begin to break down. Conversations become guarded, motives are questioned, and the bond between people starts to erode. Like a smartphone that has lost its service provider, the relationship may still exist, but its primary function—connection—has been compromised. What remains is an empty device, good only for playing games.

Playing Games: The Outcome of Lost Trust

When trust is lost, relationships often become a series of emotional games where sincerity is replaced by manipulation, miscommunication, and hidden agendas. Instead of engaging in open and honest dialogue, individuals may start to play mind games—testing each other's loyalty, withholding affection, or intentionally creating misunderstandings. These games are a defence mechanism, a way to protect oneself from further hurt or disappointment, but they ultimately prevent any real healing or reconnection.

For example, in a romantic relationship where trust has been shattered by infidelity, partners may begin to engage in passive-aggressive behaviours. They might withhold affection or attention, subtly punish one another, or create situations designed to provoke jealousy. Instead of addressing the root of the problem and rebuilding trust, they find themselves trapped in a cycle of manipulation and emotional gamesmanship. The relationship may continue, but it lacks the authenticity and connection that once made it meaningful.

Similarly, in friendships where trust has been broken—whether through betrayal, gossip, or dishonesty—the relationship can become superficial. Friends may continue to spend time together, but their interactions are laced with suspicion and unspoken tension. They may engage in polite conversation, but the depth of their bond has been lost, replaced by a sense of mistrust and guardedness. Instead of confiding in one another, they engage in a different kind of game—one of avoidance and pretence.

The Illusion of Functionality

A smartphone without a service provider may still have some functionalities – it can play games, take photos, or browse offline content. But these functions are a mere shadow of its true purpose: to connect, to communicate, to link people across distances. Similarly, a relationship without trust may still appear functional on the surface. People may continue to interact, share space, or even maintain the outward appearance of a relationship. But without trust, the relationship has lost its core function: the ability to truly connect on an emotional, intellectual, and spiritual level.

This illusion of functionality can be deceiving. It may seem as though the relationship is still intact, but in reality, it is a hollow shell, lacking the depth and connection that make relationships meaningful. Just as a smartphone without a network is reduced to a mere gaming device, a relationship without trust is reduced to a series of shallow interactions, devoid of the deeper connection that once defined it.

Rebuilding Trust: Restoring Connectivity

The good news is that just as a smartphone can be reconnected to a network, trust can be rebuilt in a relationship—but it requires effort, honesty, and a willingness to confront the issues that led to the loss of trust in the first place. Rebuilding trust is not easy; it takes time, patience, and consistent actions that demonstrate a commitment to change.

Rebuilding trust means being transparent, open, and accountable. It involves taking responsibility for one's actions, offering sincere apologies, and making amends where possible. It requires both parties to engage in honest communication, to express their feelings, and to work through their issues together. Most importantly, it requires a mutual commitment to healing the relationship and restoring the connection that has been lost.

However, just as some smartphones may never regain full functionality if the damage is too severe, not all relationships can be salvaged after trust has been broken. In some cases, the hurt may be too deep, the betrayal too significant, and the foundation of the relationship too compromised to rebuild. In such instances, it may be healthier to let go of the relationship rather than continue playing games in a broken connection.

Trust as the Lifeline of Relationships. In the end, trust is the lifeline of any relationship. Without it, a relationship is reduced to a mere facade, much like a smartphone without a service provider—a device that looks functional but has lost its true purpose of connection. When trust is lost, relationships often devolve into playing games, where authenticity is replaced by manipulation and miscommunication. Rebuilding trust is possible, but it requires effort, honesty, and a mutual commitment to healing.

Whether in friendships, family relationships, or romantic partnerships, trust is the foundation upon which meaningful connections are built. It is the invisible thread that allows us to be vulnerable, to connect, and to truly share ourselves with others. When that trust is broken, the relationship becomes hollow, reduced to a series of games that distract from the real issues. But when trust is present, relationships have the potential to be deep, fulfilling, and truly connected—just as a smartphone with a strong network connection is able to fulfil its true purpose of bringing people together.

Truth, Transparency, and Trust

In the quiet room, where healing begins,

A bond is formed beyond flesh and skin.

Not built on steel, nor measured by might,

But founded on truth, in the purest light.

Truth is the pillar, unwavering, strong,

A beacon of right, in a world full of wrong.

Without it, the whispers of doubt start to creep,

Turning hopes once bright into shadows deep.

Transparency follows, clear as the sky,

A mirror to show, not to obscure or lie;

Through this window, patients can see,

The care, the concern, and the honesty.

Trust is the thread that ties it all tight,

A sacred connection, in day and in night,

It's fragile, like glass, yet essential as air,

Once broken, it leaves hearts in despair.

For trust, when lost, is a phone with no ring,

No network or connection, no comfort, just an idle thing.

Good only for games, for masks we wear,

But empty inside, stripped of the care.

In this sacred space, between doctor and soul,

Let trust be the centre, the heart, and the goal.

For with trust, hope flourishes, deceit fades away,

And healing can happen in the light of the day.

42

The Hope Quotient: A Commitment to Never Desert the Patient

In the intricate dance between life and death, particularly within the walls of hospitals, clinics, and hospices, hope becomes a lifeline. It's the quiet, unspoken promise that even in the darkest moments, no one is alone. In the world of healthcare, hope takes on a profound significance when it is infused with a deep commitment to the patient—when the underlying message is, "No matter what happens to you, we will not desert you," and "You may be dying, but you are still important to us." This is what I call the "Hope Quotient"—the measure of a healthcare provider's commitment to ensuring that, regardless of the prognosis, the patient remains surrounded by care, dignity, and love.

The Role of Hope in Healing

Hope, for a patient, is not merely about expecting a cure or believing in a miracle. It is about finding meaning and comfort, knowing that their journey—regardless of the outcome—will not be walked alone. For many patients, especially those facing terminal illnesses or the ravages of chronic disease, the idea of hope transcends the physical. It becomes an emotional and spiritual anchor, a belief that they matter and will continue to matter until their very last breath.

In this context, the Hope Quotient is the commitment healthcare providers make to ensure that their patients never feel abandoned. This commitment is not contingent on the patient's health or ability to recover; instead, it is an unconditional vow to remain present, to listen, and to provide care and comfort, no matter the circumstances.

"No Matter What Happens to You, We Will Not Desert You"

One of the greatest fears for patients facing life-limiting illness is the fear of abandonment. Whether this fear stems from the physical absence of healthcare providers or the emotional distancing that sometimes occurs when a patient's condition becomes dire, it is a very real concern. Patients may wonder: Will my doctors still care about me if I'm no longer curable? Will my family still visit if I am bedridden and unable to communicate?

The essence of the Hope Quotient lies in addressing this fear directly. It is about reassuring the patient that, no matter what happens, they will not be deserted. This means continuing to provide attentive, compassionate care even when curative treatments are no longer effective. It means sitting with patients in their moments of fear and uncertainty, holding their hand, and offering a steady presence. It means ensuring that patients know that their worth is not tied to their ability to recover, but to their inherent humanity.

The act of not deserting a patient goes beyond physical presence. It encompasses emotional and psychological support as well. It means that the patient is not forgotten, not reduced to a number on a chart or a diagnosis in a file. It means that, even in their most vulnerable moments, they are seen, heard, and valued.

"You May Be Dying, But You Are Still Important to Us"

Death is often seen as the ultimate defeat in medicine – a sign that all efforts to heal have failed. But this perspective overlooks the true meaning of care, which is not just about curing illness but also about providing comfort, dignity, and peace. The message that "you may be dying, but you are still important to us" is a powerful affirmation of the patient's value as a human being, regardless of their physical condition.

This is where the Hope Quotient comes into play once again. It emphasises that a patient's worth does not diminish as they approach the end of life. On the contrary, this is when their need for compassionate care is at its greatest. To tell a patient that they are still important, even as they face death, is to recognise their intrinsic value as a person—beyond the disease, beyond the pain, beyond the prognosis.

It is about acknowledging that every life is significant, that every person matters, and that even in death, there is dignity. When healthcare providers express this sentiment, they give patients a precious gift: the assurance that they will not be forgotten, that their lives have meaning, and that they will be honoured and cared for until their final moments.

The Impact of the Hope Quotient on Patients and Families

The Hope Quotient does not just impact the patient; it profoundly affects their families and loved ones as well. When patients know that they will not be deserted, it alleviates some of the fear and anxiety that accompanies terminal illness. Families, in turn, find comfort in knowing that their loved one is being cared for with compassion and dignity, even when they themselves may not be present.

For families, the knowledge that healthcare providers are committed to their loved ones' well-being—regardless of the prognosis—can make all the difference in how they cope with the impending loss. It allows them to focus on spending quality time with their loved ones, rather than worrying about whether they are receiving adequate care. It also reassures them that their loved one's life is being honoured, even as it comes to an end.

Moreover, the Hope Quotient helps families navigate the difficult emotions that accompany end-of-life care. When they see that their loved one is being treated with respect, compassion, and love, it can help them come to terms with the reality of the situation. It allows them to find peace in the knowledge that their loved one is not alone, that they are still important, and that they are being cared for in the best possible way.

Hope Beyond Cure

The Hope Quotient teaches us that hope is not tied to a cure. Hope exists in the commitment to care, to honour, and to be present. It is the promise that no matter what happens, no one will be abandoned. It is the reassurance that every life has value, even in its final moments.

As healthcare providers, cultivating the Hope Quotient means embracing our role not just as healers, but as companions on the journey of life, and sometimes, death. It means understanding that our patients are more than their diagnoses—they are people with dreams, fears, and relationships. And even when we cannot cure them, we can offer them the profound gift of hope by never deserting them and affirming their importance, even as they face the end of life.

The Hope Quotient as a Pillar of Compassionate Care

The Hope Quotient is a pillar of compassionate care that transcends the boundaries of traditional medicine. It is the commitment to stay by the patient's side, to offer comfort and dignity, and to affirm their worth, regardless of their prognosis. By embodying the Hope Quotient, healthcare providers can make a profound difference in the lives of their patients and their families, offering not just medical care, but emotional and spiritual support as well.

In the end, the Hope Quotient reminds us that every person deserves to be treated with respect, care, and love, even as they approach the end of life. It is a promise that no matter what happens, no one will be abandoned—that they will always remain important to those who care for them. This, ultimately, is the true essence of hope in healthcare.

The Sublime Structure of Hope and the Sacred Hope Quotient

It's not the end that brings the tear,

But the unknown path that leads us here.

For death itself is not the foe,

But how we'll face its final glow.

In fear's deep shadow, we may tread,

Not of the stillness, but of the dread.

The pain, the loss, the dark unknown,

Can chill the heart, turn hope to stone.

Yet there, beneath, a structure stands,

A scaffold built by caring hands.

A sacred hope that lifts the weight,

Deracinating fear and fate.

It whispers softly, "You are not alone."

In life, in death, you're not on your own."

This hope transcends, it calms, it guides,

Through every storm, where fear resides.

It's not the fear of death we fight,

But how we'll journey into nigh;

Yet when Hope's quotient fills the air,

The path is clear, the heart prepared.

For sacred Hope, with tender grace,

Transforms the fear we once did face.

In every breath, it softly speaks—

"You are still loved, though growing weak."

So let Hope's structure rise and climb,

A beacon bright through endless time.

For in its strength, we find our peace,

And fear of death begins to cease.

43

The Power of Availability: How Phone and Video Calls Improve the Hope Quotient

In the modern landscape of healthcare, technology has opened new avenues for communication and support. One of the most powerful ways this has manifested is in the ability to assure patients that their doctor will be available on the phone or through a video call. This simple assurance can have a profound impact on a patient's emotional well-being and overall sense of hope. It sends a message of continuity, presence, and support, even when physical distance separates the doctor from the patient. The result is often a visible improvement in the patient's outlook— their face sparkles, they smile more easily, and their eating and sleeping patterns improve.

The Impact of Being Available

For a patient, knowing that their doctor is just a phone call or video call away can be incredibly reassuring. This availability represents more than just the convenience of access—it symbolises the doctor's ongoing commitment to the patient's care, regardless of the circumstances. In moments of uncertainty, pain, or fear, patients often crave the comfort of knowing that they can reach out to someone who understands their condition and can offer guidance, even if it's through a screen or a voice on the other end of the line.

This sense of availability addresses one of the most profound fears that patients face: the fear of being alone in their illness. When patients know that they have access to their doctor beyond the confines of scheduled appointments, it significantly boosts their sense of security and hope. This connection creates a lifeline of support that can bridge the gap between in-person visits, providing patients with a sense of continuity in their care.

Enhancing the Hope Quotient

The Hope Quotient, as discussed previously, is the measure of a healthcare provider's ability to instil a sense of hope in their patients. Hope is not just about physical healing; it's about emotional resilience, spiritual peace, and the belief that no matter what happens, they are not alone in their journey. By assuring patients that they can reach out through a phone or video call, doctors actively enhance the Hope Quotient in several important ways:

1. Immediate Reassurance: The knowledge that help is just a call away provides immediate reassurance. Whether a patient is experiencing a new symptom, feeling anxious about their condition, or simply needs to hear a calming voice, the ability to contact their doctor offers comfort and alleviates fear.

2. Continuity of Care: Regular in-person appointments may be spaced weeks apart, leaving patients feeling disconnected from their care team. The option of phone or video calls ensures that patients feel continually supported, even between visits. This continuity of care helps maintain the patient's emotional and psychological well-being.

3. Personalised Attention: Phone and video calls allow for more personalised interaction. Unlike impersonal web searches or automated helplines, these calls offer patients the opportunity to speak directly with their doctor, who understands their unique medical history and can provide tailored advice. This personal

connection strengthens the doctor-patient relationship and reinforces the patient's sense of being cared for.

4. Emotional Connection: Seeing a familiar face through a video call or hearing a trusted voice over the phone can have a powerful emotional impact on patients. It humanises the care experience and reminds patients that they are valued as individuals, not just as medical cases. This emotional connection contributes to a stronger sense of hope and well-being.

5. Empowerment: Knowing they have direct access to their doctor empowers patients to take an active role in their care. They can seek clarification on treatment plans, ask questions about their symptoms, and gain a better understanding of their condition. This empowerment fosters a sense of control over their health, which in turn bolsters their hope.

The Sparkle of Hope: Visible Improvements in Patients

The positive effects of this increased availability are often visible in patients. When patients feel secure in the knowledge that their doctor is reachable, their emotional and physical state tends to improve. The patient's face may sparkle with a newfound sense of hope, and they often begin to smile more readily. This sense of connection and security can lead to improvements in seemingly unrelated aspects of their health, such as eating and sleeping.

Improved Appetite: Anxiety and fear can suppress appetite, leading to weight loss and malnutrition. When patients feel supported and secure, their anxiety often decreases, allowing them to eat more comfortably. Knowing that help is readily available can alleviate the stress that often interferes with proper nutrition.

Better Sleep: Sleep is another area where anxiety and fear can wreak havoc. Patients who worry about their condition, especially at night, may struggle to get the rest they need. The reassurance that their doctor is only a call away can provide the peace of mind necessary for better sleep. When patients sleep better, their overall health and mood improve, creating a positive cycle of well-being.

Visible Calm and Positivity: The most noticeable change is often in the patient's demeanour. When patients know that they are not alone, that their doctor cares enough to be available even from a distance, their outlook shifts. They become calmer, more positive, and more at ease with their situation. This emotional shift can be transformative, affecting every aspect of their health and quality of life.

The Broader Implications of Technological Connectivity in Healthcare

The power of phone and video calls in enhancing the Hope Quotient is part of a broader movement toward technological integration in healthcare. Telemedicine, once considered a niche service, has become a vital component of patient care, particularly in the wake of global events like the COVID-19 pandemic. The ability to connect with patients remotely has become an essential tool in maintaining continuity of care and supporting patients in real time.

However, the true value of this connectivity lies not just in the technology itself, but in the commitment it represents. When doctors make themselves available for remote communication, they are sending a clear message: "I am here for you, no matter what." This message is a powerful antidote to the feelings of isolation and fear that often accompany illness, particularly chronic or terminal conditions.

For doctors, integrating phone and video calls into their practice requires balancing availability with the demands of their work. But for patients, this simple gesture can make all the difference. It reinforces the idea that they are not alone in their journey, that they are still important, and that their well-being is a priority, regardless of the physical distance between them and their healthcare provider.

The Lifeline of Hope Through Availability In a world where technology can sometimes feel impersonal, the assurance of availability through phone or video calls rehumanises the healthcare experience. It strengthens the bond between doctor and patient, enhances the Hope Quotient, and leads to visible improvements in the patient's emotional and physical well-being. By offering this lifeline of support, doctors can provide patients with the reassurance they need to face their challenges with hope, resilience, and a renewed sense of connection.

In the end, this availability represents more than just a convenient way to communicate—it is a powerful affirmation that, no matter what happens, the patient will not be abandoned. And in that promise, patients find the hope that allows them to smile, eat, sleep, and, ultimately, live better.

The Promise of Presence and Power of Availability

In quiet moments, frail with fear,

A voice brings comfort, soft and clear.

A doctor's word, a simple vow—

"I'll be here, then, and I'm here now."

This promise made, though small it seems,

Can lift the heart and soothe the dreams.

For in that bond, a hope takes flight,

Restoring strength in the darkest night.

The face that's seen through the video's glow,

Or voice that calls when spirits are low,

Becomes a lifeline, calm and sure,

A steady hand when none's secure.

Availability—its quiet grace,

Transforms the heart, restores the face.

A sparkle brightens weary eyes,

And sleep returns, as fear subsides.

For hope is more than fleeting light;

It's nurtured by the care in sight.

The Hope Quotient grows with ease,

When doctors offer words that please:

"You're not alone; I'm always near,

To ease your pain, to calm your fear."

And in that promise, hope ascends,

A healing power that never ends.

The structure of hope, so finely built,

With every call, the fear is stilled;

A doctor's presence, near or far,

Becomes a patient's guiding star.

44

Android and iPhone Rounds: Intrusive Tech Giants in an App-Based World

In today's increasingly interconnected world, tech giants like Android and Apple are transforming every aspect of life, including healthcare. Through apps, doctors are now granted the ability to monitor patients in real-time, no matter where they are, thanks to devices that beep, squeak, and relay a plethora of data. With such advancements, patients can be connected through wires to devices that can constantly report their vitals to doctors' phones and tablets. On the surface, this seems like an impressive leap forward in medicine—akin to watching your house through CCTV cameras while vacationing in a distant land. But such remote oversight in medicine risks the erosion of the very human connection that lies at the heart of the doctor-patient relationship.

Medicine, at its core, is not merely a profession of science but one of profound empathy and understanding. We doctors have the privilege and responsibility of caring for the Imago Dei—the image of God and to 'tinker with God's Creation' in human beings. While technology can provide valuable tools, it must never overshadow the human element that is integral to healing. The truth is, after a prolonged surgery or an intense medical ordeal, an unfortunate patient does not just need machines to beep in reassurance; they long for the warm, disarming smile of their consultant and medical team.

There have been countless instances where idiopathic fevers or inexplicable pain has subsided simply through the presence and touch of a doctor. The therapeutic power of touch—of a doctor running their fingers through a patient's dishevelled hair—transcends the capabilities of any machine. It is a connection that is deeply human and deeply healing. Machines cannot replicate the spark of compassion that ignites when a doctor touches a patient, reassuring them not just with words but with presence and care.

For a thousand years to come, there will be no replacement for human touch in medicine. The cold precision of robots and machines may assist us in surgery and diagnostics, but they cannot replicate the feel of a gallstone lodged in a bile duct, or the subtle rigidity of an abdomen with peritonitis. These sensations are uniquely human experiences, recognised not just by the hand but by the empathetic mind that interprets them. A robot cannot recognise the slight squirm on a patient's face when their inflamed appendix is palpated.

In clinical practice, the feel of a patient's body, the reactions to touch, and the subtle cues they give are often as telling as any diagnostic test. Machines and technology, though valuable, can fail to capture these nuances. The rigidity of an abdominal wall during peritonitis, the guarded expression of a patient in pain—these are clinical signs that are uniquely detected by the human hand and eye. They are not just data points to be processed but symptoms to be understood within the context of the whole person.

While the future of medicine undoubtedly involves technology, we must never forget the irreplaceable value of human touch. We, as doctors, are more than just technicians—we are healers, and healing involves far more than monitoring vital signs from afar. It is about being present, both physically and emotionally, for our patients. It is about offering not just our skills but our compassion.

Let us embrace technology, but never at the cost of the human connection that lies at the heart of medicine. The beeping of monitors may provide data, but it is the warmth of human interaction, the reassurance of a doctor's touch, and the power of empathy that will continue to heal and comfort patients for generations to come.

iPhone and Android Rounds

On hospital floors, in hallowed halls,
Where healing words and duty calls,
The rounds begin, but here's the twist—
It's not the care that's often missed.

With iPhone here and Android there,
A battle for the strongest air.
Connectivity, a fragile thread,
Where signals falter, hope is shed.

"Can you hear me now?" the doctor sighs,
As tech defeats their earnest tries.
A pixelated face, a voice unclear,
The vital touch seems far, not near.

In rooms where silence once held sway,

Now screens decide the night and day.

A glitch, a lag, a frozen screen,

And empathy remains unseen.

For though the tools are bright and smart,

They lack the warmth of a human heart.

In iPhone's sleek and Android's might,

Connection's lost in tech's cold fight.

Yet still we try, despite the flaws,

To bridge the gap, to serve the cause.

But oh, the rounds, they lose their grace,

When signals fail to keep their pace.

So let us not in gadgets trust,

For human care remains a must;

Though iPhones ring and apps abound,

True healing lies in touch and sound.

45

The Promenade of Aloneness

Aloneness, when embraced, becomes a space for self-reflection, growth, and inner peace. It is the quiet moment of a lone walker, the individual who finds solace in their own company. The promenade, in this case, is not a journey of emptiness but one of discovery. In solitude, one can find clarity of thought, a deeper connection to the world, and an opportunity to recharge emotionally and mentally.

Many great thinkers and creators have found inspiration in their aloneness. The isolation provides them with a sanctuary, a space to observe the world, to think deeply, and to channel those thoughts into something meaningful. For the surgeon, artist, or musician, aloneness is often a prerequisite for mastery, a time when the world's noise fades, and one's inner voice takes centre stage.

But the promenade of aloneness also requires balance. Too much solitude can tip the scales towards loneliness if one becomes too disconnected from the world. The trick lies in embracing the walk while remaining open to the possibility of connection, knowing when to retreat into the self and when to step back into the shared space of human interaction.

The Serenade of Loneliness

Loneliness, in contrast, is a serenade of longing. It is the haunting melody that lingers in the heart when connection feels out of reach. Unlike aloneness, loneliness is not chosen. It sneaks in uninvited, often when least expected. One can be surrounded by people, yet feel entirely alone, disconnected from the warmth of human interaction.

The battle with loneliness is a deeply personal one. It arises from the gap between the desire for companionship and the absence of it. The mind begins to fill this space with melancholy tunes, replaying past moments of joy or amplifying the void where connection once existed. The serenade of loneliness is not always mournful, but it does speak of a yearning unfulfilled.

Yet even in loneliness, there is hope. The act of battling this emotion is akin to composing a new melody – one where the longing for connection becomes a force for change. Reaching out to others, creating new relationships, or even rekindling lost connections are all ways to transform loneliness into something more bearable. Even the smallest effort to connect can break the cycle of isolation. A phone call, a visit, or even a smile to a stranger can begin to change the tune, replacing the haunting serenade with a chorus of shared experiences.

The Dance Between Aloneness and Loneliness

In life, the dance between aloneness and loneliness is inevitable. There are moments when solitude feels empowering, and others when it feels suffocating. The key to battling both lies in understanding when each emotion serves us and when it hinders us.

For some, aloneness can be a necessary retreat, a way to recharge from the demands of social interaction. For others, it is a painful reminder of the connections they lack. Likewise, loneliness can be a fleeting emotion that drives us towards meaningful connection, or it can become a persistent state that weighs us down.

The battle is not about avoiding either state entirely but learning to navigate between them with purpose. A promenade can be a time of peaceful reflection, and a serenade can be a call for connection. In embracing both, we learn to walk through life with a fuller understanding of ourselves and our needs.

Life's journey is filled with moments of solitude and connection. The promenade of aloneness offers a chance to reflect, to grow, and to find strength in our own company. The serenade of loneliness, while painful, reminds us of our innate need for connection and drives us to seek it out.

In battling aloneness and loneliness, the goal is not to eliminate either but to understand them. The balance lies in knowing when to embrace the quiet walk alone and when to reach out for a hand to hold. Through this balance, we can navigate the complexities of human emotion and find peace in both solitude and companionship.

Aloneness versus Loneliness: A Serenade and a Promenade

In quiet steps, the path unfolds,

A promenade through thoughts untold,

Aloneness walks with steady grace,

A silent smile upon its face.

The world is hushed, the air is still,

A moment's peace, a space to fill,

With whispered dreams and hopes that bloom,

A gentle calm within the room.

But loneliness sings a different tune,
A serenade beneath the moon,
A haunting cry, a longing deep,
For voices lost and hearts asleep.

It yearns for hands to intertwine,
For warmth that fades with passing time,
In crowded rooms, it lingers near.
A hollow note, a quiet tear.

Aloneness is a chosen friend.
A solace found, a means to mend,
But loneliness, it sneaks inside.
A shadow where our fears reside.

Yet in-between, the two can dance,
A fleeting step, a second chance,
To turn the ache into a song,
To find where both belong.

For aloneness brings the heart to rest,

A time to grow, a private quest,

And loneliness, though sharp its sting,

Reminds us we are tied by string.

A promenade, a serenade,

Two sides of one life's sweet parade,

And in the space where they converge,

We learn to walk, to sing, to merge.

46

Attributes that a Doctor and Team Should Possess: Truth in Lips, Courage in Blood, and Compassion in Their Heart

The world of medicine is both a science and an art, requiring a delicate balance of knowledge, skill, and humanity. A doctor, along with their team, must possess attributes that go beyond technical expertise. The best care emerges not just from well-trained hands but from truthful lips, courageous hearts, and boundless compassion. These are the traits that turn medical practitioners into healers, helping them guide patients through some of the most challenging moments of their lives.

Truth in Lips: The Integrity of Communication

Honesty is the cornerstone of the patient-doctor relationship. When doctors speak with truth on their lips, they offer their patients something invaluable—trust. Every diagnosis, prognosis, and treatment plan must be communicated with clarity and transparency. Patients deserve the truth, even when it is difficult, because it empowers them to make informed decisions about their own lives. Whether delivering good news or bad, the truth must be delivered with sensitivity and respect, keeping in mind the emotional state of the patient and their family.

Yet, truth is not merely about stating facts. It is also about honesty in action, aligning one's words with their deeds. This integrity builds confidence in the team and fosters a culture of reliability. When a doctor upholds truth in their words, they create a foundation for trust, both within the medical team and with the patients. The courage to tell the truth, even when it's hard, reflects the strength of character and professional responsibility that every medical professional must embody.

Courage in Blood: The Steadfastness in Adversity

The medical field is often rife with challenges that require more than knowledge and skill. Courage in the blood is the willingness to confront adversity head-on, to make tough decisions in the heat of the moment, and to stand by those decisions with conviction. For doctors and their teams, courage is essential in the operating room, in the face of uncertainty, and during ethical dilemmas. It's the courage to take calculated risks, knowing that the outcome could be life-altering for the patient.

Courage also manifests in resilience. Medicine can be emotionally and physically exhausting, but true practitioners find strength in their purpose. They remain undeterred by setbacks, mistakes, or the inevitable losses that are part of medical practice. It's this fortitude that enables a team to come back stronger, to continue learning, and to keep fighting for their patients, no matter how difficult the journey.

Compassion in Heart: The Essence of Healing

While truth and courage are critical, it is compassion that elevates the practice of medicine to a higher plane. Compassion in the heart is the ability to see beyond the illness and recognise the humanity in every patient. It's about understanding the fears, hopes, and emotions that accompany the physical ailments. Compassion drives doctors and their teams to not just treat the disease but to care for the whole person.

This attribute is often the balm that soothes when science reaches its limits. In situations where there are no cures, where suffering is inevitable, and where life is nearing its end, compassion can still provide comfort. It is the compassionate touch, the kind word, and the empathetic presence that often make all the difference. Compassion turns medical practitioners into trusted guides through the vulnerable stages of life, bringing peace to both patients and their loved ones.

A medical team infused with compassion operates with a shared understanding of the importance of emotional care. Whether it's in a bustling emergency room or a quiet hospice, compassion enables doctors and nurses to connect with patients on a deeper level, to listen more attentively, and to act more kindly. This connection is vital in fostering hope, dignity, and a sense of comfort even in the darkest times.

47

The Synergy of Truth, Courage, and Compassion

When a doctor and their team possess truth in their lips, courage in their blood, and compassion in their hearts, they create a powerful synergy. These attributes work together to shape not just competent practitioners but true healers. Truth provides the foundation for trust, courage fuels action in the face of difficulty, and compassion ensures that care is given with humanity and respect.

The best medical teams are those that embody these qualities in every aspect of their work. They are the ones who approach every patient with the intention to heal not just the body but the mind and spirit as well. They are the ones who understand that medicine is more than a profession – it is a calling to serve with integrity, bravery, and love.

In a world where medical advancements continue to evolve at a rapid pace, these timeless attributes remain the pillars of truly effective and humane care. They remind us that, at its core, medicine is about people—about their lives, their stories, and their well-being. Truth, courage, and compassion are the guiding stars that lead doctors and their teams through the complexities of medicine, ensuring that they not only treat but also heal.

Truth in Lips, Courage in Blood, Compassion in Heart

Let truth reside upon the lips.

Where words are clear, no fear slips.

A flame that flickers, pure and bright,

Guiding us through the darkest night.

For truth, though sharp, is never cold,

Its power vast, its purpose bold,

It speaks with honour, stands its ground,

In truth, the seeds of trust are found.

Courage flows in veins like fire.

A lifeblood born of deep desire,

To face the storm, to break the chain,

To rise again through fear and pain.

It swells within the heart's own beat,

With every step, though wounds may bleed,

For courage finds its strength in strife,

And shapes the soul that battles life.

But without compassion, all is lost.

A heart of stone will pay the cost,

For kindness heals where swords divide,

And mercy stands on virtue's side.

To feel another's grief as yours,

To open wide love's quiet doors,

Compassion makes the spirit whole,

A salve that soothes the deepest soul.

So live with truth upon your lips,

Let courage fill your fingertips,

But in your heart, let love reside.

And walk with mercy at your side.

Truth in Lips, Courage in Blood, Compassion in Heart.

48

Minimising Formality and Maximising Humanity in Healthcare: A Call for Compassionate Care

When a patient and their family enter the corridors of a hospital, they are often overwhelmed by a flood of emotions—loneliness, vulnerability, anxiety, and fear. Hospitals, for all their promise of healing, can be intimidating places, filled with unfamiliar environments, jargon-heavy communication, and bureaucratic processes that can make the experience feel cold and impersonal. In such a setting, it is crucial to minimise formality and maximise humanity. By doing so, healthcare providers can create an environment that not only addresses the physical ailments but also cares for the emotional and psychological well-being of those who seek their help.

The Isolation of the Hospital Experience

Hospitals are meant to be places of healing, but for many, they feel more like alien environments where control is wrested away from them. As soon as a patient enters a hospital, they step into a world governed by medical protocols, paperwork, and procedures. This can often make them feel like just another case number, rather than a unique individual with a personal history, fears, and hopes. For the family, watching their loved one being absorbed into this system heightens their anxiety. They are left in waiting rooms, uncertain about what lies ahead, and are often given information in technical terms that leave them more confused than reassured.

The formalities—whether they are in the form of consent forms, administrative procedures, or strict visiting hours—can contribute to the sense of alienation. While these formalities are often necessary for the efficient functioning of healthcare systems, they can inadvertently create barriers between the patient and the medical team. This is where the need to minimise formality comes into play. Hospitals must strive to streamline processes in ways that are more accessible and patient-friendly, allowing patients and families to feel that they are part of the care process rather than passive participants subjected to it.

The Power of Humanity in Healing

The act of minimising formality does not mean sacrificing professionalism or the quality of care. Instead, it means recognising the humanity in every patient and ensuring that care is delivered in a way that respects their dignity and emotions. Medical professionals must see beyond the illness and focus on the person who is affected by it. This shift in perspective can make all the difference in how a patient and their family experience their time in the hospital.

When humanity is prioritised, the hospital ceases to be just a place of clinical intervention and becomes a place of holistic healing. Simple gestures like a reassuring word, a compassionate touch, or taking the time to explain procedures in layman's terms can have a profound impact. The presence of empathy in interactions helps ease the patient's anxiety and builds a bridge of trust. It signals to the patient that they are not just a body to be treated, but a person who is being cared for in all aspects—physically, emotionally, and psychologically.

Creating a Patient-Centred Environment

To maximise humanity in healthcare, there needs to be a conscious effort to create a patient-centred environment. This involves rethinking how healthcare teams interact with patients and their families. It requires a shift from a transactional approach to care—where patients are seen as problems to be solved—to a relational approach, where patients are seen as people to be supported.

One way to achieve this is by improving communication. Medical professionals should make an effort to communicate clearly and compassionately, avoiding unnecessary jargon and speaking in a way that is understandable and reassuring. By doing so, they can demystify the treatment process and reduce the anxiety that often accompanies hospital visits. It is also important to actively listen to patients and their families, acknowledging their concerns and answering their questions with patience. This fosters a sense of partnership in the healing process, making patients feel that their voices are heard and valued.

Another important aspect of maximising humanity is recognising the emotional and psychological toll that illness takes on both patients and their families. Hospitals should have mechanisms in place to provide emotional support, whether through counselling services, patient advocates, or simply by fostering a culture of kindness and compassion within the staff. This support can alleviate the feelings of loneliness and vulnerability that so often accompany a hospital stay.

Transforming Healthcare Through Compassion

Minimising formality and maximising humanity is not just a noble ideal—it is a practical approach that can transform healthcare for the better. Studies have shown that when patients feel respected and cared for as individuals, their outcomes improve. Compassionate care can reduce stress, enhance patient satisfaction, and even contribute to faster recovery times. In this way, the human touch becomes as vital to healing as any medical intervention.

For medical professionals, embracing humanity in their practice also leads to greater job satisfaction. The ability to connect with patients on a personal level, to see the impact of their compassion, can reinvigorate their sense of purpose and fulfilment in their work. It reminds them that medicine is not just about curing diseases, but about caring for people.

In a world where medical technology continues to advance at a rapid pace, it is easy to lose sight of the human element in healthcare. But the truth is that patients and their families need more than just cutting-edge treatments – they need compassion, empathy, and understanding. By minimising formality and maximising humanity, healthcare providers can create an environment where patients feel seen, heard, and cared for as individuals. This approach not only enhances the patient experience but also fosters a culture of healing that truly honours the dignity and worth of every person who walks through the hospital doors. In the end, it is the combination of skillful care and compassionate connection that makes the journey through illness a little less lonely, a little less frightening, and a little more hopeful.

Minimise Formality, Maximise Humanity - in Day-to-day Clinical Practice

In halls where white coats often roam,

Where science builds its steady home,

Let not the walls grow cold and bare,

For human hearts are beating there.

Formality, though it plays its part,

Can mask the warmth within the heart,

A sterile word, a distant face,

Can steal from care its healing grace.

But kindness, soft in every glance,

Gives every soul a second chance,

A gentle word, a knowing smile,

Can ease the pain for just a while.

For patients are not charts to read,

Nor just a list of care or need,

They're stories lived, and lives endured,

In every hand, a hope is stored.

So let us strip the rigid frame,

And call each patient by their name,

With every step, let care be real,

And meet them where they stand and feel.

In every touch, humanity.

In every word, sincerity.

For in the space where hearts are free,

We find the root of true empathy.

Minimise the formal stance,

Maximise each chance,

To show that healing's truest art,

Begins with love, straight from the heart.

49

Beyond Cancer and Cure: Driving Home the Reality of Life and Care

The aphorism "Cure Sometimes, Relief Often, Comfort Always" has been a guiding principle in medicine, particularly in the context of serious illnesses like cancer. It reminds us that while a cure is not always possible, there are always opportunities to provide relief and comfort to patients. However, this truth must be communicated in a way that resonates deeply with both patients and their families, especially when they are facing the uncertainties that come with a cancer diagnosis. Beyond the pursuit of a cure, there is life to be lived and care to be given, and this reality must be driven home to patients and their loved ones.

The Quest for Cure: A Singular Focus

For many patients and families, the word "cancer" triggers a single-minded pursuit of a cure. This is understandable—cancer, with its reputation as a formidable adversary, often evokes fear and desperation. The hope for a cure can overshadow every other aspect of care. Medical teams, too, are often pressured to focus on curative treatments, pushing the boundaries of surgery, chemotherapy, radiation, and other interventions. While this focus on cure is vital, especially in early and treatable stages, it can inadvertently narrow the patient's view of what care truly means.

The reality is that not all cancers can be cured, and even when treatments are successful in extending life, they often come at a cost. Patients may endure significant physical and emotional suffering during aggressive treatments, and the quality of life can be compromised. For families, the pressure to continue the fight can be overwhelming, leaving little room to consider alternative approaches to care, especially when curative efforts fail.

This is where the medical community must step in—not just as providers of treatment, but as guides who help patients and families navigate the complex landscape of cancer care. It is essential to communicate that life does not end when curative treatments are no longer an option. Instead, there is life beyond cancer, and care beyond cure, and this needs to be integrated into the conversation from the very beginning.

Relief and Comfort: A Broader Perspective on Care

Relief and comfort should not be seen as lesser goals in the face of incurable illness. They are, in fact, essential components of holistic care that recognise the patient as a whole person—mind, body, and spirit. Palliative care, for instance, offers relief from the symptoms and stress of illness, enhancing the quality of life for both patients and their families. This type of care is not about giving up; it is about prioritising the patient's well-being in all dimensions, from pain management to emotional support.

Driving home the reality that there is care beyond cure involves changing the narrative around what it means to care for someone with cancer. It requires healthcare providers to shift the focus from solely prolonging life to also enriching it, regardless of the prognosis. This does not mean abandoning hope, but rather, redefining hope in broader terms—hope for meaningful experiences, hope for comfort, and hope for dignity in the face of illness.

Palliative care teams are instrumental in delivering this message, helping patients and families see that relief and comfort can coexist with active treatment. They guide patients through difficult decisions, ensuring that care aligns with the patient's values and wishes. Importantly, they help to alleviate the fear that accepting comfort-focused care means surrendering to the illness. Instead, it is about reclaiming control over how one lives, even in the presence of cancer.

The Role of Communication: Compassionate Conversations

The key to driving home the reality of life beyond cancer lies in compassionate communication. It is not enough to simply inform patients and families about their options. Medical professionals must engage in open, honest, and empathetic conversations that allow patients to express their fears, hopes, and desires. These conversations should begin early in the diagnosis and continue throughout the course of treatment, ensuring that patients feel supported at every stage.

Breaking the news that a cure may not be possible is one of the most challenging tasks a doctor faces. However, when done with sensitivity, it can be a transformative moment for patients and their families. It allows them to begin the process of acceptance and to shift their focus from fighting the disease at all costs to finding peace and meaning in the time they have left. Families, too, need to be guided through this transition, as they often bear the emotional weight of the situation and may struggle to reconcile their desire for a cure with the reality of their loved one's condition.

Providing information about palliative care and emphasising its role in enhancing quality of life is critical. Patients and families need to understand that choosing comfort care does not mean abandoning treatment altogether. Rather, it means receiving care that prioritises their comfort, dignity, and well-being, often alongside other treatments aimed at managing the disease. Through this approach, patients can continue to live with purpose and fulfilment, even in the face of a terminal diagnosis.

Reimagining Life Beyond Cancer

For many patients, life beyond cancer is not about surviving the disease but about living fully despite it. This shift in perspective allows them to focus on what truly matters—relationships, personal goals, and cherished experiences. It also opens the door to meaningful conversations about what constitutes a good life and a good death. These discussions can help patients and their families come to terms with the realities of the illness while still finding joy and meaning in their remaining time together.

Care beyond cure also extends to the family, who will continue their journey after the patient is gone. Bereavement support, counselling, and resources for coping with loss are essential components of this care, helping families navigate their grief and find healing after their loved one has passed. By addressing the needs of the family, healthcare teams can ensure that the impact of compassionate care continues long after the patient's death, leaving a legacy of comfort and support.

Conclusion: A Holistic Approach to Care "Cure Sometimes, Relief Often, Comfort Always" is more than just an aphorism—it is a call to action for healthcare providers to embrace a holistic approach to care. Patients and their families need to understand that there is life beyond cancer and care beyond cure. This message must be communicated with compassion, allowing patients to redefine what it means to live well in the face of illness. By focusing not only on prolonging life but also on enriching it, healthcare providers can help patients and families find peace, comfort, and meaning, regardless of the prognosis. In the end, it is this holistic approach that truly honours the dignity of every patient and the humanity of their journey.

The Sacred Role: Help patients make the transition from being seriously ill and fighting death to becoming terminally ill and seeking peace.

A sacred task, a solemn way,

To stand where shadows start to sway,

Between the fight for life held tight,

And Death's approach in soft twilight.

The palliative care provider's role,

Is more than healing the body whole—

It's guiding souls through battles grim,

From strength to frailty growing dim.

When illness fiercely begins to weigh,

And hope seems to be slipping far away,

The hands that once sought only a cure,

Now hold a light, both calm and pure.

For in the shift from fight to peace,

They help the heart find sweet release,

Not from the struggle to remain,

But from the grasp of endless pain.

They stand beside, with quiet grace,
To ease the fear upon the face,
To help the patient redefine,
What strength can mean as they decline.

Not giving up, but changing course,
To fight with love, with tender force,
To fight for moments, not just breath,
For dignity in facing death.

The sacred role they humbly bear,
Is helping patients to prepare—
To guide them through, with a gentle hand,
As life flows to its final stand.

For in this fight, though Death is near,
There's space for hope and space for cheer,
A palliative heart will always see,
That even in the end, we're free.

50

The Race for Quality Doesn't Have a Finishing Line: Quality in Living and Dignity in Death

The pursuit of quality, whether in living or in death, is a lifelong journey. Unlike a typical race, it has no definitive endpoint. The race for quality is a continuous process of striving to improve, to uplift, and to ensure that life is lived fully and with dignity until the very end. This concept applies not only to how we live but also to how we die. Ultimately, the quality of our experiences and the dignity with which we navigate the inevitable decline of life is what matters most.

Quality in Living: The Endless Pursuit

From the moment we are born, the pursuit of a good life begins. Quality in living encompasses the richness of our experiences, the fulfilment of our goals, and the cultivation of meaningful relationships. It is not simply about accumulating material success or external markers of achievement, but about how deeply we engage with the world around us. It is about being present, finding joy, and creating a life that aligns with our values.

However, quality in living is not something that can be achieved once and for all. It is a dynamic and evolving process, shaped by the challenges we face, the decisions we make, and the relationships we nurture. This makes the race for quality a perpetual one. As we grow older, our definition of a good life often changes. What mattered to us in our youth may no longer hold the same significance in our later years. The race for quality, therefore, is not about reaching a predetermined finish line, but about continuously adjusting and adapting to ensure that we live meaningfully at every stage of life.

In healthcare, the focus on quality in living is particularly important. Medical advancements have allowed people to live longer, but longevity without quality is hollow. The real challenge is to ensure that as life expectancy increases, so too does the quality of those additional years. Healthcare providers play a critical role in this pursuit by not only treating diseases but also enhancing the overall well-being of their patients. This requires a holistic approach that addresses physical health, emotional well-being, and social connections.

Dignity in Death: The Final Chapter

While the race for quality in living continues throughout life, there comes a point when the focus shifts toward ensuring dignity in death. Dying is an inevitable part of the human experience, yet it is often shrouded in fear and avoidance. Too often, death is seen as a defeat, a failure to prolong life. However, a more compassionate perspective recognises that death is not the opposite of life, but a natural conclusion to it.

Dignity in death means honouring the individual's wishes, providing comfort, and ensuring that they are treated with respect and compassion in their final days. Just as quality in living is about more than physical health, dignity in death goes beyond the absence of pain. It involves emotional support, spiritual care, and the preservation of autonomy. It is about allowing individuals to die on their own terms, surrounded by those they love, in an environment that feels safe and familiar.

The field of palliative care has been instrumental in advancing this understanding of dignity in death. By focusing on relieving suffering and improving the quality of life for those with serious illnesses, palliative care professionals emphasise that dying can be a meaningful experience. They provide holistic support to both patients and their families, addressing not only physical symptoms but also the emotional, social, and spiritual aspects of dying.

However, achieving dignity in death requires a cultural shift. It requires us to move away from the idea that extending life at all costs is the ultimate goal of medicine. Instead, we must recognise that there comes a time when the pursuit of quality in life must give way to the pursuit of quality in death. This means being willing to have difficult conversations about end-of-life care, advance directives, and the limits of curative treatments. It means prioritising comfort, autonomy, and emotional well-being over aggressive interventions that may prolong life but diminish its quality.

The Interconnectedness of Living and Dying

Quality in living and dignity in death are not separate endeavours. They are deeply interconnected, and how we approach one influences the other. A life lived with intention, purpose, and fulfilment naturally leads to a death that is faced with acceptance and grace. Similarly, when individuals are provided with compassionate care at the end of life, it allows them to reflect on their journey with a sense of peace and closure.

For healthcare providers, this interconnectedness highlights the importance of continuity in care. From birth to death, medical professionals have a responsibility to support their patients not just in the fight against disease, but in the pursuit of a life well-lived and a death well-died. This requires a shift in focus from simply curing illnesses to enhancing the overall quality of life. It means recognising that the goal of medicine is not just to add years to life, but to add life to years.

Conclusion: A Journey Without End: The race for quality in living and dignity in death is a journey without a finish line. It is an ongoing process of striving for the best possible experience at every stage of life, recognising that quality is not a destination but a way of being. For individuals, this means making choices that align with their values and pursuing a life of meaning, connection, and fulfilment. For healthcare providers, it means supporting patients in their pursuit of quality, not just through medical interventions but through compassionate care that honours the whole person.

Ultimately, what matters most is not how long we live, but how well we live, and how gracefully we transition when the time comes to leave this world. In the end, it is the quality of our days, not the quantity, that will define our legacy. And just as we strive for quality in living, so too must we strive for dignity in dying—recognising that both are essential parts of the human experience, and both deserve our utmost care and attention.

The Race for Quality Does not Have a Finishing Line – Our Aim is to Provide Quality in Living and Dignity in Death.

The race for quality has no end.

No final mark, no curve or bend,

It's not a sprint to cross a line,

But a journey shaped by time divine.

We strive not just to lengthen days,

But fill them full in countless ways,

For what is life, if not the chance?

To truly live, to laugh, to dance?

The aim is not in years alone,
But in the seeds of love we've sown,
In moments rich with joy and grace,
In every smile, in every face.

Quality of life is what we seek.
To lift the strong, to heal the weak,
To give each soul the space to be,
A life fulfilled, both wild and free.

And when the shadows start to fall,
We honour dignity through all—
Not fighting death, but making peace,
Allowing gentle, sweet release.

For death is not the final fear,
But living lost while we are here,
So let us live before we leave,
With open hearts and dreams to weave.

In every breath, in every day,

Let quality light up the way,

For in this race, we find our stride,

With life's true meaning by our side.

51

Pride and Humility - Duplicity, Hypocrisy, Double Standards: A Reprehensible Anathema

"I thought today I'd speak on humility, but I decided to save my sermon for a larger audience," - this statement, uttered with a touch of irony, might easily be mistaken for the words of a proud individual. However, this is precisely the sort of rhetoric one often hears from self-proclaimed god-men. Our nation certainly does not lack a vast array of such figures, and there seems to be an endless supply of them.

True humility is born from a place of security. When a person knows who they are and is confident in their purpose, they have no need to trumpet their virtues. Conversely, pride often stems from insecurity—an overcompensation to convince others (and often oneself) of one's worth. This is especially evident in leadership. A humble leader possesses quiet confidence, fully aware of their abilities and limitations. A prideful leader, on the other hand, projects an exaggerated image, constantly seeking validation.

Pride manifests in various forms: (Pride of Race, Space, Face, Place and Grace) pride of race, pride of beauty, pride of position, and pride of spiritual superiority. These different expressions of pride surround us daily, entrenched in our social structures. As someone who teaches communication skills, both verbal and non-verbal, I can often detect counterfeit humility. This superficial imitation of humility is particularly visible in public displays of piety or benevolence, which are more about self-promotion than genuine service. Whether it's a national leader or a church leader mimicking the act of washing feet, such gestures often feel ritualistic and hollow—designed to garner votes or popularity rather than to truly serve others.

Shakespeare captures the essence of pride beautifully: "He that is proud eats up himself: pride is his own glass, his own trumpet, his own chronicle" (Troilus and Cressida, Act 2, Scene 3). Indeed, pride has a way of becoming a self-consuming force. Those who engage in counterfeit humility are nothing more than exhibitionists—peddlers of pride in disguise. Just as counterfeiters do not bother replicating brown paper but rather target high-value currency, fake humility imitates what is truly priceless. Yet, such acts of false piety are often transparent and ephemeral, lacking in substance.

The ancient wisdom from Proverbs reminds us, "Pride goes before a fall" (Proverbs 16:18). History has shown us repeatedly that those who become too conceited or self-important often find themselves brought low by their own hubris. This remains a truth we witness time and again in our own lifetimes.

Humility, by contrast, is freedom from pride or arrogance. It is the quality of holding a modest or sincere view of one's own importance, arising genuinely from the heart. It is not about self-deprecation, but rather about recognising the inherent worth of others, regardless of one's own status. As the saying goes, "The face is the mirror of the mind" - चेहरा मन का आईना है. True humility shines through a person's demeanour, radiating sincerity and compassion, rather than being an act for public approval.

In a world that often values spectacle over substance, humility stands as a quiet yet powerful force – a reminder that true greatness lies not in exalting oneself, but in lifting others.

The Veil of Hypocrisy

Beneath the cloak of polished speech,

Where noble words may never reach,

Duplicity begins its dance,

A shadowed game of circumstance.

In halls where suffering cries out,

Where pain is wrapped in fear and doubt,

Some wear a mask of false concern,

While hearts of stone refuse to learn.

Hypocrisy, with a double face,

Speaks kindness laced with cruel disgrace,

One hand pretends to heal the scar,

While motives whisper who they are.

They claim to care, to stand and guide,

But selfishness they cannot hide,

For in the eyes that seek relief,

They plant a seed of bitter grief.

Double standards mark their way,

Where truth and justice fade away,

They preach of love, but sow despair.

And leave the weak without repair.

What a shame, to see such hollow men,

With power's weight held in their pen,

Yet in the face of suffering's plea,

They turn their backs on empathy.

For those who deal with pain and death,

Must carry more than shallow breath—

They need a heart that feels and knows,

The sacred trust their calling shows.

But duplicity and hollow lies,

Destroy the light behind the eyes,

In human suffering, we see,

A test of true integrity.

Let us forsake these traits of shame,

And honour every sacred name,

For in the end, it's love that heals

And truth that lifts what pain conceals.

52

The Opposite of Love is Not Hate, but Indifference

In the world of medicine, one of the most profound emotional challenges a patient can face is indifference. It is often said that the opposite of love is not hate, but indifference. This indifference, especially when shown by those entrusted with the care and well-being of patients, can be more devastating than any physical ailment. While hate still acknowledges the existence of the other person, indifference negates their very humanity, leaving them alone in their suffering.

I have witnessed this first-hand in my medical career, where indifference can manifest in a subtle, yet deeply hurtful manner. Imagine a scenario where a patient,. concerned about a recurrence of cancer in their spine after three years, asks their doctor, "Why did this happen?" And instead of receiving a compassionate response, the consultant simply walks away, as if the question had never been asked. This behaviour is not uncommon among physicians who have attained all the degrees and training the world has to offer. Despite their knowledge, their indifference to the patient's concerns is glaring. These doctors seem to consider it beneath them—infra dig—to pause, engage, and provide a thoughtful answer. Often, they delegate the responsibility to a subordinate, leaving the patient and their family to feel abandoned.

In an era where patients and their families often come to consultations armed with information from Google searches, they may already be aware that conditions like paraparesis or paraplegia, resulting from spinal metastasis, may not fully recover. They may know that the chances of returning to normal lower limb function are slim. Yet, the simple act of a doctor walking away without addressing their concerns adds a layer of emotional pain and anguish that compounds their physical suffering.

This indifference can be especially cruel because patients are seeking more than just medical answers; they are searching for reassurance, comfort, and hope. A few kind words can make all the difference. Instead of walking away, doctors could say something as simple as, "We have brought you this far, and while things are challenging, there is hope. The radiation treatment will help alleviate the metastatic pain in your spine. We are here to support you." These words, though seemingly small, carry immense weight. They offer solace, provide a sense of continuity, and reaffirm the presence of a compassionate hand guiding the patient through their darkest moments.

Indifference, in these circumstances, is a failure of empathy. It ignores the fact that medicine is not just about treating the body, but also about caring for the mind and spirit. When a doctor fails to acknowledge a patient's fears or concerns, they are not just walking away from a conversation — they are walking away from the very essence of their role as healers. It is not enough to be technically proficient; true medical care requires an engagement with the patient's emotional reality.

In the end, patients remember how they were made to feel, often more than the specifics of their treatment. A doctor's indifference can leave a lasting scar, eroding trust and leaving the patient feeling dehumanised. On the other hand, a few comforting words can create a sense of safety and connection, allowing the patient to face their illness with greater resilience.

The opposite of love is not hated, but indifference. In the medical profession, indifference can be as harmful as any disease. A doctor's responsibility extends beyond diagnosis and treatment; it includes acknowledging the fears and concerns of their patients, offering them the hope and compassion they so desperately need. In doing so, they fulfil the true calling of their profession—not just to heal the body, but to care for the whole person.

The Opposite of Love is not Hatred but Indifference

The opposite of love, we claim,

Is not the fiery hate that flames,

But indifference, a silent shade,

Where warmth of heart and hope do fade.

In hate, there's passion, sharp and clear.

A forceful feeling, strong and near,

A twisted love that turns away,

Yet still reflects a heart that sways.

But indifference, a colder guise,

Is where affection truly dies,

It's not the storm that stirs the sea,

But a flat calm where none can see.

To hate is to engage, to fight,
To struggle with a fierce delight,
But indifference is blank and still,
A void where love has lost its will.

In silence where no echo rings,
In absence where no sorrow clings,
There lies the cruellest, empty space,
Where love has vanished without a trace.

For to be left in that quiet void,
Is to be left with a heart destroyed,
No care, no anger, no disdain—
Just emptiness, a muted pain.

So let us cherish, love with fire.
And guard against the coldest mire,
For in our hearts, let warmth reside,
And drive indifference far aside.

53

Pain is Inevitable, but Suffering is Optional

Pain is an inescapable part of the human experience. Whether it manifests physically, emotionally, or psychologically, pain touches every life at some point. Yet, while pain is inevitable, suffering is a different matter. Suffering, as many have observed, is optional. This distinction is important, particularly in the medical field, where the management of pain and suffering is a crucial aspect of patient care.

Pain, by its very nature, is a signal from the body that something is wrong. It demands attention, often compelling immediate action. However, suffering is more complex. It is the emotional and psychological response to pain—the despair, the fear, the hopelessness that can accompany physical distress. While pain is a physiological event, suffering is shaped by how we interpret and respond to that pain. This is where the role of the physician becomes critical.

The onus of relieving pain and minimising suffering rests not only on the patient but also vicariously on the physician. A good physician understands that their responsibility extends beyond simply diagnosing and treating the physical source of pain. They must also address the suffering that accompanies it. This requires more than medical expertise; it demands empathy, communication, and a commitment to holistic care.

One of the key components of effective pain management is patient compliance with medication. For patients, adhering to prescribed medication regimens is crucial to controlling pain. Yet, this compliance often hinges on the relationship between the patient and the physician. If patients feel heard, understood, and supported by their doctor, they are far more likely to follow through with treatment recommendations. Conversely, if they sense indifference or detachment, compliance may falter, leading to unnecessary suffering.

This is where the concept of "low-tech, high-touch" medicine becomes essential. In an age where medical technology has reached astonishing heights, it is easy to lose sight of the fact that sometimes the most effective treatment requires nothing more than human touch. Touch is reassuring, therapeutic, and comforting. It bridges the emotional gap between the physician and the patient, conveying a sense of care and presence that no machine can replicate. The simple act of holding a patient's hand or placing a comforting hand on their shoulder can alleviate fear and anxiety, reducing suffering even when the pain itself persists.

"Low-tech, high-touch" medicine emphasises that while technology is a valuable tool, it should never replace the human connection that lies at the heart of healing. Physicians who practice this approach recognise that a warm, compassionate presence can have a profound impact on a patient's experience of pain. This touch need not be literal; it can be expressed through words, gestures, or the time taken to listen and respond empathetically. What matters is that the physician remains present, engaged, and attuned to the patient's emotional and psychological needs.

In addition to touch, communication plays a critical role in mitigating suffering. When a physician explains treatment options, sets realistic expectations, and involves the patient in decision-making, it empowers the patient to manage their pain more effectively. Patients who understand the course of their treatment and who feel that their concerns are being taken seriously are more likely to cope with pain without descending into suffering. Clear, compassionate communication can make all the difference in transforming an experience of pain into one of resilience and hope.

At its core, the distinction between pain and suffering reminds us that while pain may be beyond our control, how we respond to it is not. Physicians, through their words, actions, and presence, can help patients navigate their pain in a way that minimises suffering. By practising "low-tech, high-touch" medicine, they can provide the reassurance and comfort that often make the difference between merely enduring pain and transcending it.

In conclusion, pain is a reality of life, but suffering need not be. The physician's role is not just to alleviate pain but also to help patients manage their emotional responses to it. By fostering a compassionate, patient-centred approach to care, doctors can reduce suffering and empower patients to face their pain with dignity and strength. In this way, medicine becomes more than just a science—it becomes an art of healing, where the human touch remains the most powerful tool in the fight against suffering.

Pain is Inevitable, Suffering is Optional

Pain will come, as seasons change,

A storm that sweeps, a force untamed,

It grips the flesh, it tests the soul,

A truth of life we can't control.

But suffering is not a chain,
It's how we face and bear the strain,
A choice we make in darkened hours,
To let it crush or yield us powers.

Pain can pierce with the sharpest edge,
A wound that breaks the strongest pledge,
Yet suffering dwells in the mind,
In how we cope and seek to find.

To wallow in despair's deep well,
To let the pain tell a story,
Is to choose the weight of endless night,
Where shadows grow and steal the light.

But to embrace the pain with grace,
To face it with a steady pace,
Is to turn the burden into might,
And find a way to reclaim the light.

For pain is real, it cannot lie,
It may bring tears and questions why,
But suffering's realm is where we choose,
To bend or break, to win or lose.

So let the pain be what it is,
An inevitable, passing quiz,
And choose instead to rise above.
With hope and strength, and enduring love.

In how we meet the trials we face,
We find the power of our grace,
For pain is given, but suffering is not,
It's a lesson learned in every thought.

54

The Assault of Pain Unsettles Anyone

Pain, in its various forms—physical, emotional, or spiritual—can be a profound force of disruption in our lives. It has the power to unsettle even the strongest individuals, shaking their foundations and forcing them to confront their vulnerabilities. Pain is, after all, an assault on the body, mind, and spirit. It is relentless, unforgiving, and often unavoidable. Yet, despite its destructive capacity, pain serves a purpose: it is a signal, a warning that something is wrong, demanding our attention.

The assault of pain is universal. Physical pain may be the most tangible form, a sharp reminder that the body is in distress. Emotional pain, though less visible, can be equally devastating, leaving deep scars on the psyche. Spiritual pain, on the other hand, strikes at the very core of our being, challenging our beliefs, our faith, and our sense of purpose. No matter the type, pain is unsettling, forcing us to reckon with our limitations and our mortality.

However, pain is not merely a force of destruction. Often, it serves as a warning sign, alerting us to danger or injury. In many cases, pain prompts us to seek help, to address the underlying issue before it worsens. It is an essential part of the body's defence mechanism, reminding us to care for ourselves and to protect what is fragile. But when this warning system fails, as it does in certain diseases like Hansen's Disease (leprosy), the consequences can be tragic.

Hansen's Disease is a striking example of the crucial role that pain plays in our lives. In this condition, pain sensation is lost, leading to a disturbing array of complications. Without the ability to feel pain, individuals with Hansen's Disease are prone to injuries that go unnoticed and untreated. Over time, this can result in the loss of toes, fingertips, and other extremities. The absence of pain transforms the body into a vulnerable vessel, subject to the relentless forces of injury and decay. The characteristic leonine facies of advanced Hansen's Disease is a haunting reminder of the importance of pain as a protective mechanism. In the absence of pain, the body deteriorates, unable to defend itself against the assaults of the external world.

Yet, while pain can serve a vital purpose, there is another dimension to suffering that often goes overlooked: the suffering that arises from pleasure. It may seem paradoxical, but meaninglessness in life does not necessarily stem from weariness with pain; rather, it can emerge from exhaustion with pleasure. When life is devoid of challenge or hardship, when one is consumed by the pursuit of pleasure without purpose, a deep sense of emptiness can take root.

This is a profound truth about human nature: we derive meaning not only from our joys but also from our struggles. Pain, as unsettling as it may be, often compels us to seek meaning, to ask deeper questions about our existence. It forces us to confront the limits of our resilience, to grow and adapt in the face of adversity. Pleasure, on the other hand, can lull us into complacency, dulling our sense of purpose and leaving us adrift in a sea of meaninglessness.

This concept is reflected in the lives of those who have everything but feel nothing. They are not lacking in material wealth or comfort; rather, they suffer from a spiritual void, an existential exhaustion that comes from an overindulgence in pleasure. The absence of pain, challenge, or struggle can lead to a profound sense of disconnection from life's deeper meaning. In contrast, those who have faced pain often emerge with a stronger sense of purpose, having confronted their vulnerabilities and found strength within themselves.

In conclusion, the assault of pain is indeed unsettling, but it is also a crucial part of the human experience. Whether physical, emotional, or spiritual, pain serves as a warning sign, prompting us to address the underlying issues in our lives. Yet, paradoxically, meaninglessness often arises not from pain but from the overindulgence in pleasure. It is through pain, struggle, and challenge that we find meaning and purpose. Pain may unsettle us, but it also has the power to transform us, to deepen our understanding of ourselves and our place in the world. Without it, we risk becoming adrift in the shallow waters of a pleasure-seeking life, exhausted by the.

very pursuit of happiness.

The Assault of Pain and Total Pain

The assault of pain is fierce and wide,

It strikes where shadows often hide,

Not just a wound that skin can tell,

But a storm where deeper sorrows dwell.

Total pain, a vast expanse,

A sum of trials, not left to chance,

It weaves through flesh and reaches the soul,

A force that seeks to take its toll.

Physical pain, sharp and clear,

A constant ache, a fearsome spear,

It grips the body, makes it bow,

And leaves its mark on every brow.

Emotional pain, a silent scream.

A heavy heart where hopes may gleam,

It weighs on dreams and tugs the mind,

A deep distress that's intertwined.

Psychological pain, a haunting thought,

The battles within, so fiercely fought,

It clouds the mind with doubt and dread.

And leaves its traces where we tread.

Psychosocial pain, the strain of loss,

The sense of isolation's cost,

It fragments bonds; it severs ties,

And leaves a void where solace lies.

Spiritual pain, a quest for peace,
A search for meaning, a deep release,
It questions faith and seeks a sign,
A yearning for the divine.

Each form of pain, a bitter strain,
Together, they make up the chain.
An assault on all that we hold dear,
A test of strength, a trial severe.

Yet in this sum of many parts,
There lies a chance to heal our hearts,
To seek the light within the storm,
And find a way to be reborn.

For though pain's assault may unsettle all,
Its impact's depth we can forestall,
By facing each with courage true,
And letting strength and hope renew.

55

Meaninglessness in Life Doesn't Happen When One is Weary with Pain, but When One Becomes Exhausted with Pleasure

Pain and suffering have a purpose. Pain alerts to lurking danger. Dr. Paul Brandt, who died in 2003, is the author of 'Ten Fingers for God' and of the 'Gift of Pain'. He did pioneering work in Leprosy at Christian Medical College Hospital Vellore, India. I was privileged to hear and interact with him, and we had to learn the Extensor to Flexor tendon transfer described by Dr. Brandt to restore hand function. Leprous hands had mutilated devastation caused from loss of tactile, sensory sensation.

Life's meaning is often sought in moments of joy, fulfilment, and happiness, but paradoxically, it is the overindulgence in pleasure that can lead to a profound sense of meaninglessness. It is not the weariness from pain that robs life of its purpose, but rather the exhaustion from excessive pleasure, a phenomenon that can hollow out the soul and leave one adrift in an ocean of emptiness. This paradox challenges the assumption that happiness alone is the key to a meaningful life, suggesting instead that balance, struggle, and growth are essential components of true fulfilment.

To understand this concept, we must first explore the nature of pain and pleasure. Pain, whether physical, emotional, or spiritual, is often seen as an adversary, something to be avoided or alleviated. It disrupts our comfort and forces us to confront our vulnerabilities. But pain, despite its discomfort, is also a powerful teacher. It calls attention to what is wrong, driving us to seek solutions, growth, and healing. Pain is a catalyst for change, propelling us out of complacency and compelling us to confront our deeper selves. In this confrontation, we find purpose, resilience, and ultimately, meaning.

Pleasure, on the other hand, is often seen as the ultimate goal, the reward for a life well-lived. It is associated with happiness, satisfaction, and contentment. Yet, when pursued without balance or purpose, pleasure can become an empty pursuit, leading not to fulfilment but to exhaustion. The relentless chase for pleasure—whether through material wealth, sensory indulgence, or shallow gratification—can leave a person feeling disconnected and hollow. This exhaustion from pleasure is not the same as the exhaustion from hard work or the weariness that follows a struggle; it is a deeper fatigue, one that comes from the realisation that the things that were supposed to bring joy no longer satisfy.

The exhaustion from pleasure often manifests as a form of spiritual or existential malaise. When life becomes a continuous quest for the next thrill or comfort, it can lose its depth and meaning. The pursuit of pleasure, when it becomes an end in itself, can lead to a life devoid of purpose. This is because true meaning in life often arises not from the absence of pain or the presence of pleasure, but from the struggles, challenges, and efforts that accompany personal growth and connection with others.

The philosopher Viktor Frankl, who survived the horrors of concentration camps during the Holocaust, wrote extensively about the search for meaning in life. He argued that meaning is not found in pleasure but in purpose, and that suffering, when faced with dignity and courage, can actually enhance one's sense of meaning. In contrast, the unrelenting pursuit of pleasure, devoid of purpose, can lead to a sense of emptiness. When we seek only comfort and ease, we miss the deeper experiences that give life texture and significance.

This idea is reflected in many cultural narratives, where characters who have everything—a life of luxury, comfort, and endless pleasure—often find themselves discontented, restless, and searching for something more. It is in the absence of struggle that they begin to feel lost, disconnected from their true selves and from others. The exhaustion of pleasure does not offer the satisfaction that they expected, but rather a sense of numbness, a void where meaning should be.

On the contrary, individuals who have faced pain, adversity, and hardship often emerge with a stronger sense of purpose. They have been tested, and through their trials, they have discovered their inner strength and resilience. They find meaning in their experiences, in the connections they forge with others, and in the lessons they learn from their struggles. For them, life's challenges become a pathway to greater fulfilment, rather than an obstacle to be avoided.

In this context, the pursuit of meaning is not about avoiding pain or seeking pleasure, but about finding a balance between the two. A life that is too focused on pleasure can become shallow and empty, while a life that is only filled with pain can become unbearable. It is in the balance, in the interplay between joy and sorrow, comfort and challenge, that we find the true richness of life.

In conclusion, meaninglessness in life does not arise from weariness with pain, but from exhaustion with pleasure. When pleasure becomes the sole focus, it can lead to a sense of emptiness and disconnection, robbing life of its deeper purpose. True meaning comes not from the absence of pain or the presence of pleasure, but from the balance between the two, from the struggles and challenges that shape us into more resilient, purposeful individuals. Pain teaches us resilience, and pleasure, when balanced with purpose, brings joy. It is in the pursuit of meaning, not merely the pursuit of

Pleasure, that we find true fulfilment in life.

Meaninglessness in Life Doesn't Occur When One is Weary with Pain but When One Becomes Exhausted with Pleasure

Meaninglessness does not arise from pain,

Though weary hearts may strain and strain,

It does not come from aching nights,

Or battles fought in harshest fights.

No, it is pleasure's fleeting gleam,

When joy's illusions fade like dreams,

That makes the soul feel hollow, bare,

A sense of loss within the air.

When pleasure's peaks no longer thrill,

And empty joys the heart can't fill,

When endless chase of fleeting mirth,

Leaves one adrift without true worth.

It's not in pain where meaning wanes,

Though suffering brings its own refrains,

But in a quest for endless cheer,

Where deeper truths are lost, unclear.

Pleasure's fleeting, shallow sway,

Can leave the soul in disarray,

As joy's facade begins to slip,

And leaves a void where meaning grips.

For life's true essence, deep and real,

Is found in moments that we feel,

Not in the search for transient highs,

But in the depth where purpose lies.

So seek not just the fleeting light,

But find the truth within the night,

For meaning blooms where hearts align,

In purpose lived and love divine.

56

A Smile Uplifts All: Economising on Emotions

We've all heard the saying that it takes fewer muscles to smile than it does to frown or express anger. Scientifically, it is often claimed that a smile engages only four muscles, while anger or frustration can involve up to fourteen. While the exact numbers may vary depending on the expression, the underlying wisdom remains the same: smiling is easier, more economical, and far more beneficial to our well-being than anger.

Yes, indeed, as a plastic surgeon, I can vouch for the fact that it needs only four muscles to smile, fourteen to frown, and lose our temper!

In a world filled with stress, frustration, and challenges, we often forget the simple power of a smile. A smile is not just a facial expression; it is a universal language of warmth, connection, and positivity. When we smile, we not only uplift ourselves, but we also create a ripple effect that uplifts those around us. It is an effortless way to spread joy and kindness, requiring minimal energy yet producing maximum impact.

Anger, on the other hand, is a complex and taxing emotion. It consumes energy, strains relationships, and leaves us feeling drained. When we allow anger to take control, it affects our physical and mental health, leading to increased stress, tension, and even long-term health problems like high blood pressure. The effort it takes to frown, scowl, or express rage is not just about the number of muscles involved—it's about the emotional toll it takes on us.

The Power of a Smile

A smile is a powerful tool in human interactions. It has the ability to disarm hostility, diffuse tension, and create a sense of belonging. When we smile, our brain releases endorphins, the chemicals responsible for making us feel good. This natural boost in mood is not just a short-term effect; over time, smiling can actually reduce stress and anxiety, making us more resilient in the face of adversity.

Moreover, a smile is contagious. When we smile at someone, they are likely to smile back, creating a positive feedback loop that can transform the energy of an entire room. It is a simple yet profound way to connect with others, breaking down barriers and fostering a sense of community. Smiling requires little effort, but its impact is far-reaching.

Economising on Emotions

In today's fast-paced world, where stress and negativity are rampant, it is essential to learn how to economise on our emotions. Anger, frustration, and negativity drain our energy and lead to emotional exhaustion. By choosing to smile instead of frown, we conserve our emotional energy and use it in more constructive ways.

Economising on emotions doesn't mean suppressing our feelings or ignoring challenges. Rather, it means being mindful of how we respond to situations. It's about recognising that we have a choice in how we react. Instead of allowing anger to control us, we can choose to smile, breathe, and approach situations with a sense of calm and positivity.

When we economise on our emotions, we also create space for empathy and understanding. A smile can often open the door to dialogue and connection, even in difficult situations. It allows us to approach challenges with a sense of lightness and flexibility, rather than being weighed down by anger and frustration.

The Uplifting Effect of Smiling

Smiling not only benefits us personally, but it also uplifts those around us. A genuine smile can brighten someone's day, offering a moment of connection in an otherwise busy or stressful environment. In workplaces, schools, and social settings, a smile can create a positive atmosphere, fostering collaboration and goodwill.

The power of a smile is not just in its simplicity but in its ability to change the dynamics of human interaction. It is a gesture of kindness that transcends language and cultural barriers. In a world that often feels divided, a smile is a reminder of our shared humanity, a small yet significant act of unity.

In a world that can sometimes feel overwhelming, we must learn to economise on our emotions and choose positivity over negativity. A smile is an effortless way to uplift ourselves and others, spreading joy and creating connection. It takes far less energy to smile than to be angry, and the benefits are immeasurable. By smiling more and frowning less, we conserve our emotional resources, reduce stress, and contribute to a more harmonious world. In the end, a smile truly does uplift all.

A Smile is the Best Attire

In a world where first impressions matter, we often place great importance on our outward appearance—our clothes, accessories, and grooming. However, there is one accessory that surpasses all others in its ability to leave a lasting impact: a genuine smile. A smile is the best attire anyone can wear. It transcends fashion trends, social status, and cultural boundaries, making it a universal symbol of warmth, confidence, and kindness.

Unlike clothing, which can be expensive, a smile is free yet invaluable. It requires no shopping, no matching, and no effort beyond a simple facial movement. But its effects are profound. When we smile, we project an aura of positivity and openness, making ourselves more approachable and likeable. A smile can instantly light up a room, create connections, and make people feel at ease.

The Power of a Smile

A smile is more than just a facial expression; it is a powerful tool of communication. It conveys emotions that words sometimes fail to express—joy, empathy, gratitude, and encouragement. When we smile at someone, we send a message of goodwill and acceptance. It is an unspoken invitation to connect, to share a moment of human warmth.

Scientifically, a smile triggers the release of endorphins, the brain's natural feel-good chemicals. This not only improves our own mood but also has a positive effect on those around us. Smiling is contagious; when we smile, others are likely to smile back, creating a ripple effect of happiness. In this way, a smile can change the atmosphere in any environment, making it more positive and welcoming.

Confidence and Authenticity

A smile is also a reflection of confidence. It shows that we are comfortable in our own skin, that we are willing to engage with the world, and that we have a positive outlook on life. People who smile are often perceived as more confident, approachable, and trustworthy. In social and professional settings, a smile can be the key to forming meaningful connections and leaving a memorable impression.

What makes a smile the best attire, however, is its authenticity. A genuine smile, one that comes from the heart, cannot be faked. It is a reflection of inner contentment, happiness, and peace. When we smile authentically, we radiate positivity, and that radiance is more attractive than any piece of clothing or accessory. People are drawn to authenticity, and a sincere smile is a clear indicator of a person who is grounded and at ease with themselves.

Universality and Timelessness

One of the remarkable things about a smile is that it is universal. Across cultures and languages, a smile is understood as a gesture of friendliness and goodwill. It bridges gaps between people from different backgrounds and creates an instant connection. While fashion and attire can vary greatly across the world, a smile remains a constant symbol of positivity and kindness.

Moreover, a smile is timeless. Trends in clothing and fashion come and go, but the impact of a smile never diminishes. It doesn't matter if we are dressed in the latest fashion or in simple, everyday clothes—a smile elevates any attire. It adds a personal touch that makes us stand out, not because of what we are wearing, but because of the energy and warmth we bring into a space.

The Emotional Armour

In addition to being the best attire, a smile can also be considered emotional armour. Life is filled with challenges, stress, and uncertainties, and a smile can help us navigate through them with grace. When we choose to smile, even in difficult situations, we demonstrate resilience and strength. It is a way of facing adversity without letting it defeat us.

Smiling in the face of hardship doesn't mean ignoring reality or suppressing emotions. Instead, it is about choosing to focus on the positive, to find light in the darkness. A smile can be a source of strength not only for ourselves but also for those around us. It reassures others that things will be okay, that there is hope even in tough times.

Conclusion: A smile is truly the best attire we can wear. It is a universal expression of kindness, confidence, and authenticity that transcends material appearances. While clothes and fashion can enhance our outward appearance, it is a smile that leaves a lasting impact on others. It has the power to uplift, connect, and transform any situation. So, as we go through life, let us remember that the most important thing we can wear each day is not a brand or a trend, but a genuine smile—because it is, without a doubt, the best attire.

The Power of a Smile - Economising on Emotions – Fourteen Muscles to Frown, Four to Smile

In patient care, where hearts are healed,

The value of soft skills is revealed.

For in the art of healing's grace,

A smile adorns the face.

Four muscles form a gentle curve,

That smiles with warmth, that soothes and serves,

While fourteen strain to frown and scold,

A burden heavy, bitter, cold.

A smile, the finest attire we wear,

A simple gift, beyond compare,

It costs so little, yields so much,

A balm that softens every touch.

To economise on strained emotion,

And choose a smile, a gentle notion,

Is to offer comfort, hope, and cheer,

In every visit, far and near.

A smiling doctor, calm and kind,

Becomes a cheerleader of the mind,

A beacon of compassion's light,

That turns the darkened days to bright.

For soft skills are the heart's own key,

Unlocking trust and empathy,

In patient care, where healing starts,

A smile can mend the wounded hearts.

So let us choose the smile each day,

And let it lead us on our way,

For in each curve of kindness shown,

We build a car that's deeply known.

57

It's Nice to Be Important, But More Important Is to Be Nice: Style, Substance, and Humanity in Medicine

In the medical profession, a position of authority is often accompanied by visible symbols of importance: the white coat, the stethoscope draped around the neck, the formal attire. These visual cues signal a practitioner's role, expertise, and status in the eyes of patients and colleagues. However, while it may be "nice to be important," it is far more important to embody the values that truly define a physician—kindness, empathy, and a deep commitment to the well-being of others. In the evolving landscape of healthcare, where human interaction remains central to patient care, the fusion of style and substance, merit and mindset, is crucial.

The Trappings of Importance

A stethoscope around the neck has long been an iconic image of the physician. It is more than just a tool; it is a symbol of medical authority. In hospitals, clinics, and medical institutions, this symbol often confers an immediate sense of competence, reinforcing the idea that the person wearing it holds the key to diagnosis and treatment. The white coat, too, carries a certain weight—an emblem of cleanliness, precision, and professional distinction. Yet, these external markers of importance are, at best, superficial. They are necessary but not sufficient indicators of what makes a good doctor.

The reality is that being important in the medical profession—whether through title, position, or external symbols—is meaningless if not accompanied by a genuine commitment to kindness, empathy, and patient-centred care. The doctor's attire may confer authority, but it is the manner in which that authority is wielded that truly defines the impact on the patient. This is where the balance of style and substance becomes critical.

Style and Substance: The Doctor's Persona

Style, in the context of medicine, is not limited to physical appearance or attire. It also encompasses the way a doctor communicates, the way they carry themselves, and the manner in which they approach patient care. The way a physician interacts with patients can either create a bridge of trust and understanding or erect a barrier of distance and detachment.

A doctor who wears his stethoscope like a badge of honour but fails to listen to the patient, who prioritises his status over his bedside manner, has style without substance. Conversely, a doctor who understands that his role is not just to diagnose and treat but to guide, support, and reassure embodies both style and substance.

Substance in medicine is not just about knowledge and skill—though these are undoubtedly crucial. It is about applying that knowledge with compassion, understanding, and humility. Patients come to doctors not just for medical expertise but for care that recognises their humanity. They seek comfort, assurance, and a connection that transcends the cold clinical nature of medical interventions.

Merit and Mindset: A Holistic Approach

Merit in medicine is often defined by academic achievements, technical skill, and clinical acumen. These are the foundational pillars upon which a successful medical career is built. However, merit alone does not make a great doctor. It is the mindset and mentality with which merit is applied that differentiates a physician who is merely competent from one who is truly exceptional.

The right mindset in medicine is one that prioritises the patient's well-being above all else. It is a mindset that embraces continuous learning, recognises the limits of one's knowledge, and understands the importance of collaboration and humility. It is about seeing the patient as a person, not just as a case or a condition. It requires a mentality that values listening as much as diagnosing, and empathy as much as expertise.

Moreover, mindset is about resilience and adaptability. The medical profession is demanding, often requiring doctors to make critical decisions under pressure, manage complex emotions, and navigate the unpredictability of life and death. A physician with a strong mindset approaches these challenges with calm, grace, and a focus on doing what is best for the patient, even when the path is difficult or unclear.

The Importance of Being Nice

Being nice is often underestimated in a profession where scientific knowledge and technical expertise are so highly valued. Yet, the impact of kindness, compassion, and genuine care cannot be overstated. When doctors are kind, they create an environment of trust and safety. Patients who feel seen, heard, and valued are more likely to adhere to treatment plans, engage in honest communication, and experience better overall outcomes.

Kindness also fosters a sense of community and collaboration among healthcare teams. A doctor who is approachable, respectful, and supportive creates a positive work environment that benefits not only patients but also colleagues and staff. In an industry where burnout is a significant concern, the importance of kindness, both to oneself and to others, becomes a critical factor in sustaining a long and fulfilling career.

Additionally, kindness is not a sign of weakness, but of strength. It takes courage to remain compassionate in the face of suffering, to maintain patience in a fast-paced and often overwhelming environment, and to treat every patient with dignity and respect, regardless of their background, condition, or circumstances. Kindness, when combined with skill and knowledge, elevates the practice of medicine from a profession to a calling.

Conclusion: Style, Substance, Merit, and Mindset. In the medical profession, it is indeed nice to be important, to hold positions of authority, and to be recognised for one's expertise. But far more important is the ability to connect with patients on a human level, to embody kindness and compassion in every interaction, and to balance the external symbols of status with the internal values that define true excellence in care.

Style and substance, merit and mindset, must go hand in hand. The stethoscope around the neck may symbolise a doctor's role, but it is their heart that truly defines their impact. A physician who is both skilled and kind, both knowledgeable and compassionate, will always leave a lasting impression—one that goes far beyond the superficial trappings of importance.

In the end, being nice is not just an added bonus to medical competence; it is an integral part of what makes a doctor truly great. The ability to combine style with substance, merit with mindset, and importance with kindness is what elevates the practice of medicine and makes it a deeply rewarding and humane profession.

Nice to Be Important, More Important to Be Nice

It's nice to hold a title high,

To reach for the stars and touch the sky,

To wear success like a shining crown,

And feel the world lift you up and down.

But as we climb the peaks of fame,

Let's not forget a softer claim,

For in the quest to rise above,

It's kindness that we need to love.

To be important, yes, it's true,

Can bring accolades and praise anew,

Yet greater still, in truth's embrace,

Is how we touch each heart we face.

For in the quiet acts of grace,

In every warm and gentle place,

We find a truth that fame can't match,

A heart that reaches, not a catch.

To be nice is to show we care,

To lift another from despair,

It's in the small and simple deeds,

Where love and empathy succeed.

So while importance has its charm,

Let's not let it bring us harm;

For in being nice, we find the key,

To lives of joy and dignity.

It's nice to be important, fair.

But nicer still to always share,

A heart that's kind, a soul that's bright,

In every day, in every light.

58

The Importance of Listening Skills in Day-to-Day Medical Practice

In the realm of medicine, effective communication is pivotal to the success of patient care. Listening, often overshadowed by the emphasis on technical skills and diagnostic prowess, is an indispensable component of this communication. The act of listening—truly listening—shapes the patient experience, influences diagnostic accuracy, and enhances therapeutic relationships. Despite its critical importance, unconfirmed reports suggest that patients are interrupted every 16 seconds during history taking, highlighting a systemic issue that undermines the efficacy of medical consultations. Understanding and addressing this challenge is essential for providing compassionate and effective care.

The Art of Listening in Medicine

Listening in a medical context is far more than hearing words; it involves actively engaging with the patient's narrative, interpreting non-verbal cues, and creating a space where the patient feels heard and valued. History taking, often referred to as "His Story," is a fundamental aspect of diagnosis and treatment planning. It provides insights into the patient's condition, concerns, and the broader context of their health. To interrupt this process frequently is to disrupt the flow of information and diminish the potential for a comprehensive understanding of the patient's needs.

Effective listening entails more than passively receiving information; it requires active engagement. This means giving the patient undivided attention, reflecting on their statements, and validating their experiences. Interruptions, whether due to impatience, preoccupation, or a desire to steer the conversation toward familiar territory, compromise this engagement. They can make patients feel dismissed, leading to incomplete or skewed information and potentially affecting the quality of care.

The Impact of Interruptions on Patient Perception

Interruptions during history taking are perceived by patients in various ways. They may interpret these interruptions as a sign of the doctor's haste or impatience, suggesting a preference for swift treatment rather than a thorough understanding of their condition. This perception can erode trust and make patients feel that their concerns are not being taken seriously.

Furthermore, when doctors frequently interrupt, patients may believe that their symptoms are being dismissed or that the physician is more interested in treatments they are already familiar with, rather than exploring a holistic view of their health. This can lead to a sense of frustration and disengagement, undermining the therapeutic alliance that is essential for effective patient care.

Listening as a Diagnostic Tool

Listening carefully during history taking is crucial for accurate diagnosis. Each patient's narrative is unique and provides valuable clues that guide the diagnostic process. Interruptions can obscure these nuances, leading to missed symptoms or incomplete assessments. For instance, a patient might mention a seemingly minor symptom that, if not explored thoroughly, could be indicative of a more serious underlying condition. By allowing patients to share their stories without interruption, doctors can gather comprehensive information that enhances diagnostic accuracy.

In addition, patients often express their concerns, anxieties, and preferences through their narrative. A thorough listening approach allows doctors to address these aspects, providing not only medical solutions but also emotional support. This holistic approach is vital for effective treatment planning and patient satisfaction.

Strategies for Improving Listening Skills

1. Minimise Interruptions: One of the most effective ways to improve listening is to consciously minimise interruptions. Doctors should allow patients to speak freely and only interject when absolutely necessary to seek clarification or guide the conversation. This fosters an environment where patients feel valued and heard.

2. Employ Active Listening Techniques: Active listening involves nodding, maintaining eye contact, and providing verbal affirmations such as "I see" or "Tell me more about that." These techniques show the patient that their words are being acknowledged and considered.

3. Practice Empathy: Empathetic listening involves not just hearing the patient's words but also understanding their feelings and perspectives. Empathy can be conveyed through verbal and non-verbal cues, demonstrating genuine concern for the patient's experience.

4. Use Open-Ended Questions: Open-ended questions encourage patients to elaborate on their symptoms and concerns, providing more detailed information. This approach contrasts with closed-ended questions that may limit responses and lead to incomplete information.

5. Be Mindful of Non-Verbal Communication: Body language, facial expressions, and tone of voice play a significant role in communication. Being aware of these non-verbal cues can enhance understanding and connection with the patient.

6. Create a Comfortable Environment: Ensuring that the consultation setting is conducive to open communication can help patients feel more comfortable sharing their concerns. A private, quiet space where the patient feels secure can encourage more honest and comprehensive dialogue.

Listening as a Pillar of Medical Practice: In day-to-day medical practice, the importance of listening cannot be overstated. It is not merely a skill but a fundamental aspect of patient care that impacts diagnostic accuracy, patient satisfaction, and the overall therapeutic relationship. By addressing the issue of frequent interruptions and embracing a more patient-centred approach to communication, healthcare professionals can foster a more empathetic, effective, and respectful environment.

Listening, when performed with intent and compassion, bridges the gap between medical knowledge and patient experience, ensuring that care is both comprehensive and considerate. As medicine continues to evolve, prioritising listening skills will remain a cornerstone of effective practice, underscoring the profound truth that while it is nice to be important, it is far more important to be nice—and to truly listen.

59

The Practice of 'High-Touch, Low-Tech' Medicine

Touch is reassuring, comforting, and therapeutic. Running the doctor's fingers through the dishevelled hair of his or her patient helps allay fears, anxiety, and is a potent sedative!

"Low-Tech, High-Touch" in Clinical Practice: The Heart of Compassionate Care In the ever-evolving world of modern medicine, technological advancements have revolutionised the way healthcare is delivered. From robotic surgeries to telemedicine and artificial intelligence, the healthcare industry increasingly leans towards high-tech solutions. However, amidst this digital transformation, there is an approach to clinical practice that remains timeless: "Low-Tech, High-Touch" medicine. This philosophy prioritises human connection, empathy, and the relational aspects of healthcare over technological intervention, advocating that while machines can assist in healing, they can never replace the human touch.

The Essence of "Low-Tech, High-Touch": At its core, "Low-Tech, High-Touch" clinical practice emphasises the importance of personal interaction, patient empathy, and human intuition. In many cases, the presence of a doctor, the warmth of a comforting touch, or the simplicity of active listening can significantly contribute to a patient's healing process. The practice calls for clinicians to focus on the human experience of illness and recovery, remembering that patients are not just medical cases or diagnoses, but individuals with emotions, fears, and hopes.

This approach stands in contrast to the high-tech, often impersonal nature of modern healthcare, where patients can feel like mere data points in a sea of digital records. In such environments, the doctor-patient relationship risks becoming transactional. "Low-Tech, High-Touch" remedies this by fostering relationships built on trust and genuine care.

The Power of Touch and Presence: Numerous studies have shown that human touch can reduce pain, lower blood pressure, and alleviate anxiety. In my personal experience as a Plastic Surgeon and Palliative Care Specialist, the value of a hand held in comfort or a reassuring look has often superseded the most advanced medical interventions. One poignant example from my career involved a young girl gifting a patient a Discman and headphones. While our surgical and pharmacological measures could only partially relieve his pain, the music provided him a degree of peace that our clinical skills could not. It was a reminder that healing goes beyond the physiological—it touches the soul.

In palliative care, particularly, the importance of presence is paramount. When there is no cure, the "high-touch" approach offers solace, dignity, and emotional support. Patients facing terminal illnesses often express the desire not for more interventions, but for someone to listen, understand, and walk alongside them in their journey. As a clinician, being present in these moments—listening without judgement, offering a comforting hand—creates a space where patients feel seen and valued beyond their illness.

The Risks of a High-Tech Reliance: While technology offers incredible tools for diagnosis and treatment, over-reliance on it can create distance between doctor and patient. A surgeon, for example, might master the most advanced robotic techniques but fail to communicate compassionately with a patient who is anxious about their procedure. When technology becomes the focal point of care, we risk neglecting the essential human elements that play a crucial role in healing.

In my practice, I often witnessed patients who felt alienated by an overly technological approach. In such cases, the lack of personal interaction or the absence of human warmth could exacerbate their emotional distress. In contrast, the simple act of sitting by their side, explaining their situation in layman's terms, or acknowledging their fears would often have a more immediate positive effect than the most sophisticated medical interventions.

Moreover, excessive dependence on technology can sometimes lead to a misinterpretation of clinical data, leading healthcare providers to overlook the subtleties of a patient's condition that only human intuition could detect. Machines and algorithms, however precise, do not possess the nuanced understanding of the human body and mind that comes with years of clinical experience and personal engagement.

Low-Tech, High-Touch in Palliative Care: Palliative care, by its very nature, embodies the "Low-Tech, High-Touch" philosophy. In this field, the focus is not on curing diseases but on alleviating suffering and improving the quality of life. It requires clinicians to engage with patients at the most vulnerable times of their lives, offering empathy, understanding, and support. My transition from plastic surgery and cancer surgery to palliative care brought me closer to this philosophy and to practice it.

In palliative settings, where the emphasis is on adding life to years rather than years to life, the principles of "Low-Tech, High-Touch" can have a profound impact. Whether it's providing emotional support to families or easing the fears of dying patients, these moments of human connection often carry more weight than any medical procedure or device.

The Balance Between Technology and Touch: It is important to note that "Low-Tech, High-Touch" does not advocate abandoning technology. Instead, it encourages finding a balance. While the latest innovations in medicine undoubtedly save lives and enhance outcomes, they should never replace the doctor-patient relationship. In fact, the best clinical practice often combines the two: using technology to diagnose and treat, while employing empathy, touch, and communication to care for the patient as a whole person.

This balance is particularly important in modern clinical settings where time is a scarce resource. Doctors are often pressed to see more patients in less time, leaving little room for meaningful interaction. Yet, even within these constraints, small acts of kindness, patience, and attention can create a more compassionate clinical environment.

In the fast-paced, technologically driven world of modern medicine, the "Low-Tech, High-Touch" approach serves as a reminder of the power of human connection. Machines can diagnose and treat diseases, but they cannot offer empathy, comfort, or emotional support. As healthcare professionals, we must remember that healing is not just about curing diseases – it's about caring for the person as a whole. By embracing both the scientific and the humane aspects of our work, we can provide care that is not only effective but truly compassionate.

"Low-Tech, High-Touch" Clinical Practice is a Call to Return to the Essence of Medicine—where the Heart, Mind, and Hands Work Together to Heal.

In halls where machines hum and whir,

And endless screens our visions blur,

There lies a truth we can't forget—

The human touch is needed still.

For though the tools of modern kind
May measure, scan, and probe the mind,
No gadget, no device can feel.
The warmth of hands that help us heal.

A pulse beneath a gentle palm,
A whispered word, a voice that's calm,
These simple acts, though lacking might,
Can turn the darkest hour to light.

In medicine, it's not just steel,
But care, compassion that can heal.
A kindred look, a knowing nod,
Connects the soul, invokes a God.

Low-tech, but high in human grace,
We meet each patient face to face.
For healing's more than charts and scans,
It lives within the touch of hands.

So let the stethoscope be near,

But closer still, the heart that hears.

For in the quiet, tender care,

Lies the true art of those who dare.

To practice not with tools alone,

But with the warmth that's deeply sown.

For every life that we may see,

Deserves the touch of empathy.

60

Celebrating Imperfections: The Concept of Wabi-Sabi

In a world increasingly driven by ideals of perfection and constant improvement, the Japanese concept of wabi-sabi offers a refreshing perspective. Rooted in traditional Japanese aesthetics, wabi-sabi (侘び寂び) emphasises the beauty of imperfection, transience, and incompleteness. This philosophy provides a counterbalance to the often unattainable standards of flawlessness that dominate contemporary culture.

Wabi-sabi emerged from a blend of Zen Buddhism and Shinto influences, evolving over centuries to reflect a profound appreciation for the natural cycle of growth and decay. It finds beauty in the humble, the weathered, and the modest, celebrating the unique character that emerges from the passage of time and the inevitability of change.

At its core, wabi-sabi invites us to embrace and find beauty in the imperfections of life. This can manifest in various forms, from the irregular texture of a handmade ceramic bowl to the faded patina of an old wooden door. Each imperfection tells a story, revealing the object's history and the hands that shaped it. In this way, wabi-sabi shifts the focus from striving for an idealised state of perfection to appreciating the inherent value in the flawed and transient.

The concept of wabi-sabi also extends to the broader human experience. It encourages us to accept and embrace our own imperfections, both physical and emotional. By acknowledging and celebrating our flaws, we foster a deeper connection with ourselves and others. This acceptance fosters resilience and authenticity, allowing us to live more fully in the present moment without being preoccupied by unattainable ideals.

In Japanese art and design, wabi-sabi is evident in various forms. Traditional tea ceremonies, for instance, often feature rustic, asymmetrical tea bowls that embody the principles of wabi-sabi. These objects, far from being pristine, display signs of wear and ageing, which enhance their beauty and significance. Similarly, gardens designed with wabi-sabi in mind might feature asymmetrical arrangements and weathered materials, reflecting the natural cycle of life.

In conclusion, wabi-sabi offers a profound lesson in celebrating imperfections. By embracing the transient and the imperfect, we gain a deeper appreciation for the beauty that exists in the ordinary and the fleeting. This perspective not only enriches our appreciation of art and design but also encourages us to accept and value the inherent imperfections in our own lives.

61

Every Bad Moment Gives Pain, Every Pain Teaches Us a Lesson, Every Lesson Changes a Person

Life is an unpredictable journey, filled with highs and lows, joys and sorrows. While we all wish for moments of happiness and ease, it's often the painful and difficult experiences that shape us most profoundly. The idea that "every bad moment gives pain, every pain teaches us a lesson, and every lesson changes a person" encapsulates a fundamental truth about human growth and resilience. Pain, though unpleasant, can be a powerful teacher, guiding us toward greater understanding, empathy, and self-awareness.

Bad Moments and Pain: The Catalyst for Growth

Pain often accompanies life's most challenging moments. These experiences can range from personal loss and failure to heartbreak and disappointment. They disrupt our comfort zones and force us to confront the harsh realities of life. Yet, while bad moments bring pain, they also create opportunities for reflection. Pain strips away the superficial layers of life, exposing our vulnerabilities, limitations, and true desires.

Pain also teaches us about resilience. When faced with hardship, we often discover strengths we didn't know we had. We learn to adapt, to heal, and to move forward despite the difficulties. It is through these painful experiences that we realise our capacity to endure and grow. In essence, pain becomes the catalyst for personal growth.

Lessons from Pain: The Path to Wisdom

Every painful experience carries with it a lesson. Sometimes, the lesson is immediate and obvious, such as recognising the consequences of a poor decision. Other times, the lesson may take years to fully reveal itself, emerging only after we've had time to process and reflect on the experience. Either way, pain forces us to learn—to reassess our choices, our actions, and our beliefs.

Lessons learned from pain can teach us humility, patience, and compassion. They can help us understand the importance of forgiveness—both of others and of ourselves. Painful experiences often challenge our preconceived notions and force us to confront uncomfortable truths. This process, though difficult, helps us evolve, pushing us toward a deeper understanding of ourselves and the world around us.

Change Through Lessons: The Evolution of Self

The lessons we learn from pain do more than just provide insight – they change us. These lessons shape our character, influence our future decisions, and alter the way we perceive life. The process of change is rarely easy; it requires us to let go of old habits, beliefs, or even relationships that no longer serve us. But this change is essential for growth.

As we integrate the lessons learned from painful experiences, we often become more empathetic, more resilient, and more aware of our own limitations and potential. These changes can lead to a more authentic way of living—one that is grounded in self-awareness and acceptance. Through the process of pain, learning, and change, we become more complete versions of ourselves, capable of facing future challenges with greater wisdom and courage.

Conclusion: Life's most difficult moments often come with the greatest opportunities for growth. Pain, though challenging, serves as a powerful teacher, guiding us toward valuable lessons that shape and transform us. Every bad moment gives pain, every pain teaches us a lesson, and every lesson changes us in ways we might not fully understand until we look back and see how far we've come. While we cannot avoid pain, we can choose to learn from it, allowing it to be the force that drives our personal evolution.

62

"Death is not Extinguishing the Light but the Turning Down of the Lamp Because the Dawn has Come" - Rabindranath Tagore

Rabindranath Tagore's profound words, "Death is not extinguishing the light but the turning down of the lamp because the dawn has come," offer a poetic and philosophical perspective on the nature of death. Rather than viewing death as the end or a final darkness, Tagore invites us to see it as a transition, a passage from one state of being to another. His metaphor of turning down the lamp at dawn suggests that death is not an extinguishment of life but rather a natural part of a larger, more continuous journey.

Death as Transition, Not End

Tagore's metaphor implies that death is not an abrupt cessation of life but a gentle transition, akin to the changing of light at dawn. In this view, death is not the end of existence, but a shift from one phase of being to another. The lamp, symbolising life, is turned down because its purpose—to illuminate the darkness of night—has been fulfilled. With the arrival of dawn, a new source of light takes over, and the lamp is no longer needed.

This notion resonates with spiritual and philosophical traditions that view life as a cycle rather than a linear journey with a definitive end. In many Eastern philosophies, including Tagore's own roots in Indian spiritual thought, death is seen as a transformation or continuation, rather than an absolute end. Just as night gives way to day, life transitions into a new state through death.

The Symbolism of Light

Light is a powerful symbol in many cultures, often representing life, knowledge, and consciousness. By comparing life to a lamp, Tagore emphasises that our existence is like a light in the darkness, illuminating our way in the world. When the dawn comes, the light of the lamp is no longer necessary because a greater light—symbolising a higher understanding or a new existence—has arrived.

In this sense, death can be seen as an awakening, not a termination. The turning down of the lamp does not signify defeat or loss but a readiness to embrace something greater. The dawn represents a new beginning, a higher state of being that renders the small light of the lamp unnecessary. Just as dawn brings new possibilities and hope, death can be viewed as an opening to something beyond our current understanding of life.

A Spiritual Perspective on Death

Tagore's words are a comforting reflection on the inevitability of death. They offer a perspective that death is not to be feared, but embraced as part of the natural order of things. By seeing death as the turning down of the lamp, Tagore invites us to view it with acceptance, acknowledging that life does not end with death; rather, it transforms. The fear and sorrow often associated with death come from our attachment to the physical world and the life we know. However, if we shift our perspective and see death as a new dawn, we can approach it with peace and understanding.

This idea echoes the teachings of many spiritual traditions, where death is viewed as a return to the source, a merging with the infinite. In these philosophies, the individual soul, like the light of the lamp, returns to the vastness of the divine light. The dawn symbolises the soul's awakening to its true nature, beyond the limitations of the physical body.

Death as Part of the Journey

Tagore's metaphor also invites us to see life and death as parts of a continuous journey. Just as day and night are part of the natural cycle, so too are life and death. Life is the phase in which we shine our light in the world, navigating through experiences, learning, and growing. Death is not the end of that journey but a transition to a new phase, where the light of the lamp merges with the larger light of dawn.

This perspective can bring comfort to those facing death, whether their own or that of a loved one. It encourages us to view death not as a loss but as a part of the larger rhythm of existence. Just as we do not fear the coming of dawn after a long night, so too can we approach death with a sense of peace, knowing that it is a natural and inevitable part of the journey.

Rabindranath Tagore's metaphor, "Death is not extinguishing the light but the turning down of the lamp because the dawn has come," offers a deeply comforting and spiritually enriching perspective on death. It invites us to move beyond the fear of death and see it as a natural transition, a turning down of the lamp because a new light—dawn—has arrived. This view encourages us to embrace death as a continuation, not an end, and to trust in the natural cycles of life and existence. Through this lens, death becomes not a darkness to be feared, but a light to be welcomed, a passage into the dawn of a new beginning.

The Dawn Beyond the Night

Death is not the end we fear,

Nor the fading light that disappears.

It's just the lamp softly turned low,

As the morning sun begins to glow.

The night we've known, its stars, its dreams,

Now merge with brighter, warmer beams.

For life, though fleeting, does not cease.

It shifts to realms of quiet peace.

The dawn has come, the skies unfold,

A new horizon, bright and bold.

Where shadows fade and fears cease,

And hearts once weary rest in peace.

For death is but a gentle sigh,

As we greet the day beyond the sky.

Not an end, but a sweet reprise,

Where the soul awakes and spirit flies.

63

"We Make a Living by What We Get, We Make a Life by What We Give" - Sir Winston Churchill

Sir Winston Churchill's quote, "We make a living by what we get, but we make a life by what we give," resonates deeply with the essence of the medical profession. For physicians, this statement transcends material success, pointing to a higher calling—serving others. Beyond the pursuit of knowledge and the mastery of skills, medicine is a vocation that allows us to give something far more precious: our time, talents, and treasures to those who need it most. In this context, for a patient whose life is limited by illness, the greatest gift a physician can offer is not just medical treatment, but their time—a compassionate presence that transcends the physical.

The Privilege of Giving as Physicians

Physicians are in a unique position of privilege. The nature of their work allows them to directly impact lives, bringing healing, comfort, and sometimes even hope where there is none. The training and expertise they acquire are their talents, honed through years of dedication. These talents become treasures that can be shared with patients, particularly those less fortunate who may not have access to the best care or resources.

This privilege, however, comes with a profound responsibility. When a physician gives their talents to a patient, it is not just a transactional exchange of services for compensation. It is an act of giving that can make a difference in the quality of life of someone who is suffering. The ability to alleviate pain, to mend broken bodies, or to offer comfort in times of despair, is a powerful gift. This gift is not measured by the income earned, but by the impact made on the lives of patients.

The Gift of Time: A Physician's Greatest Offering

Among the many things a physician can give, time is perhaps the most valuable. In a world where time is often equated with productivity, taking the time to listen to a patient, to sit by their bedside, or to explain a diagnosis thoroughly can be transformative. This is especially true for patients whose life expectancy is limited. For them, time is a scarce resource, and how they spend it becomes incredibly significant.

To a patient facing a terminal illness, the gift of a physician's time can mean more than any medical intervention. It can be the difference between feeling abandoned and feeling cared for. When a physician takes the time to truly connect with a patient—listening to their fears, answering their questions, or simply being present—it can bring a sense of peace and dignity in the face of uncertainty. In such moments, the physician is not just treating a disease, but tending to the soul of the patient.

The Impact of Giving Beyond the Clinic

Churchill's words remind us that while making a living is necessary, making a life is about giving. For physicians, this giving extends beyond the walls of a clinic or hospital. It is about contributing to the greater good, whether through volunteer work, mentoring younger professionals, or advocating for those who do not have a voice. The giving of time, talents, and treasures extends to the community, where physicians can play a vital role in uplifting those who are marginalised or underserved.

This broader sense of giving is rooted in the belief that every person, regardless of their circumstances, deserves to be treated with dignity and compassion. For a physician, this might mean offering free medical camps in underprivileged areas, supporting health education initiatives, or contributing to research that seeks to address disparities in healthcare. These acts of giving enrich not only the lives of those who receive but also the lives of those who give.

Making a Life Through Giving: A Legacy Beyond Medicine

Ultimately, the legacy of a physician is not defined by the number of surgeries performed or the accolades earned, but by the lives touched through acts of giving. It is in these moments of giving—of time, of talent, of treasures—that a physician moves beyond the role of a healthcare provider and becomes a healer in the truest sense. The relationships built, the comfort provided, and the compassion extended to patients in their most vulnerable moments are what define a life well-lived.

For a patient whose days are numbered, the physician's presence can offer something that medicine alone cannot – a connection to humanity, a recognition of their worth, and a sense of peace as they navigate the final stages of life. The physician who understands this is not just making a living but making a life, both for themselves and for the patient.

Conclusion: Sir Winston Churchill's words remind us of the deeper meaning of life and work. For physicians, making a living is about the skills and knowledge that sustain them. But making a life is about giving—of time, talents, and treasures to those in need. In the practice of medicine, this giving is not just a professional duty but a privilege. And for those patients whose time is running out, the greatest gift a physician can offer is their own time, a precious commodity that, when given freely, creates a legacy of compassion and care that endures far beyond the confines of a single life.

The Gift of Life

We build our days with what we earn.

In the measured hours, the lessons learned.

But life's true light begins to grow,

In what we give, in love we show.

Not just in gold or treasures rare,

But in the time, we choose to share.

A word of hope, a helping hand,

Can heal a heart, can lift, can stand.

Talents honed in quiet grace,

When freely shared, it can change a place.

A melody to soothe the soul,

A tender touch that makes us whole.

For in each gift, the world's remade,

A brighter path for others laid.

We make a living by what we receive,

But a life worth living is in what we give.

So with our time, our gifts, our care,

Let's make a world that's just and fair.

Where kindness reigns and hearts are free,

To give and love eternally.

64

Moving Out from the Busy Operating Room to the Wilderness of Palliative Medicine: A Shift from the Comfort Zone to the Challenge Zone

The operating room, for a surgeon, is often a sanctuary of control, precision, and mastery. It is where years of rigorous training converge into decisive action, and where tangible results are achieved through skillful hands and sharp instruments. The environment is structured, with clear protocols, a well-orchestrated team, and predictable outcomes. For a seasoned surgeon, this realm becomes a comfort zone—a place where expertise and familiarity offer a sense of security and purpose. Yet, moving from the busy operating room to the wilderness of Palliative Medicine marks a profound shift from this comfort zone to what can be called the challenge zone—a space where the outcomes are uncertain, the metrics for success are intangible, and the focus shifts from curing to caring.

The Comfort Zone of the Operating Room

In the operating room, a surgeon commands a high degree of control over the situation. The problem—whether it be a tumour, a broken bone, or damaged tissue—is usually well-defined. The tools and techniques to address the problem are at the surgeon's disposal, and the end goal is clear: to repair, to restore, to remove. The environment is one of high stakes but also high rewards, where the surgeon's skills directly influence the outcome.

This structured environment becomes a comfort zone for surgeons who thrive on their ability to diagnose, intervene, and see immediate results. The adrenaline rush of a successful operation, the satisfaction of a problem solved, and the respect earned from colleagues and patients alike all contribute to this sense of comfort. Over time, the operating room becomes a place where a surgeon feels in control—confident, competent, and secure in their role.

Entering the Challenge Zone of Palliative Medicine

Transitioning into Palliative Medicine, however, is a journey into the unknown. Unlike surgery, where the goal is often to cure or fix, Palliative Medicine deals with alleviating suffering and improving the quality of life for patients with serious, life-limiting illnesses. Here, the outcomes are less defined, the problems are often complex and multifaceted, and the tools at the physician's disposal are less tangible—compassion, communication, and presence.

In the challenge zone of Palliative Medicine, the focus shifts from the concrete to the abstract. The success of an intervention is not measured by the resolution of a physical problem, but by the patient's comfort, dignity, and peace. This requires a profound recalibration of what it means to be a healer. Instead of cutting out a tumour, a physician in palliative care might be helping a patient find relief from pain, or guiding a family through difficult conversations about end-of-life choices.

The challenge zone of Palliative Medicine also demands a different set of skills—ones that are less technical but equally critical. It requires deep empathy, the ability to sit with suffering without the immediate need to fix it, and the strength to support patients and families through some of life's most challenging moments. This shift can be unsettling for a surgeon used to controlling outcomes. It demands letting go of the need for immediate results and embracing uncertainty.

The Emotional and Intellectual Challenges

The move from surgery to Palliative Medicine also involves navigating new emotional and intellectual challenges. In the operating room, surgeons are trained to focus on the task at hand, often compartmentalising emotions to ensure precision and effectiveness. But in Palliative Medicine, emotions are an integral part of the process. Physicians must be attuned to the emotional needs of their patients and their families, providing not just medical care but emotional support and guidance.

Intellectually, Palliative Medicine requires a broader understanding of the human experience. It is not just about diagnosing and treating disease but about understanding the impact of illness on a person's life, their relationships, and their sense of self. It involves grappling with existential questions, such as what it means to have a good death and how to balance the desire for more time with the need for quality of life. These are questions that have no easy answers and require a willingness to engage with uncertainty and ambiguity.

The Rewards of the Challenge Zone

Despite the challenges, the shift into Palliative Medicine can be profoundly rewarding. While the outcomes may be less concrete than in surgery, they are no less significant. Providing relief from pain, helping a patient find peace in their final days, or supporting a family through the loss of a loved one can be deeply fulfilling. The rewards in Palliative Medicine are measured not in the number of lives saved but in the quality of life preserved.

In this challenge zone, physicians often discover a deeper connection to their patients. The relationships formed in Palliative Medicine are built on trust, empathy, and mutual respect. There is a sense of shared humanity that transcends the traditional doctor-patient dynamic. This connection can be a powerful source of meaning and purpose, offering a different kind of satisfaction than the operating room provides.

Moving from the busy operating room to the wilderness of Palliative Medicine represents a significant shift from the comfort zone to the challenge zone. It requires a redefinition of what it means to be a healer, moving from curing to caring, from controlling outcomes to embracing uncertainty, and from technical mastery to emotional presence. While the challenges are great, so too are the rewards. In Palliative Medicine, physicians have the privilege of accompanying patients on some of life's most difficult journeys, offering comfort, dignity, and compassion along the way. This shift, though challenging, can ultimately lead to a deeper understanding of what it means to make a life, not just a living, through the practice of medicine.

65

Interdependence as a Higher Virtue Than Independence: A Reflection on Patient Care

---

In today's world, independence is often celebrated as the ultimate goal, a marker of strength, success, and autonomy. This cultural ideal of self-sufficiency permeates every aspect of life, including healthcare, where many patients strive to maintain their independence despite illness or disability. For many, the desire to be independent reflects a need to retain control, dignity, and self-worth in the face of physical or emotional challenges. However, while independence can be empowering, there is a greater virtue to be found in interdependence—an acceptance of mutual reliance that fosters connection, community, and shared strength.

The Desire for Independence Among Patients

For patients facing chronic illness, disability, or age-related decline, the drive to remain independent is understandable. Independence represents freedom—the ability to make decisions, care for oneself, and maintain a sense of normalcy. It allows patients to preserve their identity and dignity, which are often challenged by the limitations imposed by illness. Being independent also offers a sense of control in a situation where so much may feel out of control.

This desire for independence can be particularly strong in patients who have lived active, self-sufficient lives before illness struck. The idea of becoming dependent on others for basic needs, such as bathing, dressing, or managing medication, can be frightening and disheartening. Patients may feel that dependence diminishes their sense of self or burdens their loved ones. Therefore, many patients strive to maintain their independence for as long as possible, even when doing so becomes physically or emotionally taxing.

The Limitations of Independence

While the pursuit of independence is natural, it is not always sustainable, particularly in the context of serious illness. As a person's condition progresses, the ability to manage independently may diminish, leading to frustration, exhaustion, and isolation. Patients who cling too tightly to the ideal of independence may resist asking for help, even when they desperately need it. This can lead to unnecessary suffering, both physically and emotionally, as they struggle to manage alone.

Moreover, the emphasis on independence can create a false sense of isolation. In reality, no one is entirely independent. We all rely on others, whether for emotional support, practical assistance, or simply the interconnectedness of human life. This is especially true in healthcare, where the complex needs of patients often require a collaborative approach involving doctors, nurses, caregivers, and family members. By focusing solely on independence, patients may miss the opportunity to experience the richness of interdependence—the reciprocal support that connects us all.

The Virtue of Interdependence

Interdependence is the recognition that we are all part of a larger network of relationships, where mutual reliance is not a sign of weakness but a source of strength. In the context of patient care, interdependence is a higher virtue than independence because it acknowledges the inherent value of connection, collaboration, and community. When patients embrace interdependence, they open themselves to receiving help and support, while also contributing to the well-being of others.

Interdependence fosters a sense of belonging and shared purpose. For patients, this can mean accepting assistance from caregivers, family, and healthcare providers, while also recognising that their needs and experiences contribute to the greater whole. In an interdependent relationship, there is a balance of giving and receiving, where both parties benefit from the connection. For example, a patient may rely on a caregiver for physical assistance, but in turn, the caregiver may gain emotional fulfilment from their role, creating a mutually supportive relationship.

Interdependence in Palliative Care

In Palliative Medicine, the concept of interdependence is particularly important. As patients approach the end of life, the focus shifts from curative treatment to comfort, dignity, and quality of life. At this stage, independence often becomes less of a priority, and the need for interdependence becomes more apparent. Patients in palliative care may rely on a team of healthcare professionals, family members, and friends to manage their physical, emotional, and spiritual needs. In turn, their journey can inspire and uplift those who care for them, creating a shared experience of meaning and connection.

Embracing interdependence in palliative care can lead to a more holistic approach to healing. Rather than focusing solely on the physical aspects of care, interdependence encourages attention to the emotional, social, and spiritual dimensions of the patient's experience. This interconnected approach acknowledges that patients are not just isolated individuals but part of a larger web of relationships that shape their sense of self and well-being.

The Balance Between Independence and Interdependence

It is important to recognise that independence and interdependence are not mutually exclusive. Patients can still maintain a degree of autonomy while also embracing interdependence. In fact, balancing these two concepts can lead to a more fulfilling experience of care. Patients who are encouraged to participate in their care, make decisions, and express their preferences can retain a sense of independence, even as they rely on others for support.

Healthcare providers can play a crucial role in helping patients find this balance. By fostering an environment of respect, collaboration, and empathy, providers can support patients in maintaining their independence while also encouraging them to accept help when needed. This balance can empower patients to feel both capable and connected, reducing feelings of isolation and helplessness.

While independence is a valuable goal, particularly for patients facing illness or disability, interdependence offers a higher virtue. It recognises the strength and beauty of human connection, where mutual reliance fosters community, compassion, and shared purpose. In the world of patient care, interdependence allows for a more holistic approach, where the needs of the individual are met within the context of a supportive network. For patients, embracing interdependence can lead to a richer, more meaningful experience of care—one that acknowledges their inherent worth, not just as individuals, but as integral parts of a larger whole.

66

People Only Saw the Decisions I Made, Not the Choices I Had

Life is a series of decisions, and often, those decisions are the only visible markers of our journey. But behind each decision lies a labyrinth of unseen choices, constraints, and internal battles. The phrase "People only saw the decisions I made, not the choices I had" encapsulates the tension between the external perception of our actions and the complex realities we navigate within.

The Visible Decisions

When people look at us, they see the outcomes: the career we chose, the relationships we built, or the paths we took. These are the visible decisions, the conclusions that others can easily interpret and judge. Whether it's the decision to change careers, relocate to a different city, or even leave a relationship, each action becomes a piece of our visible narrative. Society, friends, and family often form opinions based on these decisions, labelling them as right or wrong, wise or reckless, brave or foolish. However, this external gaze rarely captures the intricate web of choices that led to the final decision.

The Hidden Choices

Beneath every decision is a maze of choices that remain hidden from public view. These choices are often influenced by factors beyond our control—personal history, family responsibilities, financial constraints, health concerns, or emotional baggage. While the final decision may appear simple, the choices we navigated to arrive at it can be fraught with complexity and compromise.

For example, consider someone who decides to leave a high-paying job to pursue a passion. From the outside, it may look like an impulsive or courageous move, depending on one's perspective. However, the person making that decision might have grappled with unseen choices: the toll of a high-stress job on their mental health, the desire for more meaningful work, or the need to prioritise family over a career. The decision to walk away is the visible outcome, but the choices leading up to it are rooted in deep introspection, sacrifice, and a balance of competing priorities.

The Weight of Judgement

When people only see the decisions we make, they often impose judgements without understanding the context of our choices. This judgement can create a sense of isolation, as others may misinterpret our decisions, believing they were made lightly or without sufficient consideration. In reality, many of our decisions are the best possible outcomes given the limited and often painful choices we faced.

For instance, a doctor might choose to leave a prestigious hospital position to focus on palliative care. Colleagues may view it as a step down from the pinnacle of a medical career, unaware of the internal conflict between staying in a high-pressure role and the deeper calling to provide compassionate end-of-life care. The decision may be labelled as a deviation from success, while in reality, it is a carefully weighed choice aligned with personal values and life circumstances.

Compassion Over Judgement

Understanding that every decision is built on a foundation of complex choices can foster compassion rather than judgement. When we recognise that the decisions others make are shaped by factors we may never fully understand, it becomes easier to empathise with their journeys. The person who chooses to stay in a difficult job may be doing so out of financial necessity, just as someone who ends a relationship may be prioritising their own emotional well-being after years of trying to make things work.

Rather than seeing decisions in isolation, we can cultivate a broader perspective that acknowledges the unseen choices, struggles, and sacrifices that accompany them. This shift in perception allows us to extend grace to ourselves and others, recognising that life is rarely as straightforward as the decisions we ultimately make.

"People only saw the decisions I made, not the choices I had," is a powerful reminder that the visible outcomes of our lives are just the tip of the iceberg. Beneath the surface lies a complex matrix of choices, often made under pressure and in the face of difficult circumstances. By acknowledging the depth and intricacy of these choices, we can move beyond judgement to a place of empathy, understanding that every decision reflects a nuanced personal journey.

The Choices I Had - The Decisions I Made

People saw the decisions I made.

Not the choices I held in my hand,

They saw me craft, cut, and stitch,

But missed the soul's quiet demand.

I loved to tinker with what God had created.

To mend the broken, to shape and restore,

But beneath the scalpel, a calling stirred—

A softer voice, one I couldn't ignore.

In the silence of suffering, I found my place.

Not in the cure, but in easing the pain,

Where life's fragility met with grace,

And healing wasn't measured in gain.

I chose to walk where others might turn,

Into the shadows where hope seems faint,

Not for the accolades or the fame,

But for the heart's quiet restraint.

Though my hands knew the art of repair,

It was in Palliative Care that I found my truth,

Not in the mending, but in simply being there,

Honouring life in its waning youth.

67

My Days Battling Covid Pneumonia: The Need for Bereavement Support During the COVID-19 Pandemic

The COVID-19 pandemic was a time of unprecedented loss, where the fragility of life was laid bare with stark clarity. The tragic irony of King Lear's words, "As flies to wanton boys are we to the gods; They kill us for their sport," echoed across the globe as millions of healthy individuals were suddenly swept away by a virus that showed little regard for age, strength, or vitality. In those dark times, if ever families needed bereavement support more than at any other time, it was during this period of overwhelming death and despair.

Governments, in a desperate and flawed attempt to control the virus, implemented lockdowns that were not only scientifically questionable but were also punctuated by almost surreal gestures—clanging steel tumblers, lighting mobiles, and sloganeering that seemed more theatrical than therapeutic. These responses, though intended to foster unity, appeared to trivialise the gravity of the situation. Beneath the cacophony of sound and light, there was a silence—an absence of the real support that bereaved families so desperately needed.

Many of my friends, who should have had years ahead of them, were taken too soon by the virus. Death came swiftly and without warning, leaving families in shock and disbelief. The traditional avenues of mourning, of gathering and comforting each other, were closed off by the very lockdowns that were supposed to save lives. The communal rituals that help us process grief were stripped away, leaving people to mourn in isolation. The bereavement was made even more unbearable by the fact that loved ones often died alone, in sterile hospital rooms, with no chance to say goodbye. This compounded the grief, turning it into something far more traumatic.

I found myself on the edge of that precipice as well. Despite being vaccinated, the virus took hold, and I began to desaturate. I contracted Covid and the near-fatal pneumonia in 2001 while working at a Palliative Care Hospital at Trissur. I was alone, lying in an ambulance, being rushed to Believers Church Medical College Hospital in Tiruvalla, one of the finest hospitals I have ever seen. Those moments, when death felt close, were a haze of medication—Remdesivir, steroids, Heparin—but they were also filled with an acute awareness of how alone I was in that room. Sixteen days later, I was discharged, a survivor of the pandemic, but my experience left me with a deep understanding of the fragility of life and the immense need for emotional support during such times.

The pandemic exposed the inadequacies in our systems of care, particularly in how we deal with grief and loss. In normal times, bereavement support is essential, but during a global crisis like COVID-19, it becomes even more critical. Families needed, and still need, support that acknowledges not just the death of a loved one but the manner in which it happened—the isolation, the fear, the unanswered questions. The traditional structures of support—family gatherings, religious ceremonies, community involvement—were shattered by lockdowns and fear of contagion. Bereavement in the time of COVID-19 was not just about the loss of life; it was about the loss of closure, connection, and communal healing.

For those of us who survived, the experience is a haunting reminder of how close we came to that same fate. But survival does not erase the trauma; it does not take away the memories of friends who died too soon or the realisation that many deaths could have been avoided. The question of whether the government's actions were scientifically sound will continue to be debated, but what is beyond debate is the deep and lasting impact on the emotional and mental health of those left behind.

In the aftermath of the pandemic, there is a crucial need to build systems of bereavement support that recognise the unique trauma of this time. We must move beyond the shallow gestures and create spaces where grief can be expressed, where the stories of those who were lost can be told, and where those who survived can find solace in their shared experiences. The pandemic has changed us all, and as we rebuild, we must ensure that we do not forget the lessons learned about the importance of human connection, even in the face of death.

My Time Battling COVID Pneumonia - 2021

The sirens wailed, the road ahead,

From Thrissur's streets, where hope had fled,

An ambulance, my breath grown thin,

Brought me to a place where life begins.

Desaturation gripped my frame,

Speechless, breathless, numb to pain,

Each moment teetered on the brink,

As fear and faith began to sync.

At Believer's Church Medical College Hospital, I found my bed.
But in my heart, a weight of dread,
The precipice of death so near,
Yet something whispered, "Do not fear."

God's hand was there, though unseen,
A power that worked in every scene,
He held me firmly, though I could feel,
The edge of life, the pull surreal.

For fifteen days, I fought alone.
But never truly on my own,
In quiet rooms, with prayer and grace,
I found my shelter, found my place.

The world outside was locked away,
But in my heart, I knelt to pray,
Devotion wrapped me like a shield.
While doctors worked and wounds were healed.

The team was brilliant, skilled, and true.

Their care was hope, their touch was new,

Yet in the stillness, there I knew,

God's presence carried me right through.

From darkness deep to morning light,

He kept me safe throughout the night.

And though alone, I felt His care,

In every whispered, heartfelt prayer.

Now healed, I stand and look behind.

At battles waged within my mind,

But grace has brought me back to see,

That God was always there with me.

Life After Life: The Evolving Paradigm

68

'Life After Life' - the Evolving Paradigm

When we think of the phrase "life after life," our minds often wander to metaphysical interpretations—thoughts of afterlives or reincarnations. But in a very real and immediate sense, life after life refers to the intricate emotional, psychological, and practical realities that unfold in the lives of those left behind when a loved one dies. For the spouse and children, and especially in the case of the death of a single parent, life after death becomes an urgent and profound continuation, one fraught with loss but also new beginnings.

The death of a family member, particularly a parent or spouse, shifts the balance of life for those surviving. The psychological ramifications of this transition are deep, and they reshape the emotional landscape of the family. The surviving spouse is not only grappling with their grief but also must shoulder new burdens—financial, emotional, and practical—that they once shared. When a single parent passes away, the emotional vacuum for orphaned children is amplified by the absence of both caretaking roles. In such scenarios, "life after life" becomes a complex paradigm of survival, healing, and adaptation.

The Role of the Surviving Spouse

For a surviving spouse, life takes on an entirely new dimension after the death of their partner. Grief can be all-consuming, a force that renders even the simplest tasks monumental. Yet, amid the personal pain, there is a broader responsibility to those still living—to the children and extended family. For many, the partner who has passed away was not just a companion but a co-parent, a financial provider, a stabilising presence in the household. Their absence creates ripples that transform the lives of those left behind.

The surviving spouse may find themselves confronting new responsibilities they had not previously assumed. If the deceased partner managed the finances, their death might force a steep learning curve on the surviving spouse, compounded by the financial stress that often follows a death, including funeral costs, medical bills, and the long-term loss of income. Beyond the financial aspects, the emotional burden can be even heavier. Children left behind are often lost in their own grief, requiring emotional support that a grieving spouse may struggle to provide. This creates a paradox: while the family requires strength to move forward, the strongest person may be the one who feels the most depleted.

The Case of Orphaned Children

The death of a single parent leaves an especially poignant void. For children, the loss of a parent is often the most significant and traumatic event they will face. If that parent was the sole caregiver, their death casts the children into a profound state of vulnerability. With no surviving parent to fill the role, the orphaned children are left without immediate emotional, financial, and practical support, often leading to a dependency on extended family members or social services.

For children, the emotional toll of losing a parent is intertwined with the fear and uncertainty about what will happen to them next. Their grief is often complicated by the sudden necessity to adapt to new living arrangements, guardians, or financial hardships. They may move into the care of relatives, fostering systems, or, in some cases, older siblings may take on the role of caregiver, significantly altering their own life trajectories. In this context, "life after life" for orphaned children is not just about surviving the loss; it's about rebuilding their future with limited resources, often requiring a resilience far beyond their years.

The Evolving Paradigm of Support

In modern times, there is an evolving understanding of how to care for those who survive the death of a loved one, particularly spouses and children. Societal, governmental, and familial support systems have become more developed, though they are not without flaws. Governments in many countries offer financial support, such as pensions or social security benefits, to surviving spouses and children. Nonprofit organisations provide counselling, educational scholarships, and emotional support. Communities are beginning to recognise the importance of mental health care for bereaved families, offering therapy and group support to help them navigate their grief.

However, it is not enough to rely solely on external support. The surviving family members must also find ways to move forward. This can involve seeking out grief counselling, relying on community and familial networks, and finding solace in shared memories of the loved one. For orphaned children, mentors, teachers, and extended family play a crucial role in helping them rebuild their lives, offering guidance and stability during the most turbulent times. They become essential figures in the evolving family structure, helping fill the void left by the deceased parent.

Healing and Moving Forward

Healing from the loss of a loved one is not a linear process. It is a journey that ebbs and flows, marked by moments of intense sorrow and occasional glimpses of hope. For the surviving spouse, moving forward often involves recalibrating their life goals. They may find solace in new relationships, or they may choose to dedicate their energy to their children, ensuring their futures remain intact despite the loss. The grieving process becomes a part of their identity, shaping their perspective on life.

For orphaned children, the path forward can be one of resilience. While the loss of a parent is a permanent scar, it does not have to define their future. Many children, with the right support, go on to lead fulfilling lives, honouring the memory of their parent in ways both large and small. The grief may never disappear, but it becomes a part of their story—a testament to their strength and capacity to endure.

The concept of "life after life" is not confined to the metaphysical or spiritual. It is a very real experience for those left behind after the death of a loved one. The surviving spouse and children must find ways to carry on, even as they grapple with profound grief and newfound responsibilities. The evolving paradigm of support—from government programmes to emotional counselling—offers pathways for families to navigate this difficult transition. Yet, ultimately, the strength to heal and rebuild comes from within, from the resilience that life demands in the face of loss.

In the death of a single parent, the story of the orphaned children begins anew. It is a story not just of grief but of courage, adaptation, and, ultimately, hope. Life continues, even after life has ended, as the living carry forward the legacy of the loved ones they have lost.

69

Hope Springs Eternal: Supporting Orphaned Children of Cancer Patients at the Regional Cancer Centre, Trivandrum

In a world often marked by adversity, the phrase "Hope springs eternal" serves as a reminder of the human capacity to endure and rebuild. Nowhere is this resilience more crucial than in the lives of children who have lost their single parent to cancer. The devastating reality of watching a parent succumb to the disease at a place like the Regional Cancer Centre (RCC) in Trivandrum leaves these children in a precarious position, emotionally and financially. As the disease claims lives, it often leaves behind young ones who must now face life without their primary caregiver and support system.

In this context, the idea of creating a support system for these orphaned children becomes not just a noble endeavour but a necessary one. Through partnerships with non-governmental organisations (NGOs), we can offer hope and stability to these vulnerable children by providing them with the education and financial support they so desperately need. By banding together, we can ensure that these young lives are not defined by loss but rather by the opportunities we create for them to thrive.

The Regional Cancer Centre in Trivandrum has long been a beacon of hope for cancer patients, offering them treatment and care during their most challenging moments. However, the effects of cancer extend far beyond the patient, impacting families, especially children, in profound ways. For a child who has lost their single parent to cancer, the world can suddenly seem like an overwhelming place filled with uncertainty and fear. The loss of a parent not only robs them of love and security but also places them at risk of poverty and a future without education. This is where the intervention of an NGO becomes critical.

An NGO focused on the welfare of these orphaned children could make a significant difference in their lives by establishing a structured programme that addresses both their immediate needs and their long-term well-being. The first priority would be to ensure that these children have access to education. Education is the key to breaking the cycle of poverty and giving them a chance at a brighter future. By providing scholarships, covering school fees, and supplying the necessary materials like books and uniforms, the NGO can remove the financial barriers that often prevent orphaned children from attending school. Furthermore, mentorship programmes could be established to offer guidance and support, helping these children to navigate the emotional and academic challenges they may face.

In addition to educational support, financial aid is essential for these children to lead a life with dignity. This could include monthly stipends to cover basic needs such as food, clothing, and healthcare. The financial assistance should also extend to vocational training for older children who may wish to pursue careers in fields other than academia. This not only provides them with a way to support themselves but also empowers them to build a future of their own choosing.

However, education and financial support are only part of the solution. Emotional and psychological support is just as important for these children. Losing a parent is a traumatic experience, and the grief that follows can be long-lasting. Counselling services, peer support groups, and access to mental health professionals would provide a safe space for these children to express their feelings and work through their grief. The NGO could partner with psychologists and social workers to offer these services, ensuring that the emotional needs of the children are met alongside their practical needs.

Building this network of support requires collaboration. The Regional Cancer Centre, with its established presence and understanding of the needs of cancer patients and their families, can serve as a critical partner. By working with the NGO, RCC can help identify children who need support and facilitate the connection between the families and the NGO. This partnership would also allow for a more holistic approach to care, ensuring that the support extends beyond the medical treatment and into the broader lives of the families affected by cancer.

Local communities can also play a significant role in supporting these efforts. Volunteers can offer their time as mentors, tutors, or companions to these children, providing them with the human connection that is so vital to their emotional well-being. Local businesses can contribute through donations or by sponsoring specific programmes. By creating a community-driven support system, we can ensure that these children are surrounded by care and compassion, even after the loss of their parent.

The challenges faced by orphaned children of cancer patients are immense, but through targeted intervention and collaboration, we can help turn their stories from one of despair to one of hope. The resilience of these children, combined with the support of an NGO and the broader community, can ensure that they not only survive but also thrive. By providing them with education, financial aid, and emotional support, we are not just helping them navigate the present but also giving them the tools to build a better future.

Hope, after all, does spring eternal. It lives in the hearts of these children and in the efforts of those who come together to help them. By working with NGOs, we can ensure that the legacy of those lost to cancer is not one of sorrow but of empowerment and opportunity for the next generation.

Hope Springs Eternal

In silent halls where shadows lay,

Young hearts bereaved; their light turned grey.

A parent lost, the world seems cold,

But hope springs eternal, brave and bold.

With hands that lift and voices kind,

We guide the young, help ease their minds.

For in their grief, a seed is sown,

A chance to rise, to stand alone.

Through every tear, a path we pave,

With love, with strength, we help them brave.

The world ahead, though steep, it seems,

We fill their hearts with hopeful dreams.

Financial aid, a bridge we build,

To see their needs and keep them filled.

No hunger, fear, nor empty hand,

Will break their stride— together we stand.

With every lesson, every care,

We teach them not to drown in despair.

Psychosocial strength we give,

To help them learn, to laugh, to live.

Emotion heals with time's embrace,

As mentors guide them through the race.

A job, a life, a future bright.

A chance to soar, to claim their right.

Hope springs eternal, like the dawn,

Through the darkest nights, they carry on.

With love and care, their spirits grow,

And in their hearts, the light will show.

70

"Let Me Make the Songs of a Nation, and I Care Not Who Makes Its Laws": The Art and Poetry of Medicine

---

Andrew Fletcher, an 18th-century Scottish patriot, once said, "Let me make the songs of a nation, and I care not who makes its laws." These words, spoken in the context of national identity and cultural power, transcend their original purpose and resonate deeply across various fields of human endeavour, especially in the practice of medicine. Fletcher's statement encapsulates the profound influence that creativity and artistry can have in shaping the very fabric of a society. Just as songs have the power to stir hearts, inspire change, and evoke deep emotions that laws cannot touch, so too does the art of medicine transcend the rigid structures of rules and protocols, becoming something akin to poetry in motion.

Medicine, in its essence, may seem like a field governed by science, much like mathematics, physics, or chemistry. These disciplines are bound by laws and equations, fixed principles that guide their application. In medicine, too, there are principles—biological facts, physiological norms, and biochemical pathways that dictate much of what we do. We rely on established protocols, diagnostic criteria, and evidence-based treatments. However, to view medicine purely through the lens of science is to miss its true depth. Medicine, unlike the hard sciences, is not just a discipline of laws and equations; it is also an art, a craft that requires creativity, intuition, and a deep connection with the human experience.

Much like a song, which can evoke a wide range of emotions from joy to sorrow, the practice of medicine touches on the full spectrum of the human condition. The surgeon's scalpel may follow the same physical principles as a physicist's experiment, but there is an artistry in the way it is wielded, a delicate balance of precision, intuition, and experience. The act of suturing a wound or reconstructing a face is not merely a technical procedure but a choreography of the hands and mind, guided by both scientific knowledge and an intrinsic sense of beauty and balance. It is in these moments, when skill intersects with intuition, that medicine becomes poetry in motion.

Consider, for a moment, the act of diagnosis. On the surface, it is a scientific process—identifying symptoms, correlating them with known diseases, and determining the best course of action. But diagnosis is also an art form. It requires the ability to listen deeply, not just to the patient's words but to the subtleties of their body language, their tone of voice, and the context of their life. A physician who is attuned to these nuances can often sense what lies beneath the surface, detecting the whispers of a diagnosis that has not yet fully revealed itself. This is where the craft of medicine shines—where science meets art, and knowledge blends with intuition.

Just as a song can capture the soul of a nation, the practice of medicine captures the soul of the individual. Every patient is a unique composition, with their own rhythms, harmonies, and dissonances. The physician's role is to listen to that music, to understand its complexities, and to create a treatment plan that resonates with the patient's needs and desires. Medicine, at its best, is a deeply collaborative process, where the physician and patient come together to compose a plan for healing—a plan that is informed by science but shaped by the art of human connection.

In this sense, the practice of medicine is far more than the application of laws or the following of equations. It is an act of creation, a deeply human endeavour that draws on both the intellect and the heart. Like a master musician, the physician must be attuned to the subtleties of their craft, always striving to create harmony where there is discord, and to bring light where there is darkness. The laws of medicine may guide us, but it is the art of medicine that heals.

Fletcher's words remind us that while laws may govern society, it is the songs—the art, the culture, the human expression—that truly shape the soul of a nation. Similarly, in medicine, while science may guide our practice, it is the art of healing that truly transforms lives. The greatest physicians, like the greatest musicians, are those who can blend technical skill with artistry, who understand that medicine is not just about curing disease but about restoring the delicate balance of body, mind, and spirit. In this way, medicine becomes a song—a powerful, resonant expression of the human experience, capable of healing not just the body but the soul.

Let Me Make the Songs of a Nation, I Care not Who Makes Its Laws

(Inspired by Andrew Fletcher's quote.)

The Art & Poetry in the Practice of Medicine

Let me make the songs, not the laws,

For in the melodies, the soul draws.

While rulers write with iron hands,

It's music that truly shapes the land.

In notes and words, the spirit soars,

It's art, not rules, that opens doors.

And in the practice of our trade,

It's poetry where healing is made.

The art of medicine, a tender song,

Where science can't always belong.

A touch, a look, a word can heal,

More than the blade or drug, we feel.

In rhythms of the heart and mind,

The pulse of life is intertwined.

Each patient tells a tale so true,

Each breath, a verse that breaks anew.

Let me sing the songs of care,

Where pain and hope meet in the air.

Where illness fades to a soft refrain,

And human kindness breaks the chain.

For in the songs we craft and play,

We find the art to heal, to stay.

Medicine, in science steeped,

Is in its heart, a song well-keeled.

So make your laws, but know this well—

It's in the songs where futures swell.

For art and poetry, hand in hand,

Guide the healer and heal the land.

71

Deluxe Death or Dignified Dying: A Reflection on End-of-Life Choices

---

The inevitability of death is a universal truth that every human must face, yet the way we approach it, prepare for it, and experience it can vary dramatically. Modern medicine, technological advances, and societal trends have introduced new complexities to how we die, raising important questions about what constitutes a good death. Among these complexities, two contrasting concepts emerge: the pursuit of a "deluxe death" – where every possible intervention is taken to prolong life at any cost – and "dignified dying", which focuses on quality of life, acceptance, and a peaceful departure.

These two approaches represent fundamentally different philosophies, rooted in divergent views on life, death, and the limits of medical intervention. As we delve deeper into these concepts, it becomes clear that dignified dying, which emphasises comfort, autonomy, and a graceful exit, offers a more humane and compassionate approach than the often-exaggerated pursuit of a deluxe death.

The Pursuit of a "Deluxe Death"

The term "deluxe death" captures the essence of our modern obsession with extending life, often through aggressive medical interventions. In this approach, the emphasis is on survival at any cost—patients may be placed on life support, subjected to multiple surgeries, or administered powerful drugs, even when the likelihood of recovery is slim. This mindset is driven by a deep-seated fear of death and a belief that medicine can, and should, prolong life as long as possible. It is also rooted in a consumerist view of healthcare, where patients and their families demand the most technologically advanced and resource-intensive treatments, hoping to beat the odds.

A patient connected by machines that beep and squeak in an unfamiliar setting is demeaning when death is imminent.

For some, the pursuit of a deluxe death may seem like a noble effort—fighting until the very end, unwilling to accept defeat. But this approach often comes with a high cost, both in terms of the physical and emotional toll on the patient and the financial burden on families and healthcare systems. Prolonging life through machines, ventilators, and invasive procedures can strip away the dignity of the dying process, transforming it into a sterile, painful, and isolating experience. The patient becomes disconnected from their loved ones, their body kept alive by artificial means while their spirit wanes.

The pursuit of a deluxe death can also prevent individuals from addressing the more profound aspects of dying—coming to terms with mortality, making peace with their lives, and saying final goodbyes to their loved ones. In the relentless focus on survival, these important moments are often lost, leaving both patients and their families with unresolved feelings of grief, regret, and unfulfilled closure.

Dignified Dying: A Compassionate Approach

In contrast, dignified dying places the emphasis not on how long we live, but on how we die. It is about accepting death as a natural part of life and focusing on quality over quantity. This approach recognises that, in some cases, less intervention can lead to a more peaceful, humane experience. Dignified dying advocates for palliative care, hospice services, and the right to refuse treatments that merely prolong suffering without improving the quality of life.

A dignified death is one where the patient is empowered to make choices about their care, where their autonomy and wishes are respected. It means giving patients the option to prioritise comfort, pain relief, and emotional well-being over aggressive treatments that offer little more than a temporary extension of life. This approach acknowledges that death, while painful for those left behind, can be a serene and meaningful passage if handled with care and understanding.

Palliative care, in particular, plays a crucial role in facilitating dignified dying. It focuses on relieving the symptoms of illness, such as pain, anxiety, and discomfort, while also addressing the emotional, spiritual, and psychological needs of the patient. Palliative teams often work closely with families, helping them navigate difficult decisions and providing support as they prepare for the inevitable loss of a loved one. This holistic approach ensures that death is not just a medical event, but a deeply personal experience that honours the individual's humanity.

The Role of Choice in Dying

One of the central tenets of dignified dying is the importance of 'choice'. A dignified death is one in which the individual has the autonomy to decide how and where they wish to spend their final days. Do they want to pursue aggressive treatments, or would they prefer to focus on comfort and being surrounded by family? Do they wish to die at home, or in a hospice where their needs can be met with dignity and respect?

Respecting a patient's choices also involves acknowledging their right to refuse treatments that do not align with their personal values or desired quality of life. It is an acknowledgement that life's worth is not measured by the number of days lived, but by the richness of those days. For some, that may mean ceasing treatment and focusing on making the most of their remaining time, without the cloud of constant medical interventions.

Cultural and Societal Influences

The tension between deluxe death and dignified dying is also shaped by 'cultural, societal, and religious *beliefs*'. In some cultures, death is seen as something to be fought against at all costs, while others view it as a natural transition that should be embraced with grace. Religious beliefs can influence decisions about end-of-life care, particularly around issues like life support, euthanasia, and palliative sedation. In some cases, societal pressure can push individuals toward deluxe death, especially when family members struggle to accept the impending loss of a loved one and demand that "everything be done."

Media portrayals of heroic medical interventions and the rise of a consumer-driven healthcare system can also create unrealistic expectations about what medicine can achieve. People are often led to believe that with enough resources and the right technology, death can be postponed indefinitely. This can lead to misguided hopes, resulting in prolonged suffering and a *dehumanising* end to life.

Finding the Balance: Towards a Dignified Death

The challenge, then, is to strike a balance between prolonging life when it can be meaningful and accepting death when it is time. A dignified death does not mean giving up hope but rather embracing a different kind of hope—one that focuses on comfort, presence, and emotional *fulfilment* in the final days. It is about valuing the human experience of dying, rather than merely extending the biological processes of life.

Healthcare professionals, families, and patients must work together to have open, honest conversations about what is most important in the final stages of life. Advance care planning, living wills, and clear communication about end-of-life preferences can help ensure that a patient's dignity is preserved, even in the face of terminal illness.

The choice between a deluxe death and dignified dying is ultimately one of values. Do we prioritise the prolongation of life at all costs, or do we focus on the quality of our final days, ensuring that we pass away with dignity, surrounded by comfort and love? While modern medicine has made great strides in extending life, it is important to remember that death is not the enemy—suffering, loss of dignity, and unnecessary pain are.

In embracing dignified dying, we acknowledge that while death may be inevitable, the way we approach it can be a deeply humane and compassionate process, one that honours both the life lived and the person who is leaving it behind.

Deluxe Death or Dignified Dying

In sterile halls, where machines hum loudly,

The battle rages, fierce and proud.

A life prolonged by force and fight,

But where's the peace in endless night?

Deluxe death, with all its gleam,

Promises more, a fleeting dream.

Wires and tubes, a desperate hold,

A heart beats on, but the soul grows cold.

Yet somewhere else, a softer end,

Where hands of love and calm descend.

No fight for time, no fear, no pain,

Just dignity in life's refrain.

A gentle breath, a whispered sigh,

In quiet peace, we say goodbye.

For death, it comes to every door,

But dignity can offer more.

No race to hold what cannot stay,

But grace to light the final way.

Not how long, but how we go,

With love and peace, the heart will know.

So choose the path with open eyes—

A peaceful end beneath the skies.

For in that final breath, we find,

Dignity leaves pain behind.

72

Measuring Pain: Tools, Challenges, and Insights - What You Cannot Measure, You Cannot Monitor. Pain is the Fifth Vital Sign

Pain, a subjective experience, poses a significant challenge for healthcare professionals trying to quantify and assess it. Unlike physical signs such as heart rate or blood pressure, pain cannot be objectively measured. This makes it essential to rely on patients' descriptions, visual tools, and scales to gain an understanding of the intensity and nature of their pain. From verbal descriptors to visual analogue scales and smiley faces, each method has its place in the complex world of pain assessment. However, the limitations and nuances of these tools reveal the complexities of understanding pain, especially when faced with different patient populations.

Verbal Descriptions: Mild, Moderate, Severe, or Excruciating

One of the most straightforward ways to assess pain is through verbal descriptions. Patients are often asked to categorise their pain as mild, moderate, severe, or excruciating. This approach, while simple, offers valuable insights into the patient's experience. The language used to describe pain carries emotional weight, allowing the healthcare provider to connect with the patient's suffering in a more empathetic way.

For example, a patient who describes their pain as "mild" may still be uncomfortable but is likely coping well, perhaps able to go about their daily activities with some effort. On the other hand, describing pain as "severe" or "excruciating" signals to the clinician that the pain is dominating the patient's life, perhaps affecting their mobility, mood, and overall well-being. These terms, though subjective, provide a crucial entry point into the patient's lived experience.

However, the limitation of verbal descriptions lies in their variability. What one patient considers "moderate" pain might be described as "severe" by another. Cultural factors, previous pain experiences, and individual pain tolerance can all influence how patients describe their pain. Despite these limitations, verbal descriptors remain a useful tool, particularly in settings where quick assessments are needed.

The Visual Analogue Scale: A Numerical Approach

The Visual Analogue Scale (VAS) introduces a more structured approach to pain measurement. Here, patients are asked to rate their pain on a scale of 0 to 10, with 0 representing no pain and 10 representing the worst pain imaginable. The VAS offers a numerical representation of pain, allowing clinicians to track changes in pain intensity over time.

The advantage of the VAS lies in its simplicity and versatility. It can be used across a wide range of patient populations and conditions, providing a quick snapshot of pain intensity. For example, a patient with chronic pain might report a pain level of 7 one day and a 4 the next, giving the healthcare provider a clear indication that the pain has decreased, perhaps due to medication or other interventions.

However, the numerical nature of the VAS also introduces challenges. Some patients, particularly those who are less familiar with numerical scales, may struggle to assign a number to their pain. Additionally, the scale does not capture the quality or nature of the pain—whether it is sharp, dull, burning, or aching. A pain level of 7 might mean something very different for a patient with a headache versus a patient recovering from surgery. While the VAS is a valuable tool for tracking pain intensity, it must be used alongside other assessments to provide a more comprehensive picture.

Smiley Faces and Colour Continuums: Tools for Paediatric Pain Assessment

Assessing pain in children presents a unique set of challenges. Children, especially younger ones, may struggle to articulate their pain in words or numbers. For this reason, alternative tools, such as smiley face scales and colour continuums, have been developed to help children communicate their pain levels.

The smiley face scale, which ranges from a happy face representing no pain to a crying face representing severe pain, allows children to point to the face that best represents how they feel. This visual representation makes it easier for children to express their pain without the need for complex language or abstract thinking. Similarly, colour continuums use shades of colour, with white representing comfort and red indicating severe pain. These tools tap into the visual and emotional world of children, making pain assessment more accessible for younger patients.

While these tools are effective for paediatric patients, they also have their limitations. Children may interpret the faces or colours differently based on their individual experiences or emotions at the moment. For example, a child might choose a sad face not because of their pain level, but because they are feeling scared or anxious. As with other pain assessment tools, smiley faces and colour continuums should be used in conjunction with observations from healthcare providers and input from parents or caregivers to ensure a holistic understanding of the child's pain.

The Nuances of Pain Assessment

Despite the variety of tools available, measuring pain remains an inexact science. The subjective nature of pain means that even the most well-designed scales and descriptors have their limitations. Cultural factors, previous experiences, and psychological states all influence how patients report their pain. For example, someone with a history of chronic pain may report their pain differently than someone experiencing acute pain for the first time. Similarly, anxiety, depression, and fear can all heighten the perception of pain, making it more difficult to assess accurately.

Additionally, pain is not a static experience. It can fluctuate throughout the day, influenced by movement, activity, and even mood. This dynamic nature of pain adds another layer of complexity to assessment. A patient who reports a pain level of 8 in the morning might experience a 3 by the afternoon, making it challenging to capture the full picture of their pain experience with a single measurement.

To address these challenges, pain assessment should be an ongoing, multidimensional process. Verbal descriptors, numerical scales, and visual tools all have their place, but they should be used in combination with clinical observations, patient history, and an understanding of the psychological and emotional factors that influence pain perception. This holistic approach allows for a more accurate and compassionate assessment of pain, ensuring that patients receive the care and support they need to manage their suffering.

The Art and Science of Measuring Pain. Measuring pain is both an art and a science. It requires not only the use of structured tools and scales but also a deep understanding of the individual patient's experience. While verbal descriptors, visual analogue scales, and smiley faces provide valuable insights into pain intensity, they are only part of the picture. Pain is a deeply personal experience, shaped by a range of factors that go beyond the physical sensation. By approaching pain assessment with empathy, flexibility, and a willingness to listen, healthcare providers can better understand their patients' suffering and provide more effective, compassionate care.

Measuring Pain - the Fifth Vital Sign, 'What You Won't Measure, You Cannot Monitor'

In the quiet space where suffering hides,

Pain speaks in whispers, or loudly confides.

To know its depth, to ease its sting,

We must find ways to track this thing.

For pain, like the other vitals we treat,

It is vital to the care we meet.

The fifth vital sign, it holds its place.

A measure of life, a sacred trace.

For children, smiley faces help explain.

The smiles or frowns that mirror pain.

A colour scale, continuum from white to red.

Explains when dangers tread.

In adults, numbers guide the way.

A scale from zero to ten.

Alerts us to treatment trends.

Map the places pain draws near.

Assuages the fear of needless fear

What we can measure, we can know.
To track its rise, or watch it go.
Without this gauge, we're lost at sea,
Unable to give the right remedy.

For every ache, each cry or sigh,
Deserves a way to quantify.
To monitor is to care,
To ease the load that some must bear.

So in our hands, let knowledge stay,
To listen, measure, heal the way.
For pain that's seen can start to mend—
The start of comfort, the patient's friend.

73

Catastrophisers and Non-Catastrophisers: The Mind's Influence on Pain Perception

Pain, as one of the most primal human experiences, is often regarded as a straightforward physiological response to injury or illness. However, the perception of pain is anything but simple. It is influenced by a multitude of factors, including the patient's mood, mindset, and the meaning they ascribe to the pain. Two distinct psychological profiles emerge when discussing how patients experience pain: catastrophisers and non-catastrophisers. These two groups process pain in vastly different ways, and understanding the distinctions between them is crucial for effective pain management.

The Catastrophiser's Response to Pain

Catastrophisers are individuals who interpret pain as a sign of impending doom or disaster. For them, pain is not just a physical sensation but a harbinger of something much worse, often interpreted as a life-threatening event. This catastrophic interpretation amplifies the pain, making it more intense and difficult to bear. The somatic expressions of pain—such as grimacing, moaning, or writhing—are often more pronounced in catastrophisers. Their emotional and psychological state exacerbates the physical sensation of pain, creating a vicious cycle where the fear of pain heightens the pain itself.

The mood of a catastrophiser plays a significant role in their pain perception. Anxiety, depression, and fear all intensify their experience of pain. Pain, for them, is not an isolated incident but part of a larger narrative of suffering and potential loss. They might ruminate on questions like, "What if this pain never goes away?" or "What if this means I'm dying?" These thoughts lead to heightened anxiety, which, in turn, increases their perception of pain. The pain becomes all-consuming, dominating their thoughts and emotions, making it difficult for them to find relief even when medical interventions are in place.

Catastrophisers are also more likely to feel helpless in the face of pain. They may believe that nothing can alleviate their suffering, which leads to a sense of despair. This hopelessness further exacerbates their pain, as the emotional toll weighs heavily on their physical experience. In extreme cases, catastrophisers may become resistant to treatment, feeling that no intervention can provide them with the relief they so desperately seek.

The Non-Catastrophiser's Response to Pain

In contrast, non-catastrophisers tend to view pain through a more pragmatic lens. For them, pain is an unpleasant sensation, but it does not signal imminent danger or death. Non-catastrophisers are more likely to see pain as something manageable, a temporary inconvenience rather than a life-altering event. Their mindset allows them to cope with pain more effectively, often experiencing less intense and more manageable symptoms.

The mood of a non-catastrophiser is typically more stable, which contributes to their ability to handle pain. Even if they feel anxious or fearful, they do not let these emotions dominate their experience. Instead, they focus on the practical aspects of pain management—whether it be through medication, relaxation techniques, or physical therapy. Non-catastrophisers are more likely to trust that their healthcare providers can help them, which fosters a sense of control over their situation.

The meaning they ascribe to pain is also different from that of catastrophisers. Non-catastrophisers may see pain as a signal from their body that something needs attention, but they do not necessarily interpret it as a sign of impending doom. They are more likely to engage in positive self-talk, reassuring themselves that the pain will pass and that they have the resources to cope with it. This positive mindset can actually reduce the intensity of their pain, creating a virtuous cycle where their belief in their ability to manage pain leads to a more bearable experience.

The Role of Interpretation: Meaning of Pain

The meaning patients attach to their pain has a profound impact on how they experience it. For catastrophisers, pain often takes on an existential dimension. They may interpret pain as a sign that their body is failing them, that their condition is worsening, or that death is imminent. This interpretation dramatically heightens their perception of pain, making it feel insurmountable. The fear of what the pain signifies can be just as overwhelming as the pain itself.

In contrast, non-catastrophisers tend to interpret pain in a more neutral or even positive light. They may see it as a challenge to overcome or as a sign that their body is responding to treatment. For example, someone recovering from surgery might view post-operative pain as a natural part of the healing process, rather than as an indication that something is wrong. This more optimistic interpretation of pain can lessen its intensity, as the individual focuses on recovery rather than catastrophe.

Psychological Interventions: Breaking the Cycle of Catastrophizing

Recognising the influence of catastrophising on pain perception has important implications for pain management. Psychological interventions, such as cognitive-behavioural therapy (CBT), can be particularly effective in helping catastrophisers reframe their experience of pain. By challenging catastrophic thoughts and replacing them with more realistic and positive ones, patients can break the cycle of pain amplification.

Mindfulness-based stress reduction (MBSR) is another powerful tool. By teaching patients to focus on the present moment without judgement, mindfulness can help them detach from the catastrophic narratives they build around their pain. This allows them to experience pain as it is, rather than as a precursor to something worse, which can significantly reduce their suffering.

For non-catastrophisers, these interventions can still be beneficial, reinforcing their positive coping strategies and helping them maintain their resilience in the face of pain. In both groups, addressing the psychological aspects of pain can lead to better outcomes and improved quality of life.

Conclusion: The Mind-Body Connection in Pain.

Pain is far more than just a physical sensation; it is deeply influenced by the mind. The distinction between catastrophisers and non-catastrophisers highlights the importance of psychological factors in pain perception. While medical interventions are essential for managing pain, addressing the emotional and cognitive dimensions is equally important. By helping patients reframe their understanding of pain and providing them with the tools to manage their thoughts and emotions, we can help them break free from the cycle of catastrophic thinking and lead more comfortable, fulfilling lives.

The power of the mind over pain should never be underestimated. When we recognise that pain is as much a psychological experience as a physical one, we open the door to more effective, holistic approaches to pain management. By empowering patients to take control of their pain through both medical and psychological means, we can help them navigate their journey with greater resilience, hope, and comfort.

Two Paths of Thought

In the mind's vast landscape wide,

Two ways of thinking side by side:

One sees storms where skies are clear,

The other moves without the fear.

The Catastrophiser walks in dread.

With shadows looming overhead.

Each minor tremor feels like a quake,

Each fragile thread, a bond to break.

They build their towers out of doubt,

And fear the worst as walls close in.

A whispered breeze becomes a storm,

Their world distorted, far from normal.

Yet on the same road, side by side,

The Non-Catastrophiser strides.

Where cracks appear, they see the light,

And search for hope in the darkest night.

They bend, but never fully break.

Find calm amidst the earth's great shake.

With steady steps, they chart the way,

Through life's rough seas, they gently sway.

For both will face the winds that blow,

But one finds peace, the other woe.

It's in the way they choose to see—

The glass is half full or empty.

So, when the tempest seems too near,

We all must choose which voice to hear.

Will we find strength or drown in cries?

Be catastrophisers or rise?

74

Don't Let What You Can't Do Prevent You from Doing What You Can Do: The Broader Approach to Pain Management

Pain, in its many forms, is one of the most challenging symptoms faced by patients, particularly in palliative care. While medical advancements have provided us with various tools and procedures to manage pain, there remains a temptation among some healthcare professionals to view invasive methods, such as neurolytic blocks or radio-ablative techniques, as the ultimate solutions. These procedures, which aim to directly interrupt pain pathways, are undoubtedly powerful tools in certain cases. However, they are not the be-all and end-all of pain management. In fact, this narrow focus on invasive techniques can overshadow the broader, more holistic approaches that can equally, if not more effectively, break the vicious cycle of pain.

The philosophy of "Don't let what you can't do prevent you from doing what you can do" is particularly relevant in this context. Just because we may not be able to completely eliminate a patient's pain through invasive means does not mean we are powerless. There is a vast array of other methods—pharmacological, psychological, and alternative—that can provide significant relief. It is in recognising the value of these diverse approaches that we can truly excel in managing pain.

The Limitations of Invasive Procedures

Invasive pain management techniques like neurolytic blocks or radiofrequency ablation can be effective in specific situations. They work by disrupting nerve pathways that transmit pain signals to the brain. In some cases, this can provide significant and long-lasting relief. However, these procedures are not without their limitations. They can be complex, carry risks of complications, and may not be suitable for all patients. Moreover, pain is not always confined to a single anatomical pathway. It often involves a complex interplay of physical, emotional, and psychological factors.

Pain can also recruit adjacent dermatomes, spreading to other areas of the body, creating a vicious cycle that is not easily interrupted by a single procedure. Thus, while invasive techniques can play a role in pain management, they should not be viewed as the only option or even the preferred option in many cases. Pain management is not a one-size-fits-all endeavour, and reducing it to a purely procedural approach risks neglecting the broader dimensions of the patient's experience.

The Power of Oral Medications

Oral medications are a mainstay in pain management and can be remarkably effective in breaking the cycle of pain. Opioids, non-opioid analgesics, anticonvulsants, and antidepressants can all be part of a well-rounded pain management plan. Unlike invasive procedures, oral medications offer the advantage of being non-invasive, easy to administer, and, in many cases, highly effective. They can provide relief across a wide range of pain conditions, from acute pain to chronic neuropathic pain.

Oral medications can also be tailored to the individual patient's needs, allowing for adjustments in dosage and combinations to optimise pain control. While they may not always offer immediate relief, as some invasive procedures do, they can provide consistent and sustainable pain management, which is often what patients need most.

The Role of 'Fellow Travellers'

One of the most critical aspects of pain management that often goes underappreciated is the role of what I like to call "fellow travellers" — non-pharmacological methods that can accompany traditional medical treatments in relieving pain. These methods might not have the direct, measurable impact of a neurolytic block, but they play a vital role in the overall experience of pain management.

Music therapy is one such fellow traveller. Music has the power to evoke emotions, shift focus, and create a sense of calm. For patients in pain, listening to music can reduce anxiety, promote relaxation, and alter the perception of pain, sometimes making the discomfort more bearable. Music's ability to engage the brain and divert attention from pain is a powerful tool that should not be overlooked.

Similarly, an aquarium can offer a soothing visual distraction, encouraging a sense of peace and relaxation. The gentle movement of fish and the sound of water can help lower stress levels, which can, in turn, reduce the intensity of pain.

Aromatherapy, too, can provide relief by engaging the senses and calming the nervous system. Essential oils like lavender, chamomile, and peppermint can promote relaxation and reduce the perception of pain. These alternative methods may seem simplistic in the face of complex medical procedures, but they can have a profound impact on the patient's well-being.

These non-invasive, complementary therapies work by addressing the psychological and emotional aspects of pain. They provide comfort and distraction, which can help to break the cycle of pain by reducing stress and anxiety. Pain is not just a physical experience; it is deeply intertwined with a patient's emotional and psychological state. By addressing these aspects, we can help patients manage their pain more effectively and improve their overall quality of life.

A Holistic Approach to Pain Management

The true art of pain management lies in the ability to integrate various methods—pharmacological, procedural, and complementary—into a comprehensive and individualised plan. We must recognise that invasive techniques are not always the answer and that there are many other ways to provide relief. By remaining open to a variety of approaches and not allowing what we can't do to prevent us from doing what we can do, we can offer our patients the best possible care.

Pain is a complex and multifaceted experience, and our approach to managing it must be equally nuanced. By embracing both traditional and alternative methods, we can break the cycle of pain and help our patients live fuller, more comfortable lives. The goal should always be to alleviate suffering, whether through a needle, a pill, or the calming presence of music or nature. In the end, it is the combination of these approaches that allows us to truly meet our patients' needs and provide them with the relief they deserve.

75

Meeting Paediatric Oncology Patients: Lessons in Courage and Hope

Meeting paediatric oncology patients is an experience that defies easy description. As a medical professional, one is trained to maintain a certain emotional distance, to approach each case with clinical objectivity. But when faced with a child battling cancer, that emotional distance quickly dissolves. The experience can be heart-wrenching, and it often feels like the weight of the world rests on your shoulders. Your voice may tremble, and you may feel choked by the enormity of the situation. Yet, in the midst of it all, these children—these little warriors—teach us some of the most profound lessons in resilience, courage, and joy.

Angels on a Mission

These children, facing what would be unimaginable for most adults, seem to carry an inner strength that defies their frail bodies. They are, in many ways, angels on a mission. They help us smile when all we want to do is cry. They teach us to laugh, even when the circumstances are dire. They are cheerful, even under the tremendous stress of their illness and treatment. Their positivity and resilience create an atmosphere of hope, even in the darkest of times.

I've never seen a child cry during my interactions with paediatric oncology patients. Perhaps they are too weak to express their pain in the way adults do, or maybe they have found a different way to cope. They seem to be wrestling with deep questions—questions that most of us would struggle to answer. Are they grappling with the "unanswered questions" that life has thrown their way, or perhaps with "unquestioned answers," truths they've come to accept without needing to understand them fully? Whatever the case, they seem to have an innate ability to focus on the present moment, to find joy in small things, and to keep fighting, no matter the odds.

The Strength of Hope

If the children are warriors, then their parents are their generals, leading the charge against a disease that strikes without warning. These parents hope against hope, clinging to every piece of good news and every small victory. And justifiably so, because the results of treatment for paediatric cancers are often among the best in comparison to other forms of cancer. Advances in chemotherapy, radiation, and surgery have significantly improved outcomes, and many children go on to live long, healthy lives.

But that hope, while powerful, is also fragile. It is built on a foundation of uncertainty and fear. The parents of these children carry the weight of the world on their shoulders, yet they continue to stand tall, to fight alongside their children, and to do everything in their power to ensure the best possible outcome. They are a testament to the power of love and the strength of the human spirit.

Wrestling with Life's Greatest Questions

The children and their families are constantly wrestling with life's greatest questions: Why did this happen? What does the future hold? Will there be a cure? These are questions that even the most experienced medical professionals struggle to answer. In many ways, the children seem to have a unique understanding of the uncertainty of life. They may not have all the answers, but they have a way of accepting the reality of their situation that is both inspiring and humbling.

Perhaps this is because, as children, they are not yet burdened by the expectations and fears that come with adulthood. They have an innate ability to live in the moment, to find joy in the small things, and to remain hopeful even in the face of adversity. Their courage, resilience, and joy remind us of the importance of staying hopeful, even when the path ahead is uncertain.

Meeting paediatric oncology patients is a profound experience that challenges everything we know about strength, resilience, and hope. These children, with their angelic spirits, teach us to smile, to laugh, and to remain cheerful, even under the most difficult circumstances. They remind us that life's greatest questions don't always have clear answers, and that sometimes, the best we can do is live in the moment, find joy in the small things, and keep fighting, no matter the odds.

Their parents, who hope against hope, inspire us with their unwavering love and determination. The advances in paediatric cancer treatment offer real hope for the future, but the journey is never easy. It is a journey of courage, resilience, and faith—one that challenges us to be better, to care more deeply, and to hold on to hope, no matter what. In the end, these children and their families teach us that even in the face of unimaginable adversity, there is always room for hope, for joy, and for love.

Children with Cancer: Warriors and Angels

Children with cancer, warriors of light,

Battling in silence, with spirits so bright.

Angels on Earth, with a mission unknown,

In their courage and strength, they have shown their own throne.

They lift my mood when shadows fall,
With smiles that break through the darkest wall.
Though frail in body, they're fierce in soul,
Guiding us gently, making us whole.

From the terrestrial, they lift me high,
To realms of the celestial,
touching the sky.
Their bravery humbles; their grace is pure,
In their presence, I find the strength to endure.

These children are warriors, angels in disguise,
With a mission of love that opens our eyes.
Though their fight is hard, their light shines bright,
A beacon of hope in the deepest night.

76

Battles of the Mind and Cries of the Heart: Addressing Total Pain in Patients

In the realm of medicine, especially in the care of those with chronic illnesses, there is a profound need to understand that pain extends far beyond the physical body. Dame Cicely Saunders, the founder of modern palliative care, introduced the concept of Total Pain, a multidimensional experience that encapsulates the physical, emotional, social, and spiritual suffering a patient endures. For many patients, their aches—the physical manifestations of disease—intensify into agony not just because of biological factors but through the battles of the mind and the cries of the heart. Understanding and addressing this complexity is crucial to easing the journey through illness.

The Nature of Total Pain

Total Pain transcends the mere physical sensation that can be treated with medication. It involves the mind's capacity to magnify suffering, the heart's cries for connection, and the spirit's yearning for meaning and resolution. Each element of pain feeds into the others. Physical pain might trigger anxiety and depression, while unresolved emotional conflicts or existential dread may exacerbate the perception of physical discomfort. Social isolation or the strain of family relationships adds another layer, compounding the suffering a patient experiences.

For a clinician, understanding Total Pain requires not only medical expertise but an attunement to the invisible battles a patient fights daily.

It means recognising that pain is often worsened by fear, loneliness, guilt, or the distress of facing one's mortality. For instance, a patient nearing the end of life may not only struggle with the pain of cancer but also the existential terror of ceasing to exist, or the guilt of feeling like a burden to their loved ones. The cries of the heart—whether for companionship, understanding, or forgiveness—are often left unheard in the sterile environment of hospitals focused on treating physical disease.

The Mind as Amplifier: Battles and Fears

Patients with chronic or terminal conditions often wrestle with mental anguish, which can intensify their physical pain. The uncertainty of the future, the loss of independence, and the potential for prolonged suffering feed into a psychological battle. This mental struggle, marked by anxiety and depression, plays a crucial role in how pain is perceived and processed. When left unaddressed, these emotional battles can turn physical discomfort into unbearable agony.

For example, a patient who fears dying alone or whose relationship with a loved one is fractured may experience worsening pain due to the mental burden of unresolved emotional issues. In this case, pain cannot be effectively treated with medication alone. The battle of the mind—the swirl of fears, regrets, and unspoken concerns—requires compassionate engagement. Clinicians must learn to ask not just about where it hurts physically but also where it hurts emotionally and spiritually. This holistic approach acknowledges that many patients experience profound suffering when they feel they lack control over their lives or fear what lies ahead.

The Cries of the Heart: Emotional and Spiritual Dimensions

The heart, often symbolising emotional and spiritual well-being, plays a pivotal role in Total Pain. For some patients, the heart cries out for meaning, for forgiveness, or for the resolution of inner conflict. Facing death, many patients are consumed by questions of legacy, purpose, and unresolved relational issues. The emotional burden of these concerns frequently overshadows even the most severe physical symptoms.

When these cries are ignored, patients may feel abandoned and unseen, which exacerbates their suffering. In palliative care, emotional and spiritual pain are as real as physical pain. A woman dying of cancer might not only ache from her disease but also from the unresolved tension between her and her estranged children. A man battling heart disease may be haunted by regrets of past decisions or spiritual doubts that have plagued him for years. These emotional cries, left unheard, often deepen their physical pain.

The process of addressing these emotional wounds is deeply personal and requires a unique sensitivity. Offering a space for patients to share their inner struggles—whether through conversation, counselling, or simply the compassionate presence of a caregiver—can help soothe the cries of the heart. This approach acknowledges that patients are not just bodies needing repair, but whole beings with emotional, social, and spiritual dimensions that demand attention.

Resolving Total Pain: Beyond Medical Interventions

Treating Total Pain involves a multidisciplinary approach, encompassing not just medical interventions but also emotional and spiritual support. The resolution of such pain often requires addressing the complex interplay between mind, body, and soul. Medical professionals, counsellors, social workers, and chaplains each play a vital role in this process.

For example, managing the physical component of pain with medication is just the first step. Understanding the emotional landscape of the patient—acknowledging their fears, grief, and hopes—helps to alleviate mental distress. Social support systems, including family and community networks, are also essential in addressing the sense of isolation and abandonment many patients feel. Lastly, addressing spiritual pain—whether it involves questions of faith, forgiveness, or the search for meaning in suffering—often requires engagement with chaplains or spiritual counsellors who can guide patients through the existential questions that arise near the end of life.

In practice, the resolution of Total Pain is not a one-size-fits-all approach. Each patient's pain is unique, shaped by their history, relationships, and worldview. A truly holistic care plan should reflect this individuality. For instance, music therapy has been shown to ease both emotional and physical pain by providing a sense of calm and connection, as illustrated by a story I recall about a young girl gifting a terminal patient with a Discman. The music provided more solace than medication could, bridging the gap between the patient's physical agony and their mental anguish.

Easing the Agony: The journey through illness is fraught with battles of the mind and cries of the heart, all of which can magnify physical pain into something more unbearable. Understanding and addressing Total Pain is essential for any clinician working with patients who suffer from chronic or terminal illness. It demands an approach that acknowledges the deep interconnectedness of body, mind, and spirit.

By addressing not just the physical but also the emotional and spiritual aspects of pain, we offer patients the opportunity to find peace and comfort, even in the face of incurable disease. The relief of suffering is as much about hearing the unspoken fears and heartaches as it is about treating the physical symptoms. Only by responding to the whole person—mind, body, and soul—can we truly alleviate the agony that arises when aches are amplified by the battles of the mind and the cries of the heart.

77

Celebrating A Sense of Gift Giving

The quote, "The way people die lives in the hearts of those who live on, and the last part of life has an importance out of proportion to its length," captures a profound truth about death and its lasting impact on those who remain behind. It emphasises that the quality of a person's final moments profoundly affects how they are remembered. This belief underscores the ethical mandate of healthcare professionals, particularly in palliative care, to ensure that every individual entrusted to them experiences a good death.

The Meaning of a Good Death

A good death is not merely about the cessation of life but about the way in which death is approached and experienced. It involves allowing patients to face death with dignity, peace, and comfort. This goes beyond physical comfort and encompasses emotional, psychological, and spiritual needs. Each death is unique, yet the commonality lies in the desire for the process to be as meaningful and pain-free as possible.

Dame Cicely Saunders, the founder of modern palliative care, introduced the concept of total pain, which acknowledges that suffering at the end of life is not just physical but can include emotional, social, and spiritual distress. Thus, providing a good death means addressing all these dimensions of suffering to ensure the patient's final moments are peaceful. In this light, the healthcare provider's role extends far beyond medical treatment—it includes creating a space where patients can feel heard, understood, and supported in their final journey.

The Last Part of Life: Importance Out of Proportion to Its Length

The final stage of life, though often short, holds immense significance. For many, it represents a time of reconciliation, reflection, and resolution. Families come together, often re-examining relationships, and patients, when allowed, may confront fears or express unspoken emotions. The brevity of this phase can be misleading, as the emotional and psychological weight it carries is often far greater than at any other time in a person's life.

For caregivers and loved ones, how a person dies can leave a lasting impression. Deaths marked by undue suffering, fear, or neglect often haunt those left behind. Conversely, a death marked by peace, dignity, and compassion can bring closure, comfort, and even a sense of fulfilment. The way a person dies often forms a cornerstone in the collective memory of the family, influencing their emotional healing process.

The Role of Healthcare Professionals in Ensuring a Good Death

Healthcare professionals, especially those in palliative care, are entrusted with the responsibility of facilitating this crucial life passage. Their role is to not only alleviate pain and discomfort but also to ensure that patients and their families are supported in every possible way. The words of the quote, "We are mandated to give a good death to all who are entrusted to us," remind medical professionals of this ethical duty. In a world that often focuses on prolonging life at all costs, the emphasis on ensuring a good death is a call to balance between life-prolonging interventions and comfort-oriented care.

For patients with terminal illnesses, aggressive treatments may no longer align with their values or desires for the remaining days. In these cases, the focus must shift from curing to healing, where healing refers to the preservation of dignity, alleviation of suffering, and fostering of emotional and spiritual peace. This transition requires immense sensitivity and communication, ensuring that patients' wishes are honoured while offering compassionate care.

Legacy and Impact on the Living

The manner of death also plays a significant role in the grief and mourning process. A death that occurs peacefully, with minimal suffering and in line with the patient's wishes, can provide solace to loved ones, offering them a sense of closure and acceptance. They are left with a memory of a life well-lived and a peaceful transition. On the other hand, a traumatic or painful death can leave behind unresolved emotions, guilt, and distress, complicating the bereavement process.

This is why the emphasis on giving a good death is not only about the individual dying but also about those who remain. It is an act of compassion that extends beyond the immediate clinical scenario, with ripples that affect the emotional and mental well-being of families for years to come. The memory of a loved one's peaceful passing can be a source of comfort, while a distressing death can lead to prolonged grief, emotional trauma, and even existential crises among those left behind.

Ensuring a good death is both a moral and professional responsibility for those in healthcare. It is a reflection of our collective humanity and our recognition of the sacredness of life's final chapter. By providing compassionate care, addressing not only the physical but also the emotional and spiritual dimensions of dying, healthcare professionals can help ensure that a person's final moments are marked by peace, dignity, and comfort.

In doing so, they not only ease the transition for the individual but also provide a lasting gift to the loved ones who remain. The way a person dies truly lives on in the hearts of those who survive, shaping memories, easing grief, and providing a legacy of compassion and care. Through this lens, the last part of life, though brief, becomes one of the most important, and healthcare professionals are uniquely positioned to make this final chapter as meaningful and peaceful as possible.

78

Medicalisation of Suffering and the Institutionalisation of Death

The Medicalisation of Suffering and the Institutionalisation of Death: Choices that Linger in Memories. In an era marked by rapid advancements in medicine, the boundaries between life and death have become increasingly blurred. Once natural processes, suffering and death are now heavily medicalised, often taking place within the sterile walls of hospitals rather than the comfort of home. As healthcare becomes more sophisticated, there is a growing tension between prolonging life at any cost and addressing the quality of life, especially during its final stages. For both patients and families, the choices made during these critical moments can linger in memory for years, shaping perceptions of life, death, and dignity.

Physicians play a pivotal role in this complex interplay, acting as guides who must navigate the delicate terrain between life-extending interventions and the acceptance of death. This essay explores how the medicalisation of suffering and the institutionalisation of death affect patients and families, and the physician's role in making these experiences less traumatic and more meaningful.

Medicalisation of Suffering: Turning Pain into a Clinical Condition

The medicalisation of suffering refers to the process by which natural human experiences, such as pain, grief, and emotional distress, are viewed predominantly through a medical lens, often reducing them to symptoms to be treated rather than human experiences to be understood. This shift has profound implications as it tends to distance the healthcare provider from the emotional and existential realities of the patient's experience.

In many cases, pain—both physical and emotional—is treated primarily with pharmacological interventions, with little emphasis on the underlying emotional, social, or spiritual suffering that often accompanies illness. As a palliative care physician, I have witnessed how excessive reliance on medications or procedures can overshadow the need for compassionate communication and emotional presence. Patients are frequently sedated or subjected to invasive procedures that may ease pain but fail to address deeper, existential concerns like the meaning of life, the fear of death, or unresolved relationships.

For instance, a patient battling terminal cancer may be flooded with pain medications but receive minimal support in confronting the fears that accompany their impending death. The medical system, driven by protocols and guidelines, often prioritises symptom management over conversations about acceptance and preparation for death. In this context, suffering becomes something to be eradicated at all costs, rather than an integral part of the human experience that requires holistic care.

The Institutionalisation of Death: A Shift Away from Home

With the advent of modern hospitals, death has shifted from the home to the institution. What was once a familial, intimate process has now become a highly medicalised event, often taking place in intensive care units, operating rooms, or hospice facilities. Families are sometimes left as spectators, watching their loved ones pass away surrounded by machines, wires, and medical staff, rather than in the comforting embrace of home and family.

While institutional care has its undeniable benefits—access to critical care, symptom management, and trained professionals—the shift away from home deaths has had emotional consequences for both patients and families. Many families report feelings of helplessness and alienation, as medical jargon, technology, and decision-making processes eclipse their role in the dying process. The sterile environment of a hospital can diminish the personal and emotional significance of death, turning it into a series of clinical events rather than a deeply human transition.

The institutionalisation of death often forces families into making hurried decisions about life-prolonging interventions—whether to insert a feeding tube, continue mechanical ventilation, or initiate resuscitation efforts. These choices, made in moments of overwhelming stress and uncertainty, often linger in memory, leaving families to question whether they acted in the best interests of their loved one or simply followed the momentum of medicalisation.

Choices that Linger in Memories: The Weight of Decision-Making

In my experience as a physician, I have seen how the decisions made during a loved one's final days can reverberate through the lives of surviving family members. One particularly poignant memory is of a man named Babu, a patient of mine who developed an aggressive recurrence of cancer after surviving for seven years post-surgery. Babu eventually passed away, but the decisions surrounding his care, from surgeries to palliative measures, had a profound impact on his family's memories of his death. His smile, as he recognised me by the familiar scent of my favourite perfume when he couldn't see in his final moments, is a memory that lives on not just for me, but for his family as well.

Decisions about end-of-life care are often made under duress, and families may carry the weight of these choices for years. Whether to pursue aggressive treatment or focus on comfort care is a decision fraught with emotional, ethical, and practical considerations. In many cases, families are torn between the desire to prolong their loved one's life and the fear of subjecting them to unnecessary suffering. When these decisions are made without adequate guidance from a compassionate and skilled physician, the consequences can be lasting guilt, regret, and trauma.

The Physician's Role: Guiding the Family

Physicians hold a unique position of authority and trust in these moments of decision-making. Yet, the role of the physician extends far beyond offering medical advice or recommending treatments. At its best, a physician's role is that of a guide—someone who helps the patient and their family navigate the difficult terrain of end-of-life care with compassion, clarity, and respect for the patient's wishes.

Effective communication is central to this guiding role. Physicians must engage in honest, empathetic discussions with patients and families about the realities of the situation. They must be willing to have difficult conversations about prognosis, the limitations of medical interventions, and the patient's preferences for how they wish to spend their remaining time. Importantly, they must also recognise when the focus of care should shift from curing to healing—acknowledging that healing does not always mean recovery, but rather addressing the emotional, spiritual, and relational needs of the patient.

In palliative care, I have found that guiding families often involves helping them come to terms with death as a natural part of life. This can mean encouraging families to spend quality time with their loved one, to talk openly about death, or to make preparations for a peaceful, dignified passing. It also means helping families to understand that not every death is a medical failure; sometimes, the most compassionate care is allowing a natural death, free from unnecessary interventions.

Compassionate Choices: A Lasting Legacy - The decisions made during the dying process can shape how families remember their loved ones for years to come. Choices that are made with compassion, clarity, and a deep understanding of the patient's wishes can offer a sense of peace and closure. In contrast, decisions driven by fear, confusion, or an over-reliance on medical technology can leave families struggling with unresolved grief.

The role of the physician is to ensure that the dying process is as dignified, humane, and meaningful as possible. This requires not just clinical expertise, but emotional intelligence, ethical judgement, and a profound respect for the sanctity of life and death. When physicians guide families through these moments with care and wisdom, they can help create lasting memories of love and respect, rather than regret and sorrow.

The medicalisation of suffering and the institutionalisation of death present significant challenges for both patients and families. As medicine continues to advance, physicians must not lose sight of the human aspects of care. Their role is not just to prolong life, but to ensure that the end of life is handled with dignity, empathy, and compassion. By guiding families through difficult choices, physicians can help shape the memories that linger—memories that honour both life and death.

79

The Paradox of Soft Skills in Palliative Medicine: A Surgeon's Perspective

Unlike the precision and hard skills needed for major ablative cancer surgeries, complex reconstructions, or the finesse required for body-sculpting procedures in plastic surgery, the practice of palliative medicine demands a different, perhaps even more challenging, skill set. In ablative cancer surgery, the focus is often on removing the disease, sometimes with aggressive measures, requiring expert knowledge of anatomy, pathology, and surgical techniques. Likewise, the delicate art of plastic surgery, particularly in free tissue transfers or replantations under an operating microscope, requires mastery of microvascular surgery, a steady hand, and the endurance for long hours of meticulous work. These are hard skills—technical, measurable, and honed through years of practice.

In contrast, palliative medicine is rooted in soft skills, which are often intangible, deeply personal, and shaped by one's empathy, communication, and emotional resilience. It is not just about treating a disease but addressing the multifaceted needs of the patient—physical, emotional, social, and spiritual. Unlike surgery, where success can be measured by clear outcomes such as tumour removal or successful tissue grafting, success in palliative care is much harder to define. It is about relieving pain, easing suffering, and helping patients and their families navigate the most difficult moments of life with dignity and grace.

The Unanswered Questions

One of the greatest challenges in palliative care lies in addressing the existential questions that patients inevitably face. As a surgeon, I have often encountered the question: "Why me, God?" This question, in its various forms, strikes at the core of human existence. It is not something that can be answered with a scalpel or sutures. It requires listening, understanding, and sometimes admitting that there are no easy answers. This vulnerability, this acceptance of the limits of our knowledge and power, is perhaps the hardest part of palliative care.

While in surgery, we fight against death and disease with every tool at our disposal; in palliative medicine, we must learn to accompany death, to walk alongside it, and to help our patients find peace in the face of it. The shift from curing to healing, from controlling to comforting, is not just a change in medical practice but a transformation in mindset. It demands humility, patience, and the ability to confront our own fears about mortality.

The Problem of Pain

Pain is another dimension where the soft skills of palliative care come to the forefront. In surgery, pain is often an expected consequence, something to be managed with medications and time. However, in palliative medicine, pain can take on a more profound meaning. It is not just physical but emotional and spiritual. The pain of facing death, the pain of leaving loved ones behind, or the pain of a life unfulfilled—all of these are issues that cannot be treated with a prescription or a procedure.

Addressing this type of pain requires deep empathy and an understanding that sometimes, the best we can offer is our presence. We may not be able to take the pain away, but we can sit with the patient in their suffering, acknowledging it and validating their experience. This requires a level of emotional engagement that is not always easy, especially for those of us trained to focus on fixing and solving problems.

The Role of Soft Skills in Palliative Care

The soft skills necessary in palliative care—communication, empathy, emotional resilience, and the ability to provide psychological and spiritual support—are often-overlooked in medical training. Yet, they are crucial in helping patients navigate the complex emotions and fears that accompany life-threatening illness. These skills do not come naturally to everyone, and they cannot be learned in a textbook. They are developed through experience, reflection, and a willingness to be vulnerable.

For a surgeon transitioning into palliative care, this can be a difficult adjustment. In surgery, we are accustomed to having control, to making decisions that have immediate and visible results. In palliative care, the outcomes are often less tangible and less immediate. The goal is not to cure but to comfort, not to fight but to accompany. This requires a different kind of courage—a willingness to face the unknown, to accept that we cannot always fix what is broken, and to find meaning in simply being there for our patients.

In many ways, palliative medicine is the ultimate test of our soft skills. It challenges us to go beyond our technical expertise and to connect with our patients on a deeper, more human level. It forces us to confront the most difficult questions of life, pain, and suffering and to find ways to provide comfort and meaning in the face of uncertainty. While the hard skills of surgery will always be crucial in the fight against disease, the soft skills of palliative care are perhaps even more important in the fight for humanity. In the end, it is these skills that allow us to truly heal, even when we cannot cure.

The Eternal Touch

For millennia, through time's vast scroll,
A simple touch has soothed the soul.
Before machines and science grew,
The human hand was a healer true.

No sterile screen, no robot's grace,
Can mirror touch or warm embrace.
No metal hand, however fine,
Can trace the tear on cheeks that shine.

A smile that lifts a heart in pain,
A stroke of hair to soothe the strain,
These gestures small, yet bold in might,
Have bridged the gap 'tween dark and light.

Beyond the scalpel's skillful art,
Lies something deeper, from the heart.
A human bond, a warmth, a grace,
That no machine can ever replace.

Though robots guide with perfect ease,
And slice through tissues, deft as breeze,
They lack the soul that fingertips.
Can share with just a brush of lips.

In palliative care's tender reign,
Where life and death walk hand in hand,
It's touch that speaks, without a sound,
To lift the spirit, love profound.

A hand held close, a patient's glance,
A silent promise in that stance.
These are the moments that remain.
When all machines have had their gain.

For love and care, in truth, transcend.
The fleeting days we may extend.
And though the world moves fast ahead,
The healing touch is never dead.

In halls of steel, or rooms of stone,

Where technology calls home,

The heart, the hand, the smile still reign—

A human touch, through joy and pain.

Love Can Touch in One Time

But as the song continues 'But lasts for a lifetime'.

Etched in Gold

Our Trust Unfold

80

Turkish Delight: A Journey of Medicine, "PAIN", and Victory in Antalya

The INCTR (International Network for Cancer Treatment and Research) conference in Antalya, Turkey, stands out as a remarkable memory in my medical career. Located 463 kilometres from Istanbul, Antalya is a beautiful Mediterranean city, steeped in history and culture. It is not far from Ephesus, a site mentioned in the Book of Revelation, seven hours away by road. This historical and spiritual proximity added a rich backdrop to the scientific discussions that unfolded during the conference.

The event brought together a diverse group of oncologists, researchers, and palliative care professionals from around the world. I had the privilege of representing the Regional Cancer Centre (RCC) in Kerala, India, where we had accomplished something extraordinary. Our hospital had become the only one in the world to manufacture both liquid and capsule morphine—a crucial medication in palliative care. It was an innovation born out of necessity, as morphine plays a vital role in managing pain for cancer patients, and its availability is a matter of life and death for those suffering from severe pain. This achievement was not just a feather in our cap but a testament to our commitment to alleviating pain and improving the quality of life for patients.

During the conference, I had the honour of presenting our work. Standing in front of an international audience, I described how we had taken the initiative to manufacture morphine in-house, ensuring that patients, especially in rural and underprivileged areas, had access to this essential drug. The response was overwhelmingly positive, and I was awarded first prize for this pioneering work.

However, the moment of triumph was preceded by a brief, unexpected challenge. During a panel discussion, a burly Briton asked me to define pain. His tone carried a hint of condescension, as though he were testing my understanding. Sensing that this question was more of a bullying tactic than a genuine inquiry, I decided to turn the situation around. I created an acronym for PAIN on the spot:

Palliative

Availability

India's

Need

I went further, elaborating on the acronym: Palliative Acceptance, Palliative Awareness, and Palliative Affordability – India's Need. I added a subtle twist, explaining that the 'I' could also stand for "International," applying to any nation grappling with the challenge of making palliative care available and affordable. My answer was well-received by the audience, although the Britisher seemed less amused. His initial attempt to intimidate had backfired, and I could sense the quiet approval of my fellow judges.

This small but significant exchange highlighted an essential truth: pain, whether physical or emotional, is a universal experience, but its management and relief vary drastically across the world. In India, we were making strides in palliative care, but much more needed to be done. Access to pain relief should not be a privilege; it should be a right. And that was precisely what we were working toward at the Regional Cancer Centre.

As a reward for my presentation, I was allowed to choose a book. I requested the Oxford Textbook of Palliative Care, one of the most comprehensive resources on the subject. True to their word, the organisers couriered the book to me promptly, and it remains a prized possession in my library to this day.

The conference in Antalya was not just about winning an award or receiving recognition. It was about advocating for better pain management and palliative care in India and globally. It was about pushing the boundaries of medical innovation to ensure that patients received the care they deserved. And it was about standing firm in the face of adversity, even when challenged in ways that felt personal.

Turkey, with its rich history and beautiful landscapes, provided the perfect backdrop for this journey of discovery and achievement. Antalya, in particular, with its blend of ancient history and modern vibrancy, felt like a fitting metaphor for the work we were doing: bridging the old and the new, the traditional and the innovative, to create something meaningful and lasting in the world of palliative care.

This trip was, in many ways, a true Turkish delight—not the sweet confection that is famous around the world, but the delight of knowing that we were making a real difference in the lives of people who needed it most. And that, in the end, is the sweetest reward of all.

Turkish Delight

In Antalya's air, where the sea meets the sky,

A story of healing, I carried high,

A tale of morphine, born from our need,

To ease the pain, to plant the seed.

In a world where suffering knows no end,
At the Regional Cancer Centre, we chose to mend.
To manufacture relief, in liquid and pill,
For those who ached when time stood still.

The stage was set in that Mediterranean town.
Where history whispered, and stars looked down,
Ephesus nearby, a symbol of might,
A chapter in Revelation, bathed in light.

Before the crowd, my voice did rise,
And soon I received the first prize,
Not for fame, but for what we'd achieved,
In the hearts of the judges, our work was believed.

The reward I sought wasn't gold or gem.
But the Oxford Textbook, a timeless tome,
Of wisdom and knowledge, for those in care,
And it came to me, with a promise so rare.

Now, years have passed, but the book remains.

A symbol of triumph through passion and pain,

A Turkish delight, that day by the sea,

Where history, science, and faith called to me.

81

Redefining Common Sense, Which is Very Uncommon

The perception that a referral to Palliative Medicine signifies the final chapter in a patient's life is a deeply entrenched but misguided notion. Even among professionals, the public, and colleagues, the idea persists that palliative care is synonymous with end-of-life care, as if patients who enter the realm of Palliative Medicine will soon breathe their last. However, this perception overlooks the fundamental essence of palliative care, which is not about death, but about enhancing the quality of life at any stage of illness. In fact, palliative care should be integrated into the treatment trajectory from day one, providing crucial support long before a patient approaches the end of life.

At the Regional Cancer Centre, where I worked, palliative care serves a vital role in the ongoing treatment of patients, and it is often necessary to dispel the myths surrounding this specialty. Pain management, for instance, is a significant focus in palliative care, and it intersects with many phases of treatment, not just the final days. Take the example of a patient suffering from mucositis, an agonising complication of cancer treatment. Liquid morphine, which is often prescribed to manage this excruciating pain, is dispensed only through the Department of Palliative Medicine. This essential medication provides relief to patients who are very much alive and actively fighting their disease, yet it is administered under the expertise of palliative care specialists.

Oral cancers, in particular, have promising survival rates, and many patients go on to live for years after their initial diagnosis and treatment. These patients benefit immensely from palliative interventions that address their pain, improve their quality of life, and support them through the rigours of treatment. Yet, the association of palliative care with death persists, creating a stigma that I frequently find myself having to challenge. Time and time again, I have been constrained to sermonise: Morphine is for the living, not for the dying. Palliative Care juxtaposes into the treatment trajectory from day one.

This statement captures the core of what palliative care truly is—a service designed to improve life, not merely to ease death. Morphine, as a symbol of pain relief, represents the broader philosophy of palliative care, which is to alleviate suffering and enable patients to live as fully as possible. Pain knows no timeline, and neither should the relief we provide for it. Whether a patient has just begun their cancer treatment or is nearing its conclusion, their comfort and well-being must be a priority.

Unfortunately, the misunderstanding of palliative care's purpose leads to delays in referrals, with many patients being referred only when their disease is far advanced, and their suffering has reached intolerable levels. This does a disservice to the patients and robs them of the opportunity to benefit from the full spectrum of care that palliative medicine can provide. Ideally, palliative care should be introduced early, working alongside curative treatments, to address symptoms and improve the patient's experience throughout their illness.

Palliative care is a holistic approach that encompasses more than just pain relief. It includes psychological, social, and spiritual support, which are essential components of comprehensive care. Patients facing serious illnesses often experience anxiety, depression, and existential distress, in addition to physical symptoms. By addressing these concerns from the outset, palliative care helps patients navigate the emotional and psychological challenges that accompany their illness.

It is crucial to educate both healthcare professionals and the public about the true nature of palliative care. It is not about giving up on treatment or preparing for death, but about enhancing life, no matter what stage of the disease a patient may be in. The goal is to ensure that patients can live as well as possible, for as long as possible, with dignity and comfort. By integrating palliative care into the treatment trajectory from the very beginning, we can ensure that patients receive the best possible care, not just when their disease is incurable, but throughout their entire journey.

In conclusion, the misconception that a referral to palliative care marks the end of a patient's life must be dispelled. Palliative care is for the living; it is about improving quality of life at every stage of illness, not just at the end. By providing relief from pain and other symptoms, and by offering emotional and psychological support, palliative care allows patients to live fully, even in the face of serious illness. It is time for both the medical community and the public to embrace palliative care for what it truly is: a vital, life-affirming part of comprehensive medical care.

82

Faith and Reason

Now faith is the substance of things hoped for, the evidence of things not seen. For by it the elders obtained a good testimony. By faith we understand that the worlds were framed by the word of God, so that the things which are seen were not made of things which are visible (Hebrews 11:1-6, The New Testament, Bible)

There have been parenthetical periods in my life when I had to toss away reason, to be blown off by the winds of disbelief and converge on faith when I became convinced of the existence of miracles wrought through wrestling in praying, importunate, and persistent intercessory.

Otherwise, the very word 'miracle' wouldn't exist in the English lexicon. Navigating through faith and reason is akin to balancing on a tightrope suspended between the seemingly opposing towers of belief and logic. Both faith and reason offer valuable perspectives on life, but the tension between them often raises questions about how they can coexist. For centuries, philosophers, scientists, theologians, and ordinary individuals have wrestled with this interplay, attempting to reconcile these fundamental aspects of the human experience. While faith often relies on intuition, trust, or belief in things unseen, reason demands evidence, logic, and critical thinking. Navigating between these domains requires an understanding that they are not mutually exclusive but can instead complement each other, enriching our understanding of the world and ourselves.

Faith, in its essence, speaks to the deeply personal and spiritual aspects of life. It calls for belief in ideas, forces, or deities beyond empirical evidence. Faith can inspire hope and provide comfort, especially in times of uncertainty, tragedy, or profound mystery. Whether faith is anchored in religious conviction, spirituality, or even in trust placed in human relationships, it transcends the immediate and the material. Faith asks us to believe in something larger than ourselves, something that may not be proven by reason alone. For instance, religious faith often includes belief in an afterlife, moral imperatives dictated by a higher power, or the existence of the soul—concepts that reason cannot readily prove or disprove.

Reason, on the other hand, is the bedrock of critical thinking, science, and rational inquiry. It involves the process of drawing conclusions based on evidence, observation, and logic. The scientific method is perhaps the clearest example of reason in action, where hypotheses are tested through experimentation, and conclusions are based on observable phenomena. Reason encourages scepticism, asking us to question assumptions and seek proof. It seeks to minimise errors in judgement by relying on what can be measured or demonstrated. Yet reason, while a powerful tool for understanding the physical world, has its limits when addressing existential or metaphysical questions, where empirical evidence is not readily available.

The apparent conflict between faith and reason has been a topic of debate throughout history. During the Enlightenment, for example, reason was elevated as the primary source of authority, with thinkers like Voltaire and Descartes championing logic and empirical knowledge over religious dogma. In contrast, many religious traditions uphold faith as paramount, viewing reason as subordinate to divine revelation or spiritual truth. This historical friction has sometimes resulted in a perceived dichotomy: either one must embrace reason and reject faith or cling to faith and dismiss reason.

However, many thinkers have posited that this is a false dichotomy. Faith and reason need not be antagonists. Instead, they can be seen as complementary approaches to understanding different dimensions of human existence. St. Thomas Aquinas, for example, argued that reason and faith are two paths leading to the same truth. He believed that reason could be used to understand the natural world, while faith illuminated truths about God and the spiritual realm. Similarly, Immanuel Kant suggested that while reason governs the realm of phenomena—the world as we experience it—faith provides insight into the noumenal, or things as they are in themselves, beyond human perception.

In more contemporary settings, many scientists, philosophers, and theologians work to bridge the gap between faith and reason. For instance, prominent figures like Albert Einstein, who once said, "Science without religion is lame; religion without science is blind," recognised the necessity of both reason and faith in forming a complete picture of the universe. The same could be said for philosophers like Søren Kierkegaard, who described faith as a "leap" that transcends rationality but does not negate it.

Faith can also serve a pragmatic role where reason has its limits. In medicine, for instance, physicians often navigate through uncertain diagnoses or treatments, where evidence-based approaches can only offer probabilities, not certainties. In such scenarios, faith—whether in the healing process, in a higher power, or in the resilience of the human spirit—can play a vital role in the patient's well-being. Similarly, individuals in professions that face life-and-death situations, such as palliative care, may turn to faith to provide emotional sustenance when reason alone cannot offer all the answers.

The interplay of faith and reason is also essential when confronting life's ultimate mysteries, such as death, the existence of a soul, or the meaning of life. Reason, while invaluable in exploring the physical and material aspects of these phenomena, often reaches its limits when addressing the intangible or transcendent. Faith steps in to fill these gaps, offering solace and answers where empirical data cannot tread. But this does not mean that reason must be abandoned. The best navigation of life's challenges often involves a thoughtful integration of both reason's insights and faith's assurances.

In conclusion, navigating through faith and reason is less about choosing one over the other and more about understanding when each is appropriate. Faith offers a way to deal with life's mysteries and uncertainties, providing meaning, hope, and a sense of connection to something greater. Reason, on the other hand, offers a disciplined and reliable method for understanding the physical world and for making decisions based on evidence. The most fulfilling and insightful life may be one that honours both dimensions, recognising the strengths and limitations of each. By holding both faith and reason in balance, we can approach life's most profound questions with humility, openness, and a deeper sense of understanding.

Faith and Reason

Two paths diverge, yet often meet,

One feels the ground beneath one's feet,

The other soars on wings unseen,

Through realms where logic has never been.

Reason, steady, sharp, and clear,

Seeks truth in all that we hold dear,

With questions deep and answers bright,

It shines its lantern through the night.

But Faith, a flame that never dies,
Leaps high, beyond where reason flies,
It whispers softly in the soul,
Of mysteries that make us whole.

Reason asks the "how" and "why,"
Faith trusts the unseen, the sky.
Where doubts may crowd and shadows fall,
Faith holds the heart above it all.

Together, though they seem apart,
They weave the wisdom in our hearts,
For what is life without the two?
A dance of both is what rings true.

Reason leads, but Faith believes,
In what the mind alone conceives,
And in the end, they share one quest:
To seek the good, to find what's best.

83

Competence, Confidence, and Compassion: Navigating Best- and Worst-Case Scenarios in Medicine

In the realm of medicine, competence is often considered the foundation upon which a physician's skills are built. It is what enables a doctor to diagnose accurately, prescribe effective treatments, and perform procedures with precision. Competence is the result of years of rigorous study, hands-on experience, and continuous learning. Yet, while competence helps a doctor do their best in ideal circumstances, it is confidence and compassion that equip them to handle the most challenging and worst-case scenarios. Together, these qualities form the triad that defines a truly exceptional physician—one who is prepared not only to deliver excellent medical care but also to provide comfort, reassurance, and hope during times of crisis.

Competence: The Foundation of Excellence

Competence is the bedrock upon which all medical practice rests. Without it, even the most well-meaning doctor would be unable to deliver effective care. Competence in medicine involves the ability to recognise symptoms, interpret diagnostic tests, and make decisions based on the best available evidence. It also involves surgical skill, technical expertise, and familiarity with the latest research and treatment protocols.

A competent doctor can handle a wide range of cases, from the routine to the complex. This competence builds trust with patients and colleagues alike. When a doctor is competent, they provide the best possible chance for recovery or improvement, whether treating a common cold or performing intricate surgery. Competence ensures that the physician's technical abilities are at their peak, allowing them to offer accurate diagnoses and effective treatments. However, in worst-case scenarios—situations where uncertainty, fear, and emotional distress dominate—competence alone is not enough.

Confidence: The Power to Act Decisively

When faced with worst-case scenarios—severe trauma, terminal illness, or life-threatening complications—confidence becomes the essential quality that allows a physician to act decisively. Confidence is rooted in competence, but it goes beyond technical knowledge. It involves the ability to remain calm under pressure, make quick decisions in life-or-death situations, and inspire trust in both patients and colleagues.

A confident doctor can navigate crises with composure, even when the outcome is uncertain. Confidence helps a doctor stand firm when difficult decisions must be made, such as choosing between high-risk surgeries or shifting focus to palliative care. In such moments, doubt or hesitation can be disastrous. Confidence allows the physician to move forward with conviction, guiding the medical team and providing a sense of security to patients and their families.

Moreover, confidence is crucial in instilling hope. In worst-case scenarios, patients and families often look to their doctor for assurance. A confident physician can communicate difficult truths without causing unnecessary despair, offering realistic hope while preparing the patient for potential outcomes. This balance of realism and optimism is critical in maintaining trust and managing expectations during difficult times.

Compassion: The Heart of Healing

While competence ensures that a doctor can provide the best care, and confidence allows them to act decisively, compassion is what makes a physician truly exceptional, particularly in worst-case scenarios. Compassion is the ability to connect with patients on a human level, to understand their fears, anxieties, and hopes, and to provide emotional and psychological support in addition to medical treatment.

In critical moments—when a diagnosis is terminal, or a surgery has failed—patients and their families often feel overwhelmed by grief, fear, and uncertainty. Competence and confidence can provide a path forward medically, but it is compassion that provides comfort and solace. A compassionate physician recognises that their role is not only to heal the body but also to ease suffering, to listen, and to provide care that respects the dignity of the patient, even when a cure is no longer possible.

Compassion also plays a critical role in decision-making during worst-case scenarios. It allows the physician to consider the patient's values and wishes when making difficult choices about end-of-life care or aggressive treatments. A compassionate doctor will take the time to explain options clearly, respecting the autonomy of the patient while offering guidance rooted in medical expertise. Compassion ensures that care is patient-centred, focusing not just on prolonging life but on improving the quality of the patient's remaining days.

84

The Convergence in Crisis: Competence, Confidence, and Compassion

In worst-case scenarios, these three qualities—competence, confidence, and compassion—must work together. Competence ensures that the doctor has the knowledge and skills necessary to offer the best possible treatment. Confidence allows the doctor to act swiftly and decisively, even in the face of uncertainty. Compassion ensures that the doctor remains attuned to the emotional and psychological needs of the patient and their family, offering comfort, empathy, and dignity.

For example, consider a physician working in a trauma centre. Competence allows them to quickly assess a critically injured patient, identifying internal bleeding or other life-threatening conditions. Confidence enables the doctor to make fast decisions—whether to operate immediately or stabilise the patient first—without hesitation. But compassion is what allows the physician to sit with the patient's family afterward, explaining the situation with empathy, offering support, and preparing them for all possible outcomes.

In palliative care, where the focus is on alleviating suffering rather than curing illness, the interplay between these qualities becomes even more evident. Competence ensures that pain and symptoms are managed effectively. Confidence gives the physician the strength to discuss difficult topics like death and dying with clarity and sensitivity. Compassion allows the doctor to walk with the patient through their final journey, providing not only medical relief but also emotional and spiritual support.

A competent doctor can offer the best possible care in ideal circumstances. But when faced with the worst-case scenarios—life-threatening illness, traumatic injuries, or terminal diagnoses—it is confidence and compassion that enable them to provide not just treatment but comfort and hope. These qualities—competence, confidence, and compassion—are not isolated traits but must converge to offer holistic care. Together, they allow a physician to navigate both the best and worst of medical situations, ensuring that patients receive the most effective, humane, and compassionate care possible. In the end, it is this convergence that defines not just a good doctor, but a truly exceptional one.

85

A Physician's Care: A Convergence for the Greater Common Good

Parallel lines don't meet! Medicine is often seen as a complex science—an intricate web of diagnoses, treatments, and technical precision. However, the practice of medicine is equally an art that demands the blending of skills, values, and human empathy. A physician's care should never resemble parallel lines that never meet—segregating treatment from compassion, technical knowledge from communication, or cleverness from common sense. Instead, effective care requires the convergence of multiple qualities: cleverness, communication, common sense, competence, and confidence. These five qualities should intersect in service of the greater common good, ensuring that every patient receives holistic and humane care.

Cleverness: The Key to Innovation

Cleverness in medicine is not merely about intellectual brilliance or outsmarting diseases but the ability to think creatively when faced with difficult situations. A clever physician often transcends standard medical protocols and finds innovative solutions tailored to individual patient needs. This cleverness becomes especially vital in cases where conventional treatments fail or are inadequate. However, cleverness must always be tempered with humility, as the most creative solutions should not merely reflect the brilliance of the physician but should serve the ultimate goal of alleviating suffering and improving patient outcomes.

Communication: Bridging the Gap

Good communication forms the backbone of trust in the doctor-patient relationship. Without it, even the most accurate diagnoses or the most skilled surgeries can fall flat. A physician must communicate effectively with patients, families, and the larger medical team to ensure that everyone is on the same page. Communication bridges the gap between the physician's clinical knowledge and the patient's lived experience. It helps to build rapport, alleviate anxiety, and provide clear explanations of medical conditions and treatment options. In palliative care, for instance, where emotional and psychological support is as important as medical intervention, communication becomes a form of healing itself. The physician who speaks with empathy listens actively and responds with care, offering more than just treatment—a sense of reassurance and trust.

Common Sense: The Wisdom of Practicality

Common sense may seem like an obvious component of good medical care, but in a world driven by technology and data, it can sometimes be overlooked. While advanced diagnostic tools and specialised treatments have their place, they should never overshadow the physician's ability to apply practical, real-world wisdom to each case. Common sense can prevent overtreatment or excessive interventions when simple, effective solutions are at hand. For instance, recognising that a patient's quality of life might not improve with aggressive treatment requires the kind of practical wisdom that common sense offers. In the end, it is this grounded approach that allows a physician to make decisions that are both medically sound and, in the patient's best interest.

Competence: The Foundation of Care

Competence is non-negotiable in the practice of medicine. It involves not just the acquisition of knowledge but also the application of that knowledge with precision, accuracy, and responsibility. A competent physician is one who remains updated with the latest advancements, techniques, and guidelines, but also knows when to rely on tried-and-true methods. Competence is the foundation upon which all other qualities must rest. Without it, no amount of cleverness, communication, or common sense can be effective. The patient's trust hinges on the physician's ability to make accurate diagnoses, perform surgeries with precision, and prescribe treatments that work.

Confidence: The Power to Act

Confidence in a physician is crucial—it inspires trust, ensures decisive action, and fosters a sense of security in patients. However, it must be differentiated from arrogance. Confidence should stem from competence and experience, not from an inflated sense of self-importance. A confident physician is willing to make tough decisions, often under pressure, without wavering. At the same time, they are open to collaboration, second opinions, and learning from mistakes. Confidence allows a physician to provide leadership in difficult situations and to convey a sense of calm to anxious patients and their families.

Convergence for the Common Good

The convergence of cleverness, communication, common sense, competence, and confidence ensures that a physician's care is holistic. When these qualities work in harmony, they lead to outcomes that benefit not just the individual patient but society at large. A physician who operates with these principles fosters an environment of trust, safety, and innovation in the healthcare system. This, in turn, elevates the standard of care for all.

For example, during the COVID-19 pandemic, the convergence of these qualities in physicians worldwide resulted in swift adaptations to unprecedented challenges. Cleverness led to rapid innovations in treatment protocols. Clear communication was vital in keeping the public informed and in managing patient expectations. Common sense dictated that preventive measures like social distancing and vaccination were essential. Competence ensured that front-line workers could respond effectively to the crisis, while confidence in their decisions helped manage an overwhelming surge of cases.

A physician's care should never be like parallel lines that never meet—detached, dispassionate, or purely technical. Instead, it should be a convergence of cleverness, communication, common sense, competence, and confidence, working together for the greater common good. When these qualities meet, they create a form of care that is not only scientifically sound but also deeply humane. In the end, it is this holistic approach that enables physicians to fulfil their ultimate purpose: to heal, to comfort, and to serve.

86

From Five-Year Survival to Disease-Free Period: A Journey in Cancer Treatment

In the realm of cancer care, the concept of survival has evolved tremendously over the past decades. Not so long ago, the five-year survival mark was considered the gold standard – a crucial milestone indicating the likelihood of a patient remaining alive for five years following a cancer diagnosis. However, as medicine has advanced, so too has our understanding of what it means to "survive" cancer. Today, the focus has shifted from merely surviving to achieving a "disease-free period," aiming for long-term remission or complete eradication of the disease.

This progress is the result of a confluence of innovations across various fields of medicine—surgery, chemotherapy, radiation therapy, and now, cutting-edge modalities such as immunotherapy, gene therapy, targeted therapy, and the advent of robotic surgery. These modalities are increasingly taking centre stage, offering hope where traditional approaches may have fallen short.

The Evolution from Surgery to Robotic Surgery

Surgery, historically the first line of defence against cancer, has undergone significant transformations. Initially, cancer surgery was often radical and disfiguring, with the primary aim being to remove as much of the tumour as possible, sometimes at great cost to the patient's quality of life.

Over time, the introduction of reconstructive techniques, particularly in plastic surgery, has helped mitigate the physical and emotional impact of these procedures.

The advent of robotic surgery marks a pivotal point in the evolution of surgical oncology. Robotic-assisted surgeries allow for greater precision, less invasiveness, and quicker recovery times. The technology provides surgeons with enhanced dexterity and vision, enabling them to perform complex procedures that would be challenging or impossible with traditional methods. For patients, this means less post-operative pain, shorter hospital stays, and a faster return to normal activities.

Despite these advances, surgery alone is often insufficient for treating cancer, particularly in cases where the disease has spread. This is where the combination of surgery with adjuvant therapies—such as chemotherapy and radiation—has historically played a role.

Chemotherapy: The Traditional Workhorse

Chemotherapy has been the backbone of cancer treatment for decades, targeting rapidly dividing cancer cells throughout the body. While it has undoubtedly saved countless lives, its non-selective nature means it also harms healthy cells, leading to significant side effects such as nausea, hair loss, and immune suppression. The toxic effects of chemotherapy have driven researchers to seek more targeted treatments—ones that can attack cancer cells while sparing the healthy ones.

Although chemotherapy continues to be an essential component of cancer care, it is increasingly being integrated with newer, more advanced therapies. Today, we are witnessing a paradigm shift where treatments are becoming more personalised and focused on the specific genetic and molecular profiles of a patient's cancer.

The Rise of Immunotherapy and Targeted Therapy

Immunotherapy represents one of the most groundbreaking developments in cancer treatment. Unlike chemotherapy, which directly targets cancer cells, immunotherapy harnesses the body's immune system to recognise and attack cancer cells. Drugs known as checkpoint inhibitors have revolutionised the treatment of several cancers, including melanoma, lung cancer, and bladder cancer, by essentially "releasing the brakes" on the immune system, allowing it to mount a stronger attack against the disease.

Similarly, targeted therapy has changed the landscape of cancer treatment by focusing on specific molecular targets within cancer cells. These therapies are designed to interfere with the cancer's ability to grow and spread, making them more effective and less toxic than traditional chemotherapy. For example, drugs that target the HER2 receptor have dramatically improved outcomes for patients with HER2-positive breast cancer.

The combination of targeted therapies with immunotherapy, often referred to as "precision medicine," has shown great promise, providing highly individualised treatment plans based on the unique characteristics of each patient's cancer. This represents a significant leap forward from the one-size-fits-all approach that has dominated cancer treatment for so long.

Gene Therapy: The Next Frontier

Gene therapy is another rapidly emerging field in cancer treatment. By modifying or replacing faulty genes within cancer cells, gene therapy aims to correct the underlying causes of cancer at the genetic level. Techniques such as CRISPR and CAR T-cell therapy are making waves, particularly in the treatment of certain blood cancers where conventional therapies have failed.

CAR T-cell therapy, for instance, involves engineering a patient's own T cells to better recognise and destroy cancer cells. This form of treatment has shown remarkable success in treating certain types of leukaemia and lymphoma, providing hope for patients who have exhausted all other options.

The Road Ahead: Combining Modalities

As we look to the future, the trend in cancer treatment is increasingly towards combination therapies that integrate multiple modalities—surgery, chemotherapy, immunotherapy, targeted therapy, and gene therapy—in a synergistic manner. This multidisciplinary approach maximises the chances of eradicating the cancer while minimising the risks and side effects associated with any single treatment.

The goal is no longer just to extend life but to ensure that patients live longer, healthier lives free from the burden of cancer. By shifting the focus from mere survival to achieving a disease-free period, we are fundamentally changing the narrative around cancer care. The integration of innovative technologies, such as artificial intelligence and personalised medicine, further holds the potential to improve outcomes and enhance the quality of life for cancer patients.

We have come a long way from simply measuring success by the five-year survival mark. Today, the era of immunotherapy, gene therapy, targeted therapy, and robotic surgery has ushered in a new chapter in cancer treatment—one that prioritises quality of life, individualisation, and long-term disease-free periods. As we continue to push the boundaries of what is possible, there is renewed hope that cancer will one day be a manageable, if not curable, disease for all.

The journey is far from over, but the progress made thus far is a testament to human ingenuity, perseverance, and the relentless pursuit of better outcomes for cancer patients worldwide.

87

NASH: The Four Modes of Life-Takers and the Dilemma of 'Acts of God'

In understanding how lives are tragically lost, especially from an insurance perspective, there is a stark classification known as NASH: Natural, Accident, Suicide, and Homicide. These four categories have become a fundamental way to categorise life-ending events, from everyday tragedies to preventable deaths. But while NASH covers the majority of life's tragic ends, there remains a nebulous category that insurance companies use as an escape hatch—the so-called "Act of God." This term, designed to absolve companies of paying claims in extreme circumstances, has proven to be an elusive and often heartless mechanism, especially when lives are lost to disasters like the COVID-19 pandemic.

Natural Death: The Inevitability of Time and Disease

Natural death is perhaps the most accepted mode of passing, defined by the inevitable processes of ageing, illness, or congenital health issues. It is the closure that life anticipates, albeit in various ways. For insurance companies, natural death is usually a simpler case to resolve, with policies written explicitly to cover such losses. Yet, there are grey areas where natural causes blur into the realm of the "Act of God." For example, during the COVID-19 pandemic, many succumbed to a virus that insurers classified as an uncontrollable event, leaving families without financial recourse. The cold detachment of insurers has left loved ones grappling not only with grief but with the bureaucratic cruelty of denied claims.

Accident: The Randomness of Tragedy

Accidental death is the most unpredictable of the NASH categories. It could happen in an instant—through a car crash, a fall, or an industrial mishap. Insurance companies do offer payouts for accidental deaths, yet they often rely on the fine print to absolve themselves in specific instances. If an event can be categorised as an "Act of God"—an earthquake, tsunami, or even a pandemic—companies may argue it was not a true accident but an unforeseeable disaster, beyond human control.

This distinction is critical because while accidents should be covered, certain incidents get shunted into the "Act of God" category. Natural disasters or viral outbreaks are events insurers claim cannot be foreseen or mitigated. Yet, how is this distinction made, and where is the human element? Accidents can often be traced back to human negligence or error, yet labelling them as divine intervention often benefits no one but the corporations.

Suicide: The Unseen Struggle

Suicide is a deeply personal and tragic form of death, often arising from prolonged mental health struggles, social isolation, or financial despair. For families left behind, suicide brings both emotional devastation and, often, financial ruin. Many insurance companies include clauses that do not cover suicide, especially within the first few years of a policy. This denial leaves families grappling with the dual burden of loss and a lack of support. In some ways, the rejection of claims in the case of suicide mirrors the callousness with which insurance companies handle "Acts of God."

Moreover, the pandemic itself saw a spike in suicides, attributed to isolation, fear, and financial collapse. Yet, insurers quickly bundled these cases under pandemic-related exclusions, minimising the payout. It reveals a pattern: when people need support the most, large corporations shut down the avenues of assistance, opting for financial security over human compassion.

Homicide: The Ultimate Breach of Trust

Homicide, the deliberate act of ending another's life, is as old as human conflict. In terms of insurance, homicides tend to lead to more straightforward payouts, though complications arise when motives are questioned, or when the person responsible for the death is a beneficiary. Investigations can drag on for months, leaving families in financial limbo.

Interestingly, homicides caused by negligence or manslaughter, often linked to industrial accidents or large-scale corporate malfeasance, can sometimes be categorised as "Acts of God." This happens when companies deflect blame onto uncontrollable circumstances, rather than acknowledging human error. This again highlights the convenient use of divine intervention as a shield for corporate irresponsibility.

The "Act of God" Escape Clause

The concept of "Act of God" remains one of the most frustrating clauses in insurance policies. It acts as a blanket term for any event that seems beyond human control—earthquakes, floods, pandemics, and other catastrophes. Yet, as you rightly point out, many of the CEOs and decision-makers in these corporations are atheists. For them, "Act of God" is merely a legal tool, a way to protect profits, rather than a genuine appeal to divine forces.

COVID-19 has starkly revealed this hypocrisy. When millions died, not through negligence but through a naturally occurring virus, insurance companies labelled it an "Act of God" and washed their hands of responsibility. Yet, how do these same executives, who do not believe in a higher power, justify using God as their defence? It is a perverse contradiction. Families, like those of your 25 classmates who passed, found themselves abandoned at their most vulnerable moment.

Final Thoughts: NASH and the Ethics of Responsibility

NASH—natural, accident, suicide, homicide—provides a framework for understanding death, but it is incomplete without recognising the loophole that corporations use to deny responsibility: the "Act of God." In reality, many of the tragedies classified under this term could be mitigated, controlled, or predicted with proper human oversight. The pandemic was a moment of reckoning for insurance companies, yet they responded by evading responsibility rather than stepping up.

For families, the financial devastation that follows such denials compounds their grief. It is time to question whether such an escape clause has any place in modern society, especially when the so-called "Acts of God" often result from human inaction or irresponsibility. Whether in natural death, accident, suicide, or homicide, the need for ethical responsibility must be paramount, rather than the whims of corporate profiteering.

88

Treating 'A Patient, Not a Paper': A Reflection on Patient-Centred Care in a Technologically Driven World

In modern medicine, we increasingly rely on technology to generate metrics—digits, values, and scans—that help us make clinical decisions. Yet, as these tools advance, we risk reducing our patients to mere abstractions: a set of numbers, a list of diagnoses, or an image on a screen. Technology can tell us a lot about disease, but it cannot tell us who the patient is. It is the shadows cast by these scans that often obscure the light of human experience.

I had the privilege of treating a patient who exemplified this tension between human care and technological advancement. Diagnosed with lung cancer at the age of 94, he had already exceeded the average lifespan by many years. He endured chemotherapy and radiation with remarkable resilience. Despite his courage in the face of medical adversity, what wounded him most was not his illness but the constant rebuke of his family, who could not forgive him for being a lifelong smoker.

When he was transferred to my care, his condition was mild; he was dyspnoeic but still alert and engaged. He approached me with a question that was both disarming and deeply human: "Can I smoke, Beloved Doctor? I've read your write-up against tobacco. In eight months, I'll be hitting my hundred to the gallery!" The question caught me off guard—not because I hadn't been asked it before, but because it came from a man who, against all odds, had defied his prognosis to reach the remarkable age of 94, now looking forward to crossing the century mark.

I could have recited the well-worn medical advice about smoking cessation, but in that moment, I realised that this was not about prolonging his life by a few more weeks or months. It was about the quality of life he had left. This man, who had already lived through nearly a century of experiences, was not asking me for a lecture on the dangers of tobacco. He was asking for the freedom to live out his final days with dignity, doing something that gave him comfort. So, I told him, "Please, sir, smoke."

That simple permission triggered an emotional response I did not anticipate. He hugged me and wept. It wasn't just the permission to smoke; it was the validation of his humanity, the acknowledgement that his wishes mattered, even if they flew in the face of medical orthodoxy.

On discharge, the patient returned to his home, resumed his simple routines, and smoked a few more cigarettes before passing away peacefully at the age of 100 years and three months. He died in the house he had built, on the cot he had slept in for years—a place that was a testament to the life he had lived. I learned of his passing while I was at Incheon Airport in Seoul, South Korea, and I was struck by the grace of his departure.

This experience stands as a powerful reminder that treating 'a patient, not a paper' means seeing beyond the data, the scans, and the protocols. Technology may inform us about disease, but it can never replace the profound connection that comes from understanding a person's values, desires, and dignity. The patient is not their illness, their scan, or their lab report. They are a human being whose life extends far beyond the reach of our medical expertise.

The story of this centenarian lung cancer patient underscores the essence of palliative care, where the focus shifts from curing to healing. Healing, in this context, is not about eradicating disease but about honouring the patient's autonomy, their emotional well-being, and their right to a peaceful death. It is about recognising that, sometimes, our role as physicians is not to prolong life at all costs but to ensure that the life left is worth living.

As we continue to integrate technology into every facet of medical care, we must be vigilant not to lose sight of the person behind the patient. Scans, lab results, and numbers are vital tools, but they can never capture the entirety of a human life. True healing comes when we see the whole person—when we listen, understand, and, most importantly, care.

89

The Conspiracy of Silence

The "Conspiracy of Silence" in patient care refers to the often unspoken and suppressed truths between medical professionals, patients, and their families regarding the severity of an illness, the prognosis, or the imminence of death. This silence, although sometimes driven by the intention to protect, can lead to unintended consequences—preventing patients from preparing emotionally, spiritually, and practically for the end of life and depriving them of the opportunity to make informed decisions about their care. It is a multifaceted issue that touches on communication barriers, cultural expectations, and the psychological discomfort many health professionals feel when faced with difficult conversations.

One of the primary reasons for this silence is the discomfort around discussing mortality. Medical professionals are often trained to view death as a failure, especially in highly specialized fields such as oncology or surgery. The focus is predominantly on curing, extending life, and managing symptoms, leaving little room for discussions around the inevitability of death. This "curative mentality" sometimes leads to an over-optimistic presentation of outcomes, even when the medical reality is much grimmer. Many clinicians hesitate to break bad news, fearing that they may crush the patient's spirit or leave them feeling hopeless.

Additionally, the conspiracy of silence may also arise from cultural and familial dynamics. In certain cultures, there is an emphasis on shielding the patient from the knowledge of their terminal condition.

Family members may request that the truth be withheld, believing that full disclosure would cause unnecessary distress. This creates a delicate ethical dilemma for healthcare providers—balancing the family's wishes with the patient's right to know their condition. Such practices are common in some parts of Asia and the Middle East, where families may decide not to inform a patient diagnosed with terminal cancer or an incurable disease.

Impact on Patient Autonomy

The silence, while intended to protect, often has the opposite effect—it strips the patient of autonomy and informed choice. By withholding critical information, doctors and families inadvertently deprive patients of their right to understand the full scope of their illness and to make decisions that align with their values, preferences, and life goals. For instance, a patient may choose to prioritize quality of life over aggressive treatment in their final days if they are fully informed. Without knowing their prognosis, they may opt for interventions that extend life but do so at the expense of unbearable suffering, missed opportunities to say goodbye, or unfulfilled personal wishes, such as resolving family conflicts or pursuing spiritual solace.

This silence also hampers a patient's ability to plan for their death—a moment as significant as any in life. Palliative care physicians emphasize that death is a part of the continuum of life and should be approached with dignity, not dread. Being open about the reality of the situation allows patients to emotionally prepare and to seek comfort in their own ways, whether that's through religious rituals, writing letters to loved ones, or arranging final affairs. By keeping these discussions shrouded, healthcare providers and families may inadvertently cause emotional harm and exacerbate feelings of isolation and confusion in the patient.

Consequences for Healthcare Providers

For healthcare providers, participating in this conspiracy of silence can be emotionally taxing. Medical professionals, especially those in high-stress, life-saving fields, often deal with an internal conflict between the desire to save lives and the reality that, at times, they must shift toward offering comfort rather than cure. This unspoken avoidance of reality may foster feelings of guilt or failure in clinicians, which can lead to burnout or moral distress. A doctor who cannot speak openly about a terminal prognosis may feel that they are complicit in a lie, even when their intentions are noble. Over time, this internal conflict can erode the sense of purpose and clarity in a medical career, contributing to emotional exhaustion and even leaving the clinician emotionally distant from the patient.

Breaking the Silence: The Role of Palliative Care

Palliative care as a speciality has emerged to address many of the issues inherent in this conspiracy of silence. By focusing on the whole patient—physical, emotional, social, and spiritual—rather than merely the disease, palliative care embraces open communication about the realities of illness and death. The cornerstone of palliative medicine is honesty and empathy, where patients are provided with realistic options and supported in making decisions that improve their quality of life. The emphasis shifts from merely prolonging life to enriching the time patients have left in ways that are meaningful to them.

Breaking the silence in patient care doesn't mean abandoning hope—it means redefining it. Instead of framing success solely in terms of survival, hope can be reframed as achieving peace, resolving conflicts, or enjoying precious moments with loved ones. Palliative care teams are trained to navigate difficult conversations and empower patients to confront their illness in ways that are emotionally supportive. This approach helps reduce feelings of abandonment in patients as their disease progresses and instils a sense of shared understanding between the patient, family, and medical team.

The Ethical Imperative

Ethically, the conspiracy of silence in patient care challenges fundamental principles such as autonomy, truth-telling, and informed consent. Patients deserve to know the truth about their condition, even when it's uncomfortable or distressing. From an ethical standpoint, withholding such information is paternalistic and undermines the trust that is critical to the patient-doctor relationship. While navigating these conversations requires great sensitivity, it is a professional obligation to ensure that patients have the opportunity to make decisions that are aligned with their values, no matter how difficult those choices may be.

To break this conspiracy, healthcare providers must be trained not only in technical skills but also in the art of communication. These discussions need not be harsh or abrupt; rather, they should be handled with compassion, allowing for the patient's emotional responses and guiding them through the difficult journey of understanding their prognosis. Institutions should promote an environment that supports these honest conversations, encouraging transparency and sensitivity across all levels of patient care.

The conspiracy of silence in patient care is a deeply ingrained issue, often perpetuated by cultural norms, personal discomfort, and a medical culture that prioritizes curative treatments over conversations about mortality. However, the growing recognition of palliative care as an essential part of medicine is slowly breaking down these barriers. Patients deserve to know the truth about their illness, not to frighten or diminish hope but to empower them to live their final days on their own terms. By fostering open communication, physicians can provide care that truly respects the dignity and autonomy of the patient, ensuring that the end of life is approached with grace, understanding, and peace.

The Conspiracy of Silence

In sterile rooms where whispers dwell,

Between the pulse and quiet swell,

A silence forms, both sharp and kind,

Where truth and fear are intertwined.

The doctor's lips, though skilled and wise,

Hold back the storm beneath calm eyes,

For words of death, once set in flight,

Can dim the day, erase the light.

But silence, though it wears a veil,

Is like a tide that cannot fail.

It washes hope, it stirs the shore,

It leaves the patient wanting more.

The truth unspoken, kind but cruel,

Makes honesty the rarest tool.

In saving hearts, in easing pain,

We often build a cage of strain.

The patient waits with searching gaze,
For what the silence dares not say,
And in that void, they lose their right
To face the dark, to find the light.

But there is grace in breaking through,
In letting harshest winds blow true,
For in the knowing, peace can grow,
A softer strength in letting go.

So let us speak, let silence die,
Let truth and love hold every sigh,
For in the telling, life remains—
More than a cure, more than the pain.

90

An Inquiring Mind and an Observing Eye Find Matter for Improvement

These traits equip individuals with the ability to perceive opportunities for improvement in various facets of life.

An inquiring mind embodies curiosity and the desire to seek knowledge, understand complexities, and challenge the status quo. This intellectual curiosity drives individuals to ask questions, explore unknown territories, and solve problems. For instance, scientific breakthroughs often stem from researchers questioning established norms and relentlessly pursuing new answers. Similarly, entrepreneurs continuously refine their business models by asking how they can better serve their customers.

An observing eye complements an inquiring mind by providing the keen attention to detail required to notice subtle deficiencies or areas of potential enhancement. Observation is not just about seeing but about interpreting and understanding the underlying patterns and dynamics. Artists, for instance, succeed by observing their environment and expressing intricate details through their work. In the business world, a leader with an observing eye might identify inefficiencies in workflows that lead to more streamlined operations.

When these two traits combine, they form a powerful engine for improvement. Consider the example of technology development: Engineers with inquiring minds ask how technology can be made more efficient or user-friendly. Their observing eyes then catch specific issues in current designs or processes, leading to innovations that significantly improve performance and usability. The same principles apply in everyday life, where a curious and observant individual might identify gaps in knowledge or skill sets and seek ways to fill them, thereby continuously enhancing their personal and professional capabilities.

Moreover, this combination fosters a culture of continuous improvement in organisations and communities. When leaders and members consistently question how things can be better and pay attention to the finer details, they create environments that thrive on innovation and adaptability. Schools, workplaces, and even social settings benefit from such cultures, witnessing cumulative advancements over time.

In sum, the synergy between an inquiring mind and an observing eye can transform mediocrity into excellence. By persistently seeking knowledge and paying close attention to details, individuals and organisations can identify numerous opportunities for improvement, driving progress across all areas of life. This mindset not only paves the way for personal development but also contributes significantly to the broader quest for societal advancement.

91

Addressing the 'Aching Void'

The concept of the "aching void" speaks to a profound sense of emptiness or loss, often arising from personal or collective experiences such as grief, disconnection, or existential contemplation. This void can manifest in various ways: a feeling of isolation, an inability to find meaning, or a yearning for connection. Addressing this emptiness requires a multifaceted approach that encompasses emotional, psychological, and social dimensions.

Understanding the Nature of the Void

The aching void often stems from significant life transitions, such as the loss of a loved one, the end of a relationship, or even a major life change like retirement. These experiences can leave individuals grappling with feelings of inadequacy, nostalgia, or confusion about their identity and purpose. It's essential to recognise that this void is a natural response to loss and is not inherently negative; it can serve as a catalyst for growth and self-discovery.

Emotional Expression and Acknowledgement

One of the first steps in addressing the aching void is emotional expression. Suppressing feelings of loss can lead to more profound despair and isolation. Writing, art, or talking with friends and loved ones can provide outlets for these emotions, allowing individuals to process their feelings more fully. Acknowledging the void—rather than avoiding it—can pave the way for healing. Therapy, whether through professional guidance or support groups, can also be invaluable in facilitating this acknowledgement and helping individuals navigate their emotions.

Seeking Connection

Human beings are inherently social creatures, and connection is crucial in filling the void. Reaching out to others—whether through friendships, family ties, or community engagement—can combat feelings of isolation. Volunteering or participating in group activities can foster a sense of belonging, reminding individuals that they are part of a larger tapestry of humanity. These connections not only provide emotional support but also remind individuals of their inherent worth and the value they bring to others.

Finding Meaning and Purpose

Addressing the aching void also involves a search for meaning and purpose. This journey can be deeply personal and often requires introspection. Engaging in activities that align with one's values—such as pursuing hobbies, education, or career goals—can help individuals reconstruct their identity in the wake of loss. Spirituality or philosophy can offer frameworks for understanding suffering and existence, guiding individuals toward a deeper comprehension of their experiences.

The Role of Creativity

Creativity can be a powerful tool for addressing the aching void. Artistic expression—be it through music, writing, painting, or other forms—allows individuals to channel their emotions and experiences into something tangible. This process not only aids in personal healing but can also resonate with others, creating connections through shared experiences of loss and recovery.

Building Resilience

Finally, cultivating resilience is key to navigating the aching void. Resilience does not imply a lack of struggle but rather the capacity to endure and emerge stronger. Developing coping strategies, fostering a growth mindset, and embracing flexibility in the face of change can empower individuals to confront their voids. Mindfulness and meditation practices can enhance self-awareness, helping individuals stay present and engaged rather than overwhelmed by feelings of emptiness.

Addressing the aching void is an ongoing process that requires time, patience, and intentional effort. By embracing emotional expression, seeking connection, finding meaning, and harnessing creativity, individuals can navigate their experiences of loss and emptiness. Ultimately, while the aching void may never fully disappear, it can transform into a space of growth and renewed purpose, leading to a richer, more fulfilling life.

92

Energising Domiciliary Care, Scripting the First Dedicated Palliative Care Policy Passed by the Government of Kerala, and Supervising Oral Morphine Production: A Pioneering Journey

---

Throughout my career in medicine, particularly in the fields of Plastic Surgery and Palliative Care, I have encountered numerous challenges that required innovation, resilience, and compassion. Among my most significant contributions, three stand out: energising domiciliary care, scripting the first dedicated Palliative Care Policy, and supervising the production of oral morphine. These initiatives were not just professional accomplishments; they were transformative efforts aimed at improving the quality of life for patients suffering from terminal illnesses. Through them, I was able to address the limitations of healthcare access, the suffering caused by pain, and the need for systemic policy changes in Palliative Care.

Energising Domiciliary Care: Reaching the Unreachable: Domiciliary care—delivering healthcare to patients in their homes—was a concept I embraced passionately during my time at the Regional Cancer Centre (RCC). In my early years as a surgeon, I witnessed first-hand the difficulties faced by terminally ill patients who were unable to travel long distances to receive care. Many lived in remote districts like Idukki and

Wayanad, areas with poor infrastructure and limited access to specialised healthcare facilities. These patients, often battling cancer or other life-limiting illnesses, were in dire need of not only medical care but also emotional and palliative support.

Recognising the barriers they faced, I spearheaded efforts to energise domiciliary care by launching a dedicated Tele Clinic. With the support of a UK-based charity, Help the Hospice, and the collaboration of local partners like the Sisters of Destitute, I established a system where patients could receive consultations remotely. Using ISDN (Integrated Services Digital Network) technology, we connected with patients via a telecamera and a large monitor. This allowed me and my team to assess their condition, adjust treatment plans, and offer emotional support from a distance, thus mitigating the physical and financial strain of travelling.

The tele-clinic model was a lifeline for patients who would have otherwise suffered in isolation. It provided continuity of care, particularly in terms of pain management, which was often the most pressing issue. We set up a network of hospice beds at Karuna Bhavan in Adimali, ensuring that oral morphine was available to control pain effectively. Although this work went largely unrecognised in India, it was applauded internationally. I had the honour of receiving an award from HE President Tony Tan in Singapore, a testament to the impact of our efforts. More importantly, the patients and their families expressed deep gratitude for the comfort and

93

The Expanding Mandate: Care Beyond Cure

Palliative care has traditionally focused on patients with terminal illnesses, providing comfort and quality of life when a cure is no longer possible. However, the scope of palliative care is rapidly expanding to encompass a broader population, including the elderly, psychiatric patients, individuals with dementia, and those who are physically or intellectually challenged. These groups are often marginalised or neglected, yet they require comprehensive, compassionate care to maintain dignity and a sense of well-being. This essay explores how the mandate of palliative care is evolving to meet the needs of these diverse populations.

Care of the Elderly

The ageing population is increasing globally, bringing with it a host of challenges related to chronic illness, frailty, and declining cognitive function. Elderly individuals often experience multiple comorbidities, such as heart disease, diabetes, and arthritis, which impair their quality of life. Palliative care for the elderly focuses on symptom management, psychosocial support, and helping them maintain autonomy as much as possible.

One of the key issues elderly patients face, is polypharmacy, the use of multiple medications, which can lead to adverse effects and decreased quality of life. Palliative care provides a more holistic approach by focusing on comfort and reducing unnecessary treatments.

Importantly, palliative care helps elderly individuals navigate complex end-of-life decisions, emphasising dignity and respect during their final stages of life.

Furthermore, social isolation, a common issue among the elderly, can lead to depression and anxiety. Palliative care teams work to integrate social support systems, encouraging meaningful interactions and a sense of belonging even in the later stages of life.

Care of Social Discards

In society, there are groups of people who are often considered "social discards"—those who have fallen through the cracks of social systems, including the homeless, those living in extreme poverty, or individuals with long-term substance abuse problems. These populations are particularly vulnerable and often lack access to appropriate healthcare.

Palliative care for social discards is rooted in the principle of equity, recognising that every individual, regardless of social or economic status, deserves dignified care. Providing palliative care to these groups may involve addressing not only physical pain but also significant emotional and psychological distress. Many of these individuals have complex trauma histories, and palliative care practitioners are trained to offer a compassionate, non-judgemental approach.

In some cases, the care provided is not only medical but also social, helping individuals reconnect with families, secure housing, or access basic human needs. This highlights palliative care's broader responsibility, not just to manage symptoms, but to advocate for the fundamental dignity and rights of the marginalised.

Care of Psychiatric Patients

Psychiatric patients, particularly those with severe and chronic mental illnesses, are often-overlooked in traditional healthcare settings. These individuals may suffer from schizophrenia, bipolar disorder, or major depressive disorder, conditions that can complicate physical illnesses and make medical management more difficult.

Palliative care for psychiatric patients requires a multidisciplinary approach. Mental health professionals collaborate with palliative care teams to manage both psychiatric symptoms and the physical issues that may arise from other chronic illnesses. A central focus of care is ensuring that these individuals do not experience unnecessary suffering due to neglect, stigma, or lack of understanding about their psychiatric condition.

Ethical dilemmas often arise in the care of psychiatric patients, particularly around issues of autonomy and decision-making capacity. Palliative care emphasises the importance of understanding the patient's wishes while balancing safety and well-being. Creating an environment where psychiatric patients feel heard, valued, and supported is a key aspect of expanding palliative care to this group.

Care of Patients with Dementia

Dementia is one of the most common reasons individuals require palliative care in old age. Alzheimer's disease and other forms of dementia gradually rob individuals of their cognitive abilities, leading to a loss of independence, personality changes, and profound confusion. Palliative care for dementia patients involves managing symptoms like agitation, pain, and difficulty swallowing, while also supporting families as they cope with the gradual decline of their loved ones.

Since dementia can last for many years, palliative care in this context often focuses on long-term comfort rather than immediate end-of-life care. It requires an understanding of the patient's evolving needs and a commitment to reducing suffering over time. Family caregivers also benefit from palliative care services, as they frequently face burnout and emotional distress while caring for a loved one with dementia.

One of the biggest challenges in dementia care is communicating with patients who may have lost the ability to express themselves. Palliative care teams use various methods, including non-verbal communication and close observation, to assess pain and discomfort, ensuring that even those who cannot articulate their needs receive compassionate care.

Care of the Physically and Intellectually Challenged

Individuals with physical and intellectual disabilities often face a lifetime of medical challenges, compounded by societal stigma and neglect. Palliative care for these individuals is essential, as they frequently endure chronic pain, limited mobility, and a reduced quality of life. The goal of palliative care in this population is to enhance comfort, independence, and dignity.

For physically challenged individuals, palliative care includes pain management, rehabilitation services, and the provision of assistive devices to improve mobility. Intellectual disabilities may complicate communication about pain and other symptoms, necessitating a specialised approach that involves caregivers and advocates in the decision-making process.

One of the central tenets of palliative care for the disabled is *respect for autonomy*. Even individuals with profound disabilities have the right to make decisions about their care. Palliative care teams work to involve patients as much as possible in the planning and implementation of their care, ensuring that their preferences and values are respected.

Palliative care's expanding mandate reflects a growing recognition of the importance of addressing not only physical symptoms but also the social, psychological, and spiritual needs of vulnerable populations. Whether caring for the elderly, the marginalised, psychiatric patients, those with dementia, or the physically and intellectually challenged, palliative care practitioners emphasise dignity, compassion, and holistic support. As palliative care continues to evolve, it stands as a critical component in ensuring that all individuals, regardless of their circumstances, can live with comfort, respect, and meaning during their final stages of life.

94

The Currency of Vision: A Life Beyond Mediocrity

Imagine a world where life operates like a bank, and the only currency of exchange is vision—the clarity of thought, ambition, and purpose. In such a world, many people would go to bed with anxious thoughts, fearing that their metaphorical cheques might bounce. Vision, unlike money, is not something you can accumulate by simply working through routines. It requires boldness, imagination, and the courage to see beyond the ordinary. Those without it would find themselves running low on this currency, their dreams stifled by fear and self-doubt.

In this vision-driven world, mediocrity would be the currency of antiquity. To live without vision is to accept the status quo, to repeat what has already been done, and to dwell in the past. Mediocrity thrives in comfort zones, where people take the path of least resistance, never striving for more. It's the outdated mode of existence where innovation is stifled, and progress stalls.

Without vision, people are left holding empty cheques—promises of potential that will never be fulfilled. True success in life requires more than just going through the motions. It demands that individuals see possibilities others might overlook, that they dare to aim higher than the ordinary. Visionaries, in this metaphorical bank of life, are the wealthiest. They are the ones who inspire change, spark creativity, and lead the world into the future.

Ultimately, living without vision is living a life devoid of purpose. While many might fear their cheques being returned due to a lack of vision, it is only those willing to cultivate and invest in their dreams who can transcend mediocrity and thrive in a world that demands more than just survival—it demands growth.

95

Rainbows and Horizons in Health Care

In the realm of health care, the metaphors of "rainbows" and "horizons" serve as powerful symbols for hope, healing, and the pursuit of better health outcomes. Rainbows represent the promise of recovery and the beauty that can emerge from adversity, while horizons embody the potential for progress and innovation in medical practices. Together, these symbols encapsulate the aspirations and challenges faced by health care providers, patients, and the broader community.

The Rainbow: Symbol of Hope and Healing

Rainbows often appear after storms, signifying the possibility of renewal and transformation. In health care, this symbolism resonates profoundly. Patients facing illness or injury frequently navigate turbulent experiences—pain, fear, and uncertainty. The journey toward healing can feel overwhelming, yet the prospect of recovery often shines like a rainbow on the horizon.

For healthcare professionals, nurturing hope in patients is essential. It involves not only treating physical ailments but also addressing emotional and psychological needs. Practices such as empathetic communication, holistic care, and supportive environments can help cultivate a sense of hope. The presence of supportive family members and community resources can also enhance the healing process, creating a collective commitment to recovery.

Moreover, rainbows in health care can symbolise the diversity of treatments and therapies available. Just as a rainbow is composed of various colours, modern medicine incorporates a wide array of approaches—conventional, complementary, and alternative. Integrative care models that combine these modalities can offer patients a more personalised path to wellness, enhancing their chances of recovery and satisfaction.

The Horizon: Vision for the Future

While rainbows signify hope, horizons evoke the forward-looking vision that drives healthcare innovation. As the medical field continually evolves, professionals strive to push boundaries and explore new possibilities. This includes advancements in technology, research, and patient-centred care models.

Telemedicine, for instance, has expanded access to care, breaking geographical barriers and providing services to underserved populations. Innovations in artificial intelligence and data analytics promise to enhance diagnostic accuracy and treatment efficacy, paving the way for more personalised health care. These advancements illustrate the horizon of possibilities that lie ahead, transforming how care is delivered and experienced.

The horizon also reflects the importance of public health initiatives that aim to improve population health. Addressing social determinants of health—such as education, economic stability, and access to healthy food—can lead to systemic changes that enhance community well-being. By envisioning a healthier future, healthcare providers can work collaboratively with policymakers and communities to create environments that support optimal health for all.

Bridging the Gap

Navigating between the rainbow of hope and the horizon of innovation requires a balanced approach. It involves recognising that while advancements in healthcare are crucial, the human element remains at the core of the healing process. Empathy, compassion, and communication are essential to bridging the gap between technological progress and patient-centred care.

Furthermore, fostering a culture of inclusivity within healthcare can ensure that diverse voices and experiences are heard and valued. Engaging patients in their care decisions and promoting health literacy can empower individuals to take charge of their health journeys. In this way, healthcare becomes a partnership, where both providers and patients work together toward common goals.

The metaphors of rainbows and horizons in health care illuminate the dual nature of healing: the immediate hope that guides individuals through challenging times and the visionary aspirations that drive progress in the field. By embracing both elements, health care professionals can create a more compassionate, innovative, and equitable system that not only addresses the needs of today but also anticipates the possibilities of tomorrow. In doing so, they not only heal individuals but also nurture the health of entire communities, paving the way for a brighter, healthier future.

96

The Tripartite Concept of Personhood: Spirit, Soul, and Body

Apostle Paul, with wisdom deep,

Did speak of man as whole and steep:

In spirit, soul, and body's frame,

We're formed as one, yet not the same.

The spirit soars, to God it's tied,

In faith and hope, it doth abide.

The soul within, emotions reign.

It bears the joys, the tears, the pain.

The body stands as earthbound clay,

But through its strength, we live each day.

These three, though one, in harmony,

Shape all we are, our destiny.

For those who care, in love they see,
This tripartite humanity.
In Palliative's tender art,
They heal the body, soul, and heart.

With equity and empathy,
They strive for true equality.
No soul ignored, no pain dismissed,
In every care, their hands persist.

They surge ahead with hope anew,
For in each man, this truth holds true:
To heal the body's fleeting stay,
The soul and spirit light the way.

97

The Doctor as a Cheerleader: Inspiring Hope and Healing

The image of a doctor as a cheerleader might seem unconventional at first glance. We typically associate physicians with scientific precision, clinical detachment, and methodical decision-making. However, the deeper role of a doctor often transcends medical expertise, extending into the realm of emotional support, encouragement, and the fostering of hope. In many ways, a physician can be seen as a cheerleader for their patients—not in the sense of blind optimism, but as someone who motivates, inspires, and bolsters the patient's will to persevere through the challenges of illness.

The role of doctors as cheerleaders in their patients' journeys, proclaiming how they balance optimism with realism, and why fostering hope is as vital as any treatment or surgery.

More Than Just Medicine, it is the emotional support patients need, and doctors are cheerleaders in this area.

When people seek medical care, they are often in a vulnerable state, facing pain, uncertainty, and fear. Whether it is a diagnosis of cancer, the uncertainty of a complex surgery, or a chronic illness requiring lifelong management, patients look to their doctors for more than just a prescription or procedure. They look for reassurance, hope, and guidance through their suffering.

In my experience as both a surgeon and palliative care physician, I've found that clinical knowledge alone cannot always carry a patient through the trials of illness. Sometimes, what patients need most is emotional support—a belief that there is light at the end of the tunnel, that they are not alone in their journey, and that they possess the strength to face whatever comes next. This is where the role of the doctor as a cheerleader becomes critical.

A cheerleader in the medical context doesn't just motivate by offering hollow platitudes or unrealistic expectations. Instead, they act as a steady, positive force, reminding patients of their inner strength, resilience, and capacity to cope. This support can help alleviate fear, increase compliance with treatment, and improve overall well-being, all of which can positively impact clinical outcomes.

Balancing Realism with Optimism

One of the most challenging aspects of being a physician cheerleader is finding the balance between realism and optimism. On the one hand, it's crucial to be honest with patients about the severity of their condition, the limitations of treatment, and the likelihood of outcomes. False hope can be damaging, leading to disillusionment and eroding trust in the doctor-patient relationship. On the other hand, focusing solely on the grim realities of an illness can leave patients feeling hopeless and demoralised, which can hinder their mental and physical healing.

This balance is delicate but necessary. A doctor must learn to offer optimism while remaining grounded in reality. For example, in the case of a cancer diagnosis, the physician can convey that while the prognosis may be uncertain or challenging, there are still options for treatment, comfort, or quality of life improvement. The message is not "everything will be fine," but rather, "we will face this together, and there are ways to make the most of this journey."

In palliative care, where the primary goal may not be curing the illness but managing symptoms and improving quality of life, this balance is even more critical. Patients and their families must understand the limitations of what medicine can do, but they also need to hear that their dignity, comfort, and relationships can still be preserved. This message of hope, in its most authentic form, can be deeply healing, even if it doesn't mean recovery.

Building Trust Through Cheerleading

For a doctor to be an effective cheerleader, there must first be trust between the physician and the patient. Cheerleading isn't about empty enthusiasm – it's about building a relationship founded on empathy, communication, and understanding. Patients need to feel that their doctor sees them not just as a case to be solved but as a whole person with emotional, social, and psychological needs.

In my years of practice, I've found that patients respond best to doctors who listen deeply, validate their fears and feelings, and offer encouragement in ways that are meaningful to the individual. Some patients need a doctor to be a steady, calming presence, while others respond better to a more energetic, motivational approach. The key is understanding what kind of support each patient needs and adapting the "cheerleading" style accordingly.

This trust-building often involves taking the time to explain procedures, clarify treatment options, and allow space for patients to express their concerns and desires. When patients feel heard and understood, they are more likely to believe in the doctor's reassurances, follow through with treatment plans, and maintain a positive outlook, even in the face of adversity.

The Role of Cheerleading in Recovery

The psychological and emotional state of a patient can have a profound effect on their physical health. Numerous studies have shown that patients who feel optimistic and supported tend to have better outcomes, whether that's faster recovery times, improved pain management, or better compliance with treatment. The role of the doctor in fostering this state of mind cannot be understated.

Consider the case of post-operative recovery. As a plastic surgeon, I have often dealt with patients facing lengthy, painful recoveries after significant surgeries. It's in these moments, when physical healing is slow and patients can easily become discouraged, that the doctor's role as a cheerleader becomes most evident. Offering encouragement, setting small achievable goals, and celebrating even the tiniest milestones can help patients remain motivated through difficult rehabilitation processes.

In chronic conditions, where full recovery may not be possible, the doctor's cheerleading role becomes one of helping patients find meaning and purpose despite their limitations. For instance, a patient with a degenerative neurological condition may never regain full mobility, but the doctor can help them focus on what they can do—perhaps spending time with loved ones, pursuing hobbies, or managing symptoms effectively. By focusing on what remains rather than what's lost, physicians can help patients maintain a sense of agency and dignity.

The Cheerleader in Palliative Care: A Different Kind of Hope

In palliative care, the cheerleading role takes on a different form. Here, it is not about motivating patients to fight against disease, but rather about helping them to live fully in the time they have left. As physicians in this field, we become cheerleaders for the quality of life, helping patients focus on comfort, emotional well-being, and personal goals as they near the end of life.

One of the most powerful lessons I've learned in palliative care is that hope is not exclusive to survival. Even when a cure is no longer possible, hope can exist in other forms—the hope for a peaceful death, for reconciliation with loved ones, for the preservation of dignity, and for the alleviation of suffering. As cheerleaders in this context, doctors provide a sense of direction and possibility, guiding patients and families through the final stages of life with grace and compassion.

The doctor's role as a cheerleader may not fit the traditional mould of medical practice, but it is an essential aspect of patient care. Beyond diagnosing illnesses and prescribing treatments, doctors are uniquely positioned to inspire hope, provide emotional support, and guide patients through some of the most challenging experiences of their lives. By balancing optimism with realism, building trust, and focusing on the holistic needs of the patient, physicians can act as cheerleaders, offering more than just physical healing—they offer hope, resilience, and a sense of possibility.

In a world where illness often feels like a battle, doctors can stand alongside their patients as their greatest champions, helping them find the strength to endure and the courage to face whatever lies ahead.

98

Poetry Reading in Palliative Care Conferences Doubly Dublin: The Use of Poetry in Palliative Care Conferences

Both the Bournemouth and Limerick Palliative conferences were unforgettable, as the post-dinner was an elderly gentleman sat high on a stool after dinner, reading poetry in a sombre voice. Many wept and me too! Poetry, by its very nature, delves into the depths of human suffering, mortality and the meaning of life. It focuses not just on physical symptoms, but also on emotional, psychological, and spiritual dimensions of care. Conferences centred around this specialty aim to advance medical knowledge, share best practices, and explore the intricacies of compassionate care. But in recent years, these gatherings have also embraced something unexpected yet profoundly fitting—poetry. Poetry, with its power to distil emotions and experiences into a few evocative lines, offers a unique language for expressing the inexpressible. For professionals in palliative care, poetry becomes a valuable tool to process and communicate the complexities of end-of-life care. It allows clinicians, caregivers, and patients alike need to articulate the nuanced realities of suffering, hope, love, and loss.

In the formal setting of a conference, where clinical and academic discourse dominates, the inclusion of poetry creates a bridge between science and the human spirit, grounding discussions in the very essence of care: humanity.

Poetry as Reflection and Catharsis

For many healthcare professionals, palliative care can be emotionally taxing. Physicians, nurses, and caregivers witness patients and families grappling with death, fear, and sometimes despair. In such a setting, the clinical tools available—medications, procedures, even conversations—can often fall short of addressing deeper existential questions. Here, poetry becomes a mirror reflecting the emotions that many professionals might struggle to express in technical language.

At conferences, the reading or sharing of poetry offers a cathartic outlet. A carefully chosen verse can encapsulate the ineffable emotions tied to the work. For example, a simple poem might evoke the shared grief of witnessing a patient's suffering or celebrate the small victories of adding life to days rather than days to life. By using metaphor and imagery, poetry helps to acknowledge and process the emotional weight, offering attendees a space to confront their own feelings of vulnerability.

Poetry as a Tool for Empathy

Empathy is central to palliative care, and poetry can deepen this empathy by helping caregivers see the world from different perspectives. Poems written by patients, for instance, bring their inner world to life, conveying the fear, isolation, or even the acceptance that accompanies a terminal diagnosis.

When these are shared at palliative care conferences, they remind clinicians that patients are more than just cases - they are individuals with rich emotional lives, confronting their mortality in ways that transcends the clinical.

For caregivers, hearing a patient's or family member's poem can foster a deeper connection to their work. It offers a rare glimpse into the subjective experience of illness and dying, highlighting the emotional truths that clinical data often obscures. This deeper understanding can improve the care provided, as caregivers are reminded of the importance of seeing beyond symptoms and diagnoses to the human being in front of them.

Fostering Resilience and Compassion Through Poetry

Palliative care is as much about healing the caregivers as it is about healing the patients. Burnout is common in a field where professionals regularly confront death. In this context, poetry at conferences serves another vital role - it promotes resilience. By addressing themes of suffering, hope, and the cycle of life and death, poetry offers solace to those who bear witness to the inevitable mortality of their patients. It allows them to connect with universal human experiences, fostering a sense of shared purpose and community in the face of overwhelming emotions.

Moreover, poetry can be a vehicle for compassion, not just for others, but for oneself. Many palliative care professionals are driven by an intense sense of duty, often neglecting their own emotional needs.

The communal experience of sharing poetry—whether reading a classic poem that speaks to the fragility of life or listening to a colleague's original verses—offers a moment of reflection, helping caregivers reconnect with their own humanity and practice self-compassion.

Bridging the Gap Between Science and the Humanities

Palliative care lies at the intersection of science and the humanities. While clinical expertise is essential for managing symptoms and providing care, the holistic approach that palliative medicine champion demands an understanding of the human condition, which transcends the purely medical.

This is where poetry has a unique role to play. In the rigid structure of a medical conference where protocols, trials, and evidence-based practices are the focal points; poetry offers a counterbalance. It reminds the attendees that medicine is not just a science—it is an art.

Incorporating poetry into conference proceedings elevates the dialogue beyond symptom management and treatment protocols. It challenges the participants to engage with the philosophical questions that often, questions arise in palliative care: What does it mean to live well? What constitutes a good death? How can we, as caregivers, create meaning in the face of mortality. Poetry, in its fluidity, allows for exploration of these questions in a way that scientific presentations cannot enriches the overall discourse and adding depth to the exchange of ideas.

A Shared Language for a Global Audience

Palliative care conferences bring together professionals from diverse cultural, religious, and linguistic backgrounds. backgrounds. Poetry has the advantage of being a universal form of expression that transcends these differences. A poem's reliance on metaphor, rhythm, and emotion allows it to speak across languages, resonating with people regardless of their cultural context. At international conferences, where participants may come from different healthcare systems and face unique challenges. Poetry offers a shared language of empathy and compassion.

Moreover, poetry's flexibility makes it adaptable to different cultural perspectives on life, death, and suffering. By including poems from various traditions, conference organisers can honour the diverse beliefs and practices of the global palliative care community. In doing so, they foster a more inclusive and holistic approach to the discipline, enriching the global dialogue on care at the end of life.

In the field of palliative care, where the focus is on holistic well-being, the inclusion of poetry in conferences serve as a reminder that medicine is both an art and a science. Poetry offers a means to express the emotions and experiences that words often fail to capture in clinical settings. It allows caregivers to reflect, process grief, foster empathy, and connect with both their patients and their own inner worlds. As palliative care continues to evolve, poetry will likely play an even greater role, providing a space for shared humanity in the face of life's most profound challenges.

Ireland is perhaps the most exciting country I've visited a few times. I love Ireland because it's emblem is the harp present in all international conferences? You see a sweet teenager playing the harp. The Guinness Beer has an inverted harp as its logo as one is prohibited from using the official Irish logo! Staying in Hotel Ballsbridge opposite the American Embassy was interesting as there were protestors before it on a daily basis. Trinity College was just 10 minutes' walk from where I stayed, I used to while away time there, wondering about Jonathan Swift of *Gulliver's Travels* and Oscar Wilde. Another utter literary genius alumni Dallán Forgaill, who wrote 'Be Thou my vision, O Lord of My Heart' was again Irish, the immortal hymn which inspired and was a favourite of Ida Sophia Scudder, who founded Christian Medical College, Vellore, Tamil Nadu in 1900, and Dame Edith Mary Brown, who founded Christian Medical College, Ludhiana, Punjab (1894).

99

Immodestly Yours

I could do the country proud under Kleig Lights, being the Flag Bearer of India at Dublin while attending a world cancer summit. Shaking hands with HE Tony Tan President of the island nation of Singapore, receiving an award is unforgettable. The time in an assignment to start Palliative Care activities in Ethiopia, taking classes at the Black Lion (Tikur Anbessa Specialised Hospital (TASH), a university teaching hospital in Addis Ababa, Ethiopia that serves as the country's main referral hospital) for medical students was a unique moment of recognition. An award for professional excellence and service to society from the erstwhile Maharaja of Travancore late Sri Uthradom Tirunal Marthanda Varma was a moment of crowning glory. I could melt into the crowd in Dhaka or Colombo, marvel at the Egyptian museum seeing surgical instruments used before Christ, attending an INCTR conference and Pain congresses at Houston and Cape Town in 2014, when I could see the country weep when Phil Hughes, a promising Australian cricketing all-rounder, was hit by a beamer and died of internal carotid dissection. At the IAHPC conference in Seoul, South Korea, however, I found it difficult convincing the attendees that our Home Care Team at Regional Cancer Centre, Trivandrum could do Ascitic or Pleural tap in the home setting!

As a 'wild card entry' into debate competition in International Conferences, I have secured a prize. As the recipient of the prize, I could choose, usually an expensive book! Presently, my wonderful wife Prof. Rachel Cherian Koshy, and yours truly, Cherian Koshy, are Faculty (Anaesthesiology and Surgery) at SUT Academy of Medical Sciences,

Trivandrum, and our wonderful daughter Dr. Kripa Elizabeth Cherian and her husband Dr. Aditya John are Faculty at Christian Medical College, Vellore, Tamil Nadu, with their wonderful sons (David and Joshua). Our son Dr. Karun Koshy Cherian, his lovely wife Dr. Reenu Elizabeth Cherian, are Faculty at Christian Medical College, Ludhiana, Punjab, with their wonderful daughter Stefania Rachel Cherian. Looking back, I think and thank Dominus meus et Deus meus, as through it all I have made stepping stones from stumbling blocks, and milestones from stones thrown!

100

Knowledge is Power, Unity is Strength, but Attitude is Everything

---

This was the theme of the Cancer summit I attended in Dublin, where I was chosen to be the flag bearer for India. In life, the values of knowledge, unity, and attitude play essential roles in shaping our experiences, growth, and achievements. "Knowledge is Power," "Unity is Strength," and "Attitude is Everything" are more than just expressions—they encapsulate key elements that determine how we navigate the world. While knowledge equips us with the tools to understand and solve problems, unity provides the collective strength to accomplish bigger goals. However, it is our attitude that determines how effectively we utilise both knowledge and unity, making it the most crucial element for personal and collective success.

Knowledge is Power

Knowledge is a fundamental force that empowers individuals and societies. It allows us to understand the world, to innovate, and to overcome obstacles. Whether it is academic knowledge, technical skills, or life experience, possessing knowledge gives us the power to make informed decisions, solve complex problems, and drive progress. In every field—be it science, business, or medicine—knowledge has been a key factor in transforming society.

For example, medical advancements have significantly improved life expectancy and quality of life, all thanks to scientific knowledge. In the same way, entrepreneurs rely on market knowledge to build successful businesses. Access to information and the ability to apply it effectively can transform individuals, leading to opportunities that would otherwise remain out of reach.

However, knowledge alone does not guarantee success. One can be knowledgeable but still fail to make an impact if they lack the right attitude. Knowledge must be coupled with humility, openness to learning, and the willingness to apply it for the greater good. Otherwise, knowledge may remain untapped potential.

Unity is Strength

While knowledge empowers individuals, unity amplifies the power of groups. Working together with a shared vision, people can accomplish far more than they could on their own. Unity brings together diverse talents, perspectives, and resources, making collective efforts stronger and more resilient. History is full of examples that demonstrate the importance of unity, from civil rights movements to national liberation struggles, where people united under a common cause to bring about meaningful change.

Even in day-to-day life, unity plays a vital role in creating supportive communities and productive work environments. When people collaborate effectively, they can overcome challenges, solve problems more efficiently, and achieve common goals. For example, in a team setting, no matter how talented individuals are, it is only through working together that they achieve optimal results.

Yet, like knowledge, unity requires the right attitude to thrive. Unity without mutual respect, cooperation, and trust is fragile and can easily collapse. Attitude plays a crucial role in maintaining harmony and fostering a sense of belonging and purpose within groups. Thus, while unity is strength, its strength depends on the positive attitudes of the individuals within the group.

Attitude is Everything

Attitude, more than anything else, shapes how we interact with knowledge and unity. It is the lens through which we view our challenges, relationships, and opportunities. A positive attitude empowers us to make the most of our knowledge and work effectively with others. In contrast, a negative attitude can undermine even the most knowledgeable person or the most united team.

For example, a person with a growth mindset who views challenges as opportunities for learning is more likely to overcome obstacles and achieve success. Their positive attitude enables them to persist in the face of adversity, apply their knowledge effectively, and contribute meaningfully to group efforts. On the other hand, someone with a pessimistic or rigid attitude may struggle to see solutions, give up easily, or clash with others, ultimately limiting their potential.

Moreover, attitude is contagious. A leader with a positive attitude can inspire a team to stay motivated, work together, and overcome challenges. In contrast, a negative attitude can spread discontent, eroding both individual and collective efforts. This is why attitude is often considered the most important factor in determining success—it can either amplify the power of knowledge and unity or diminish it entirely.

"Knowledge is Power, Unity is Strength, but Attitude is Everything" encapsulates a powerful truth about life. Knowledge equips us with the understanding and skills to navigate the world, and unity provides the collective force to achieve great things together. However, it is an attitude that determines how effectively we use both knowledge and unity. A positive attitude allows us to apply our knowledge wisely and work harmoniously with others, ultimately leading to success and fulfilment. Therefore, while knowledge and unity are essential, it is an attitude that truly drives progress and shapes our outcomes.

Knowledge is Power, Unity is Strength, but Attitude is Everything

Knowledge, a beacon in the dark,

A spark that ignites the questing mind.

It shapes our world with every thought,

Lifting the veil from the unknown and blind.

With wisdom gained, we rise and grow,

Navigating where others fear to go.

Unity, the force of many hearts,

A woven fabric stronger than one thread.

Together we stand, together we strive,

With shoulders aligned, all paths ahead.

For strength in numbers is a timeless creed,

When we unite, we can succeed.

But above it all, one thing remains,

The lens through which we see the day—

Attitude, the silent being that is us

We are also human beings without fuss,

That shapes the course, molds the clay.

For you can have knowledge, you can be strong,

But without the will, you'll go wrong.

It's in the way we face the fight,

The stance we take in wrong or right.

For power fades, and strength can break,

But attitude is what we make.

In it lies the key to everything—

The spark, the unity, the dream, the wings.

Afterword

For millennia, the human touch has been a profound and irreplaceable element of healing and care and will continue to be so for millennia! Despite the remarkable advancements in technology, no machine, no matter how sophisticated, can replicate the emotional and empathetic bond that is communicated through non-verbal gestures such as a smile, a comforting hand on a shoulder, or the gentle stroke of hair. These subtle, yet powerful, acts of kindness and compassion have been intrinsic to caregiving since the dawn of humanity, and they will remain irreplaceable for millennia to come.

The touch of a human being carries an emotional weight that machines simply cannot duplicate. Consider the act of holding a hand or offering a warm, empathetic smile to a patient in distress. These simple gestures convey a sense of understanding and comfort that transcends words. They build trust, offer solace, and remind the sufferer that they are not alone in their pain. This non-verbal communication—the essence of human care—goes beyond the sterile precision of technology. It is a transfer of warmth, emotion, and connection, something a cold, mechanical hand cannot offer. A robot, no matter how advanced, cannot run its metal fingers through the dishevelled hair of a person in suffering, nor can it offer the intimate reassurance needed to uplift their spirits.

Beyond the surgeon's scalpel and sutures, there is skill, solace, serenity, and serendipity.

Robotic technologies like the da Vinci Xi, widely regarded as one of the most advanced multiport surgical systems, have revolutionised medicine. They offer unparalleled dexterity, precision, and consistency in performing intricate procedures. Surgeons can now rely on machines to assist them in complex operations with extreme accuracy, thereby reducing human error. Robots, guided by the steady hands of surgeons, can navigate through delicate tissues and make precise incisions with precision far beyond what the human hand alone can achieve. Yet, despite this astounding progress, there is something fundamentally missing.

For all their skill, robots cannot replicate the visceral experience of human touch. The sensation a surgeon feels when grasping a gallstone between their thumb and index finger is a tactile experience that no machine can mimic. Similarly, a machine may take a patient's temperature with scientific precision, but it cannot compare to the intuitive knowledge conveyed when a surgeon places the back of their hand against the patient's skin. These moments—these tangible, physical connections—are the heart of human care.

This is where palliative care becomes a significant counterpoint. It exemplifies the notion that while technology can enhance care, it cannot replace the human element. Palliative care, in its essence, is "low-tech but high-touch." It focuses on improving the quality of life for patients with serious illnesses, often when curative treatments are no longer possible. The practice does not hinge on complex machines or robotic systems but on the simple acts of presence, listening, and touch.

The power of human presence in palliative care cannot be overstated. Holding a patient's hand, offering a smile, or simply sitting in silence as they process their grief and pain are moments that endure in the hearts of those who receive them. These small acts of compassion can make an enormous difference in the final stages of life, providing a sense of dignity, comfort, and peace. Palliative care embraces the belief that while life may be finite, love, empathy, and human connection are eternal. To echo the sentiment from the song “My Heart Will Go On,” love can touch us “one time but last for a lifetime,” leaving an indelible mark that technology cannot replace.

In a world increasingly dominated by machines, the irreplaceable value of human compassion must be preserved. While robots may excel at surgical precision, and while technology will continue to advance at breathtaking speeds, there will never be a substitute for the healing power of a human touch. The future may be full of cutting-edge technologies that improve surgical outcomes and prolong life, but the deepest moments of healing—the ones that truly matter—are those in which one human connects with another, not through machines, but through the age-old medium of care, compassion, and love.

‘Living’ Before ‘Leaving’

To live before you leave, that’s the way.

Where each breath whispers, “stay another day.”

Not chasing time but savouring the space,

Finding grace in the slowest pace.

It’s not the years but the moments we hold,

In warm hands, stories patiently told.

Not counting the steps to an unseen door,

But dancing with the steps we’ve taken before.

A touch, a smile, a soft embrace,

The power of presence, a gentle face.

For healing is not in curing alone,

But in how deeply our hearts are known.

To live before you leave is to truly be,

To laugh, to cry, to love, to see.

That life's true measure isn't length or might,

But the flicker of kindness in the fading light.

And when it's time to say goodbye,

The soul will rise, but love will not die.

For in living fully, before we part,

We leave the world our beating heart.

The Heart Remembers

Friendship isn't written in perfect lines,

Not a script where everything aligns.

It's found in the spaces where we don't agree,

Yet choose to stay, letting each other be.

It's not about echoing every word,
But listening deeply to what's unheard.
Understanding doesn't need a shared stance,
But an open heart and a second chance.

Forgiveness lives where mistakes reside,
It heals the wounds, though scars may abide.
We don't forget, but we learn to let go.
For friendship's strength is in the flow.

And even when time pulls us apart,
When distance stretches, quiets the heart,
The memories linger, soft and bright,
A touchstone of warmth in the darkest night.

Though the voices fade and the calls grow few,
What we shared remains, always true.
For friendships are more than the moments we see—
They're the echoes that last eternally, free.

Happiness Multiplies

Happiness is a fleeting breeze.

A gentle touch of morning light.

It whispers softly through rustling trees,

A gift that grows when shared in flight.

Hold it close, and it may fade.

A fragile bird with wings so bright.

But let it soar, unafraid,

And watch it multiply in flight.

In laughter shared, in kindness spread,

In every smile and every tear,

Happiness grows when hearts are led.

To lift each other, year by year.

For joy, like love, is never less,

No matter how much you give away.

It blooms in every shared caress.

And lights the darkest, longest day.

So spread your joy, let others see.

The warmth and light that fill your soul.

For happiness, in giving free,

Becomes a fire that makes us whole.

Life Management

Be honest when in trouble's snare,

Let truth be the armour you wear.

Though storms may rage and skies turn grey,

Honesty will light your way.

Be simple when wealth fills your hand,

For riches are like shifting sand.

In humble hearts, true treasures lie,

Not in gold that can pass by.

Be polite when authority reigns,

Power's weight can forge harsh chains.

But kindness in command is rare,

A gentle touch shows you care.

Be silent when anger ignites,

For words can wound with bitter bites.

In quiet reflection, wisdom grows.

And peace returns when the fire slows.

This is life, a delicate art.

Guided by a mindful heart.

With these virtues as your guide,

You'll find the balance deep inside.

Truth to Be Accepted

When you search and seek in vain,

For answers to ease the pain,

When every path turns cold and bare,

And you feel lost in endless despair—

It's not a problem to unwind,

Nor a puzzle for the mind.

Some things, no matter how we try,

Are truths that simply occupy.

For in the silence, wisdom calls,

Through quiet halls where reason falls.

Not every riddle has a key,

Some truths are just meant to be.

So lay down your weary fight,

Not every shadow hides the light.

Embrace what is, let go of doubt,

For peace is what acceptance brings about.

In life, not all things are to mend,

Some journeys come without an end.

But in the stillness, you will find,

Truth is the calmness of the mind.

Gifts of Life

Birth is a gift, a seed gently sown,

By parents' hands, through love we've grown.

They mould our hearts with care and grace,

In their embrace, we find our place.

Education is a teacher's hand,

Guiding us through learning's land,

With every lesson, minds take flight,

Turning ignorance into light.

A job, a company's prized trust,

Turning effort into just,

With hands that labour, minds that strive,

We find our purpose, dreams alive.

A wife, life's gift, a partner true,

In joy and sorrow, she walks with you

Through every storm, her love will stand,

Together you journey, hand in hand.

But friends, oh friends, are gifts divine,

Scattered by God's loving design.

They are the stars in life's vast sky,

Guiding you when roads run dry.

Each gift is woven in life's thread

Binding us where dreams are led.

Cherish these blessings, near and far,

For they are the lights that make us who we are.

Further Reading

1. Arthrodesis of Interphalangeal Joints and Fixation of Phalangeal Fractures in Trauma-Preliminary Report of a Simple Technique - Indian Journal of Plastic Surgery,, Cherian Koshy,1989, 22 (2) pp 99- 102

2. 'Use of Ionized Air in Burns Management' – Preliminary Support, Cherian Koshy, Norman Guido Indian Journal of Plastic Surgery, 1989, 22 (2) pp 65-67

3. Experience in the Management of Air Crash victims,© Dr Cherian Koshy, Proceedings International Symposium on Surgical Emergencies, Feb: 1994, Al Hasa, Kingdom of Saudi Arabia

4. Compassion, driving force of palliative care- Dr Cherian Koshy, HELP for the HILLS-16 May 2012, 5:27 New Indian Express

5. People will keep on hoping, no matter what the odds. For example, I keep buying lottery tickets—hope springs eternal. This expression was coined by Alexander Pope (An Essay on Man, 1732) and quickly became proverbial

6. Learning from each other: cross-cultural insights on palliative care in Indian and Australian regions- International Journal of Palliative Nursing, Pam McGrath, Cherian Koshy -2005, October 15th (10) 499-509

7. To be or not to be—that is the question" is the first line of arguably the most famous speech in Shakespeare's Hamlet. In this soliloquy from Act 3, Scene 1, Hamlet contemplates death and what comes after it.

8. Richard Leider (2020). "The Power of Purpose." Purpose Project.

9. - Discusses the distinction between career and calling and provides tools for individuals to find their purpose in life

10. Dan Cumberland (2018). The Meaning Movement Blog: "What's the Difference Between a Career and a Calling?"

11. - An in-depth exploration of how a calling is fundamentally different from a career, with practical advice on how to discover and pursue one's calling.

12. Bangalore: A Century of Tales from City and Cantonment by Peter Colaco.

13. Colaco's book offers a detailed look into the social life of Bangalore, tracing the city's transformation, including the rise of its nightlife and pub culture.

14. Pub Culture and Urban Youth in Bangalore: Social Dynamics and Health Risks"

15. This paper from the -Journal of Urban Sociology examines the relationship between Bangalore'

16. emerging pub culture and its impact on youth behavior, including increased instance accidents due to alcohol consumption.

17. Quality of Life in Cancer – The Emerging Arbiter, The National Medical Journal of India, Cherian Koshy, Rachel Cherian Koshy 1998, Vol 11, No1, p 48 – 49

18. Tobacco Related Cancers- Portends for the Future, Health For the Millions, Cherian Koshy, Rachel Cherian Koshy, Sept – Oct 1998, p 18 – 19

19. Vile, Vicious Vapid – the Tobacco Smokescreen, Cherian Koshy, Rachel Cherian Koshy, Kerala Medical Journal Vol 40, No 2, p 26 – 29

20. The Thyroid in Rhyme- (Invited Paper), Cherian M Koshy, Kerala Surgical Journal, 1997, Vol 4, No 2, p 95

21. Breast Cancer in Rhyme, Cherian M Koshy, Kerala Medical Journal, Vol 38, No 2, p 27

22. At Home in Palliative Care, in Hospice Information Bulletin, 03.2004 Volume 2 No 4, published by St Christophers Hospice, London, and Help the Hospice

23. Palliative Care in Indian Journal of Palliative Care Cherian Koshy2007 | JanuaryJune | Volume Issue 1, page: 22

24. Cost of Treating Cancer Pain in India- A look at some underlying issues Dr Cherian Koshy, Book Chapter in 'Freedom from Pain' I K International Publishing house Pvt Ltd page 121

25. Palliative Care in J of Palliative Medicine, Vol 11, No 4, 2008, p 636- 637 ©Mary Ann Liebert 1nc Journal of Palliative Medicine. May 2008, Vol. 11, No. 4: 636-637

26. 'The Palliative Care Movement in India, another Freedom Struggle or a silent Revolution' Indian Journal of Palliative Care, Volume 15, issue 1, 2009 p 10-13

27. Tele-Clinic in Palliative Care' – Unique window of opportunity to deliver quality specialist Palliative Care, Singapore Palliative Care Congress proceedings, Palliative Medicine, 2010/24(2): 207

28. 'Deluxe Death' or Dignified Dying?, Cherian M Koshy, in Journal of Palliative Medicine, Volume 17,No2, 2014, ©Mary Ann Liebert Inc,p 246

29. Comprehensive Care planning in Palliative Care, Dr Cherian Koshy, in Indian Journal of Palliative Care April 2016, published by Wolters Kluwer-© Mednow, p 186

30. Music and Medicine International Seminar on Psychosocial issues in health care with special emphasis on Psychosocial Oncology, Dr Cherian Koshy, Conference Proceedings March 1997, Regional Cancer Centre, Trivandrum

31. Validation of the Malayalam version of Leeds assessment of neuropathic symptoms and signs pain scale in cancer patients in the Regional Cancer Centre, Thiruvananthapuram, Kerala, India, Dr S Ansar, Dr Cherian Koshy Original Paper, Volume 23, Issue 3, 2017, pages 393-299

32. Rainbow of Palliative Care activities carried out through a Primary Health Centre' ©Dr Binoy S Babu, Dr Cherian Koshy April 2016, Indian Journal of Palliative Care

33. Disenfranchised Grief Does it exist in cancer-Cherian Koshy in ©Proceedings on the Palliative Care Congress at Limerick, Ireland

34. Home Care Services in the Department Palliative Medicine-Dr Cherian Koshy © Proceedings of 6th Asia Pacific Hospice Conference at Seoul Korea

35. Oral Morphine Manufacture at the INCTR (International Network for Cancer Research and Treatment), Dr Cherian Koshy © Proceedings Antalya, Turkey, March 22nd to March 24th 2009,

36. Tele Clinic Services at the Regional Cancer Centre, Kerala India -Dr Cherian Koshy ©Proceedings of International Conference on

Public Health and Palliative Care at Dhaka, Bangladesh January 11 – 13 2011

37. 'Home Care Services of Regional Cancer Centre' - Dr Cherian Koshy, UICC, World Cancer Congress Proceedings July 2006, Washington DC

38. Involved in drafting the first Palliative Care Policy of its kind in the World passed by the Government of Kerala, India and later the SOP, (Standard Operating Procedures for Narcotic Use) *vide* GO (P), 109, /2008/H&FWD, (GO (P) No,109/2008/H&FWD dated 15th April 2008

39. On Death and Dying- 50th Anniversary Edition, 2014, ElISABETH KÜBLER ROSS- Scribner Reissue Edition

40. Avulsion injuries of extremities, Cherian Koshy, K Ramakrishnan Nair,© Indian Journal of Plastic Surgery, 1987, 20, (2) 80 – 83

41. ' BREAKS' Protocol for breaking Bad news, Dr Vijayakumaran Narayanan, Dr Cherian Koshy,2010, Indian Journal of Palliative Care, Volume 16, issue 2, p 61 -1 67

42. Metastatic Bone Disease, in Australasian Journal of Cancer, Vijakumaran Narayan, Cherian Koshy, Volume 8, No 4, 2007

43. Doka, K. J. (1989). Disenfranchised Grief: Recognizing Hidden Sorrow. Lexington Books.

44. - This foundational text explores the concept of disenfranchised grief and offers ways to understand and support those experiencing it.

45. 2. *Doka, K. J. (2002). Disenfranchised Grief: New Directions, Challenges, and Strategies for Practice. Research Press.

46. - A continuation of Doka's earlier work, this book delves int…

47. Harris, J. R., Lippman, M. E., Morrow, M., & Osborne, C. K. (Eds.). (2016).* Diseases of the Breast (5th ed.). Wolters Kluwer.

48. - This comprehensive textbook is considered a definitive reference for clinicians and researchers in the field of breast cancer. It covers all aspects of breast cancer diagnosis, pathology, treatment, and ongoing research.

49. Love, S. M. (2015).* Dr. Susan Love's Breast Book (6th ed.). Da Capo Press.

50. - A highly accessible book written by renowned breast cancer surgeon Dr. Susan Love. This book serves as a guide for patients and their families, offering detailed yet un...

51. Here are five key references on thyroid cancer, spanning clinical research, diagnosis, treatment, and patient care:

52. Warsofsky, L., & Van Nostrand, D. (2016). Thyroid Cancer: A Comprehensive Guide to Clinical Management (3rd ed.). Springer.

53. - This book is a leading reference for the management of thyroid cancer, providing a comprehensive review of diagnosis, treatment options, surgical techniques, and molecular advancements in the field.

54. Cooper, D. S., & Doherty, G. M. (2020).* The Thyroid: A Fundamental and Clinical Text (11th ed.). Wolters Kluwer.

55. . Kloos, R. T., Eng, C., Evans, D. B., & Francis, G. L. (2012).* Thyroid Cancer: A Multidisciplinary Approach (1st ed.). Demos Medical Publishing.

56. - Surrogate Advertising: A Study on the Impact of Banned Products in India"* by Ritu Sood and Anupam Sharma. This article discusses how surrogate ads, especially those for alcohol and tobacco, affect public perception and behavior, with special reference to youth.

57. - *"Tobacco Advertising and Promotion: Impact on Youth Smoking"* by John Pierce et al. This research explores how tobacco advertising, including indirect means, influences youth smoking initiation.

58. - *"Ethics and Regulation of Tobacco Advertising in Sports Sponsorships"* by B.M. Forster and H.J. Grize. This paper looks into the use of sports events like the Wills Trophy to advertise tobacco products and the ethical concerns surrounding it.

59. - *"Surrogate Advertising and Consumer Response in India: A Policy Perspective"* by Ashish Gupte. This piece focuses on the evolution of surrogate advertising in India and its broader effects on the population.

60. - *"The Role of Sports Sponsorship in the Promotion of Tobacco and Alcohol: The Case of the Wills World Cup"* by J.R. Reynolds and D.T. Goldstein. This study highlights how sports events, including cricket tournaments, have been used by companies to subtly promote harmful products.

61. - *"Impact of Advertising on Children: Tobacco and Alcohol Surrogate Promotions"* by R. Prasad. A comprehensive study focused on the effects of surrogate ads on younger au

Bibliography

1. https://www.indeed.com/career-advice/finding-a-job/job-vs-calling-vs-career

2. https://psychcentral.com/pro/the-difference-between-curing-and-healing-the-mind

3. https://www.ihi.org/insights/why-knowing-difference-between-curing-and-healing-matters

4. https://www.thehindu.com/news/cities/bangalore/Pilot-error-caused-1990-Bangalore-air-crash-report/article16302972.ece

5. Arthrodesis of Interphalangeal Joints and Fixation of Phalangeal Fractures in Trauma-Preliminary Report of a Simple Technique - Indian Journal of Plastic Surgery, , Cherian Koshy,1989, 22 (2) pp 99- 102

6. 'Use of Ionized Air in Burns Management' – Preliminary Support, Cherian Koshy, Norman Guido Indian Journal of Plastic Surgery, 1989, 22 (2) pp 65-67

7. https://www.plasticsurgery.org/reconstructive-procedures/cleft-lip-and-cleft-palate-repair

8. https://www.researchgate.net/publication/273959501_'Time_Gentlemen'_Bangalore_and_its_drinking_cultures

Nair, Janaki. The Promise of the Metropolis: Bangalore's Twentieth Century. Oxford University Press, 2005.This book discusses the transformation of Bangalore from a colonial city to a post-colonial metropolis and the accompanying changes in its social fabric, including the rise of urban nightlife and pub culture.

Nair, Tara. "Urbanization, Social Change, and the Public Sphere: The Case of Bangalore." Economic and Political Weekly, vol. 45, no. 33, 2010, pp. 77–84.

9. https://www.webmd.com/beauty/cosmetic-procedures-scars

10. https://my.clevelandclinic.org/health/treatments/21525-body-countouring

11. Friedman, Oren. "Psychological Stress of Aesthetic Surgeons and the Celebrity Factor." Aesthetic Surgery Journal, vol. 34, no. 3, 2014, pp. 423-430.

12. Swanson, Eric. "The Pressure of Perfection: Stress Among Plastic Surgeons." Plastic and Reconstructive Surgery, vol. 138, no. 2, 2016, pp. 375-385.

13. Nguyen, Peter T., and Susan A. Clark. "Balancing Act: How Interviewers Manage Challenges and Threats During the Selection Process." International Journal of Selection and Assessment, vol. 28, no. 1, 2020, pp. 12–25.

14. Davis, Laura M., and Robert E. Thompson. "Stress and Cognitive Load in Interviewers: How Challenges Influence Selection Outcomes." Journal of Occupational Health Psychology, vol. 25, no. 1, 2020, pp. 45–58.

15. World Health Organization (WHO). (2019). Workplace Equity for Health Professionals: Guidelines for Reducing Bias in Selection and Promotion. WHO Publications.

16. Reply to Right to Information Query , No, 1186,/2008/AAO?RCC

17. Hanahan, Douglas, and Robert A. Weinberg. "The Hallmarks of Cancer." Cell, vol. 100, no. 1, 2000, pp. 57–70.

18. Fearon, Eric R., and Douglas Hanahan. "The Molecular Basis of Cancer." Journal of Clinical Oncology, vol. 12, suppl, 1994, pp. 116s–130s.

19. Tobacco Related Cancers- Portends for the Future, Health For the Millions, Cherian Koshy, Rachel Cherian Koshy, Sept – Oct 1998, p 18 – 19

20. Vile, Vicious Vapid – the Tobacco Smokescreen, Cherian Koshy, Rachel Cherian Koshy, Kerala Medical Journal Vol 40, No 2, p 26 – 29

21. https://aspph.org/news/external-relations/misinformation-and-disinformation/

22. Lee, J. Y., & Kim, H. J. (2021). "Robotic Surgery in Oncology: Current Status and Future Directions." Annals of Surgical Oncology, 28(4), 2193-2201.

23. American Cancer Society. (2020). "Cancer Statistics, 2020." CA: A Cancer Journal for Clinicians, 70(1), 7-30.

24. Jordan, V. C., & O'Regan, R. (2020). Breast Cancer: A Comprehensive Guide to Diagnosis and Treatment. Springer

25. Harris, E. R., & Nguyen, P. L. (2021). "The 'Commando Operation': Defining and Standardizing Composite Resections in Multidisciplinary Teams." Surgical Innovation, 28(2), 134-142.

26. Kushner, H. S. (1981). When Bad Things Happen to Good People. Avon Books.

27. Sweeney, J. P. (2004). Cancer Is So Limited (poem).

28. A widely circulated poem, Sweeney's "Cancer Is So Limited" poignantly captures the limitations of cancer, listing things like "it cannot cripple love, it cannot shatter hope, it cannot corrode faith." This poem is often featured in cancer care settings for its uplifting message.

29. Kalanithi, P. (2016). When Breath Becomes Air. Random House.

A neurosurgeon who confronts terminal cancer writes a poignant memoir about the limitations of cancer in controlling one's sense of purpose and the value of life, even in its final stages.

30. Frankl, V. E. (2006). Man's Search for Meaning. Beacon Press. This classic work explores the psychological battle for meaning in the face of suffering, trauma, and despair, based on Frankl's experiences in Nazi concentration camps. It provides insight into how the mind can transcend suffering through finding purpose.

31. Kübler-Ross, E. (1969). On Death and Dying. Scribner. Kübler-Ross examines the five stages of grief and the mental battles individuals face when confronting death. This book explores emotional responses to trauma, loss, and the existential cries of the heart during times of profound transition.

32. Lewis, C. S. (1961). A Grief Observed. Faber & Faber.: After the death of his wife, Lewis chronicles his deep grief and the emotional battles he faces, questioning faith, love, and the human condition. It's a raw and honest reflection on the heart's cries in times of great sorrow.

33. Tolle, E. (2005). A New Earth: Awakening to Your Life's Purpose. Penguin Group.

34. Charon, R. (2001). "The Patient-Physician Relationship." The New England Journal of Medicine, 344(15), 1157-1160.

35. Levine, M. (2015). "The Art of Medicine: The Doctor-Patient Relationship." The Lancet, 385(9981), 2366-2367.: This piece reflects on the importance of the emotional and psychological aspects of the doctor-patient relationship in achieving positive health outcomes.

36. (1 Samuel 16 , 14 – 16) Old Testament , NIV Bible , David plays the harp to ward off King Saul's distress

37. Music and Medicine International Seminar on Psycho-Social issues in health care with special emphasis on Psycho-social Oncology, Dr Cherian Koshy, Conference Proceedings March 1997, Regional Cancer Centre, Trivandrum

38. Doka, Kenneth J. (1989). Disenfranchised Grief: Recognizing Hidden Sorrow. Lexington Books.This foundational text introduces the concept of disenfranchised grief, discussing types of grief that society fails to acknowledge or validate

39. Attig, Thomas. (2010). How We Grieve: Relearning the World (Revised Edition). Oxford University Press.- Attig explores the process of grieving, focusing on various types of grief, including disenfranchised grief, and how individuals can find meaning after loss

40. https://thebetterindia.com/330112/nipah-virus-dr-anoop-kumar-diagnosis-bats-kozhikode-kerala/

41. Interprofessional Collaboration and Teamwork in Healthcare: A Review

    Authors: Christina M. D'Amour, Michel Ferrada-Videla, et al.

    ournal: Human Resources for Health, 2017, 15(1), 19.Summary: Reviews literature on interprofessional collaboration, emphasizing its role in enhancing patient care.

42. The Impact of Fragrance on Patient Anxiety and Satisfaction in Clinical Settings Authors: Laura M. Thompson, Michael J. Reynolds Journal: Journal of Clinical Psychology in Medical Settings, 2020, 27(3), 345-355. Summary: Investigates how pleasant fragrances, such as a doctor's perfume, can reduce patient anxiety and increase overall satisfaction during medical consultations.

43. Scent and the Therapeutic Alliance: Enhancing Doctor-Patient Relationships Through Olfactory Cues Authors: Karen E. Lawson, Timothy G. Miller Journal: Medical Humanities, 2021, 47(2), 123-130. Summary: Explores the role of scent as a non-verbal tool in strengthening the therapeutic alliance between doctors and patients.

44. The Soul of Medicine: Tales from the Bedside Author: Pauline Chen, Publisher: Viking Press, 2019. ISBN: 978-0735226784 Description: Combines personal narratives with medical insights to highlight the importance of addressing the spiritual and emotional needs of patients in clinical practice.

45. Learning from each other: Cross cultural insights on Palliative Care in Indian and Australian regions, Pam Mc Grath, Hamish Holewa, Cherian Koshy in International Journal of Palliative Nursing, 2009, Vol 15, no 10 -An Essay on the Goodness of God, the Freedom of Man and the Origin of Evil: Author: Gottfried Wilhelm Leibniz-Publisher: Translated by George H. Whicher, Cambridge University Press, 1989.ISBN: 978-0521422793-Description-Leibniz's foundational work where he introduces the concept of theodicy, arguing that the existing world is the "best of all possible worlds

46. The Problem of Pain-Author: C.S. Lewis, Publisher: Harper One, 1940.:ISBN: 978-0060652928: Description: C.S. Lewis explores the nature of pain and suffering, offering a Christian perspective on why a good and powerful God allows evil.

47. Theodicy: Essays on the Goodness of God and the Presence of Evil :Author: Marilyn McCord Adams, Publisher: University of Chicago Press, 1999., ISBN: 978-0226732570- Description: Adams offers a comprehensive analysis of various theodicies, emphasizing the moral and existential dimensions of evil.

48. Redefining Health Care: The Paradigm Shift to Palliative Care, Author: Atul Gawande, Publisher: Picador, 2019.ISBN: 978-1524742485, Description: Discusses how palliative care is reshaping the healthcare landscape by prioritizing patient-centered approaches and quality of life over purely curative measures.

49. Paradigm Paralysis in Scientific Research: Causes and Consequences, Authors: Jennifer A. Smith and Thomas R. Lee, Journal: Science & Education, 2020, 29(5), 643-659., Summary: Examines the factors leading to paradigm paralysis in scientific communities and its impact on research progress.

50. "Death by Design: The Suicide Tourism Dilemma", Author: Dr. Emily S. Carter, Publisher: Oxford University Press, 2020., ISBN: 978-0190878516, Description: Explores the ethical and legal challenges posed by suicide tourism, analysing case studies and proposing policy recommendations.

51.

52. "Global Perspectives on Suicide Tourism: Cultural and Psychological Insights, Authors: Karen E. Lawson, Timothy G. Miller Publisher: Palgrave Macmillan, 2022.ISBN: 978-1138079605, Description: Examines suicide tourism through diverse cultural lenses, exploring how cultural attitudes towards death influence the phenomenon.

53. Tele-Clinic in Palliative Care' – Dr Cherian Koshy, Unique window of opportunity to deliver quality specialist Palliative Care, SPCC(Singapore Palliative Care Congress) proceedings, Palliative Medicine, 2010/24(2): 207

54. "Truth, Transparency, and Trust: Navigating Ethical Challenges in Doctor-Patient Relationships" Author: Dr. Jessica A. Martinez, Institution: University of California, Los Angeles, Year: 2022 URL: Description: A doctoral dissertation exploring the ethical frameworks that support truthfulness and transparency in building trust between doctors and patients.

55. "The Impact of Transparent Communication on Patient Trust and Satisfaction" Author: Dr. Michael T. Johnson, Institution: Harvard University, Year: 2021 URL: Description: Investigates how transparent communication strategies influence patient trust, satisfaction, and overall healthcare experiences.

56. Niemann, A., & Stangier, U. (2017). Hope as a Concept in Palliative Care: A Narrative Review. In Palliative Care: A Patient-Cantered Approach (pp. 123-138). Wiley-Blackwell.

57. Kirk, T. R., & Millar, K. (2016). Hope in Palliative Care: A Systematic Review of the Literature. In Palliative Care: A Patient-Centered Approach (pp. 1-16). Wiley-Blackwell.

58. Frost, J., & Massoudi, B. Connected Health: Improving Patient Experience through Technology. Routledge, 2017. Discusses the impact of technology, including smartphones, on patient engagement and care delivery.

59. Wong, D. T., & Lee, H. K. "Evaluating the Impact of Digital Rounds on Clinical Practice: A Systematic Review." BMC Medical Education, vol. 20, no. 1, 2020, pp. 1-9., A systematic review examining the limitations and challenges of digital rounds compared to traditional clinical rounds.

60. American Medical Association. "Clinical Rounds: The Importance of Face-to-Face Patient Care." 2021.,This report outlines the benefits of traditional clinical rounds and the importance of direct patient interactions for quality care.

61. Hawkley, Louise C., and John T. Cacioppo. "Loneliness Matters: A Theoretical and Empirical Review of Consequences and Mechanisms." Annals of Behavioural Medicine 40, no. 2 (2010): 218-227

62. Kabat-Zinn, Jon. Wherever You Go, There You Are: Mindfulness Meditation in Everyday Life. New York: Hyperion, 1994.Summary: Focuses on the positive aspects of mindfulness and solitude,

63. Lewis, C.S. The Four Loves. New York: Harcourt, Brace, 1960.:Summary: Lewis explores four kinds of love (affection, friendship, eros, and charity) and argues that compassion and truth are essential elements of love. He also discusses courage as necessary for practicing love in a broken world.

64. Sacks, Jonathan. To Heal a Fractured World: The Ethics of Responsibility. New York: Schocken Books, 2005.

65. Frankl, Viktor E. Man's Search for Meaning. Boston: Beacon Press, 1946.: Summary: Frankl argues that finding meaning in life requires courage to face suffering, truth to guide one's actions, and compassion to connect with others, showing how these virtues interact to support human resilience.

66. Gawande, Atul. Being Mortal: Medicine and What Matters in the End. New York: Metropolitan Books, 2014.: Summary: Gawande critiques the over-formalization of healthcare systems, especially in end-of-life care, advocating for more personal, compassionate interactions focused on the patient's values and well-being.

67. Fadiman, Anne. The Spirit Catches You and You Fall Down: A Hmong Child, Her American Doctors, and the Collision of Two Cultures. New York: Farrar, Straus, and Giroux, 1997.

68. Summary: This case study reveals the cultural hypocrisy and duplicity in Western medicine, where the healthcare system fails to recognize

and respect the medical practices and beliefs of marginalized communities

69. Erich Fromm. The Art of Loving. New York: Harper & Row, 1956.: Summary: Fromm, a psychoanalyst and social philosopher, explores the nature of love, emphasizing that love is an active process. He argues that indifference, characterized by passivity and disengagement, is the opposite of love because love requires care, responsibility, and involvement.

70. Viktor E. Frankl. Man's Search for Meaning. Boston: Beacon Press, 1946.

71. Summary: In this seminal work, Frankl explores how individuals can find meaning in life, even in the midst of suffering. He argues that while pain is inevitable, the way we respond to it can determine whether we experience deep suffering or discover meaning in adversity

72. Joanna Bourke. The Story of Pain: From Prayer to Painkillers. Oxford: Oxford University Press, 2014.: Summary: Bourke traces the history of how pain has been understood and treated, and how its assault on the human body and psyche has been described throughout different cultural contexts. She emphasizes that pain profoundly unsettles an individual's identity and the way they interact with the world.

73. Viktor E. Frankl. Man's Search for Meaning. Boston: Beacon Press, 2006.: Summary: Frankl, a Holocaust survivor, explores the importance of finding meaning in life, even amid suffering. He discusses how pleasure-seeking can lead to a lack of fulfilment when not grounded in deeper value

74. Ron Gutman. Smile: The Astonishing Powers of a Simple Act. New York: Crown Publishing Group, 2011.: Summary: This book

explores the science behind smiling and how a simple smile can influence our happiness, health, and relationships.

75. Stevens, A. J. "The Importance of Being Nice: A Study on Workplace Relationships." Journal of Organizational Behaviour 29, no. 3 (2008): 289-304.: Summary: This article discusses the impact of kindness on workplace dynamics and productivity, suggesting that being nice leads to healthier work environments.

76. Rogers, Carl. "The Therapeutic Relationship: The Role of Listening." Journal of Humanistic Psychology 19, no. 3 (1979): 3-16. Summary: This article addresses the importance of listening in building a therapeutic alliance and facilitating effective patient interactions.

77. Kahn, E. A. The High Touch Revolution in Health Care: The New Paradigm for Health Care Delivery. Health Professions Press, 1998.: Summary: Kahn explores the principles of high-touch medicine and the importance of personal connection in patient care, contrasting it with high-tech approaches

78. Kawasaki, Guy. The Art of Wabi-Sabi: How to Find Beauty in Imperfection. Portfolio :Summary: Kawasaki discusses the philosophy of Wabi Sabi in the context of modern living, providing insights on how to cultivate a mindset that embraces flaws and the beauty of aging.

79. Schwartz, Jeffrey. The Mind and the Brain: Neuroplasticity and the Power of Mental Force. HarperCollins, 2002.=Summary: Schwartz explores how neuroplasticity is influenced by relationships and environments, demonstrating how our brains function in interdependence with social contexts and interpersonal interactions.

80. Schwartz, Barry. The Paradox of Choice: Why More Is Less. Harper Perennial, 2004.Summary: Schwartz examines how the abundance

of choices in modern life can overwhelm individuals, leading to indecision and dissatisfaction. The book explores the psychological processes behind making choices and how decision-making can be improved by limiting options

81. Koenig, H. G., King, D. E., & Carson, V. B. (2012). "Handbook of Religion and Health." Psychiatric Clinics of North America, 35(3), 437-445.Reviews key findings from the "Handbook of Religion and Health" and discusses their relevance to clinical practice

82. Institute of Medicine (US) Committee on Spirituality and Health in Society. (2009). Religion, Spirituality, and Health: A Framework for Education and Practice. National Academies Press.Provides a comprehensive framework for integrating spirituality into healthcare education and practice.

83. Mills, C. (2018). Insurance and Risk Management. Routledge., Discusses risk assessment and management strategies in insurance, with sections dedicated to natural disasters and acts of God.

84. Whispered Secrets: Medical Ethics and the Conspiracy of Silence by Dr. Laura Thompson Description: Delves into ethical dilemmas faced by healthcare professionals when deciding whether to disclose or withhold critical information from patients.

85. Smith, T. R., & Johnson, L. M. (2019). "Integrating Creative Arts in Palliative Care: The Impact of Poetry Readings." Palliative & Supportive Care, 17(2), 213-220. , Analyses the impact of poetry readings on patient well-being and professional development in palliative care conferences.

www.ingramcontent.com/pod-product-compliance
Lightning Source LLC
LaVergne TN
LVHW041008150826
845672LV00001B/9

* 9 7 9 8 8 9 6 1 0 8 1 4 6 *